Pra

'The magic in this necessary and beautiful book is how deftly Spargo-Ryan shines her light on life's dark materials to offer comfort and inspiration to the rest of us. A must read.' – Sarah Krasnostein, author of *The Trauma Cleaner* and *The Believer*

'Anna Spargo-Ryan writes with the kind of searing insight and beauty that both shatters your soul and also pieces it back together. I hope she never stops.' – Clementine Ford, author of *Fight Like A Girl* and *How We Love*

'With humour, generosity and courage, Anna Spargo-Ryan narrates an experience that is so often impossible to put into words. By taking us inside therapy sessions, hospital wards, and cars, rooms and self-talk that act as entrapment, we are given an opportunity to learn, to empathise and to love. *A Kind of Magic* should be read by anyone wanting to understand mental illness, and for anyone with mental illness wanting to be understood.' – Kylie Maslen, author of *Show Me Where it Hurts*

'*A Kind of Magic* has achieved something quite marvellous – it is somehow both as funny as it is suffused with grief; just as it manages to balance its gentle wisdom with moments of wonderful silliness, and to convey something of the mental and bodily experience of psychosis and panic in a manner that's neither abstracted nor voyeuristic, but rather vitally, pulsingly alive. And it's a page-turner, to boot. This is a book brimming with character as well as life, all the more striking for the painful material from which it has been built.' – Fiona Wright, author of *Small Acts of Disappearance* and *The World Was Whole*

Also by Anna Spargo-Ryan

The Gulf
The Paper House

A Kind of Magic

A memoir about anxiety, our minds, and optimism in spite of it all

Anna Spargo-Ryan

ultimo press

Published in 2022 by Ultimo Press,
an imprint of Hardie Grant Publishing

Ultimo Press
Gadigal Country
7, 45 Jones Street
Ultimo, NSW 2007
ultimopress.com.au

Ultimo Press (London)
5th & 6th Floors
52–54 Southwark Street
London SE1 1UN

NATIONAL LIBRARY OF AUSTRALIA

A catalogue record for this work is available from the National Library of Australia

A Kind of Magic
ISBN 978 1 76115 073 9 (paperback)

10 9 8 7 6 5 4 3 2 1

Cover design Alissa Dinallo
Cover images Teardrop by Minur / Shutterstock; Paint splodges by ana & yvy / Creative Market
Typesetting Kirby Jones | Typeset in 12.5/18 pt Adobe Garamond Pro
Copyeditor Ali Lavau
Proofreader Rebecca Starford

Printed in Australia by Griffin Press, an Accredited ISO AS/NZS 14001 Environmental Management System printer.

MIX
Paper from responsible sources
FSC www.fsc.org FSC® C009448

The paper this book is printed on is certified against the Forest Stewardship Council® Standards. Griffin Press holds FSC® chain of custody certification SGSHK-COC-005088. FSC® promotes environmentally responsible, socially beneficial and economically viable management of the world's forests.

Ultimo Press acknowledges the Traditional Owners of the country on which we work, the Gadigal people of the Eora nation and the Wurundjeri people of the Kulin nation, and recognises their continuing connection to the land, waters and culture. We pay our respects to their Elders past and present.

If Anna Spargo-Ryan were capable of
supplying a pithy biography,
she wouldn't have written this entire book
about herself.

This book was written on the stolen lands of the
Boon Wurrung people of the Kulin Nation.

I acknowledge the Traditional Custodians and pay my respects
to Elders past and present.

paytherent.net.au
djirra.org.au
indigenousliteracyfoundation.org.au

For better mental health care
universal access
compassion
action
love

But out in the field, experience has no chapter headings or paragraph breaks or ellipses in which to catch your breath … it just keeps coming at you.

— Zadie Smith, 'Peonies'

I change, then, without ceasing.

— Henri Bergson, *Creative Evolution*

Anna Spargo-Ryan doesn't seem at all like a miserable person.

— *The Age*

Author note

Hey pal,

I hope that you're well. Or, if you're not, that you can feel my bubble of love around you. Not in a weird way.

The following pages contain some experiences and events that might be distressing to read. It has always been important to me to be frank and open (some might say 'too open') about my mental illness, but that might not be where you're at. As this book discusses psychosis, anxiety, trauma, depression, suicide and therapeutic processes, I wanted to check first that you were in the right place to read it.

This is not intended to be a trauma dump. I long for it to bring you feelings of camaraderie, companionship and empathy. But I also have no wish to pretend that life with mental illness is less serious than it is. Sometimes, it is vile and vulgar. And so, sometimes this book is vile and vulgar, even while it's reaching out its hand to hold yours.

Ready?

If you decide to push ahead with reading about brains and feelings, turn to page 3.

If you decide to get under your comfiest blanket and stream episodes of a show you like, close the book.

Part 1

APRIL

The first thing I notice about my new therapy appointment is that I've worn the wrong shoes. I've done everything else correctly: washed my hair, used deodorant, selected an age-appropriate shirt, practised my calm and knowledgeable voice. But *thongs*? To a medical centre?

They slap as I follow my new therapist along the hallway – *slap slap slap* – disturbing the sick people.

'Sorry,' I say, calmly and knowledgeably. 'Thongs are so loud!' I laugh so she knows it's a joke. The thongs are an aberration. We both know I'm totally fine and just seeing a new therapist for no reason.

I need her to know that I am good at therapy. I know the names of all the disorders and their symptoms. I have clinical terms for describing my feelings. One time I went to hospital because my head was caving in, and I knew so much about mental illness that they asked if I was a nurse. Also, I'm extremely well adjusted. Has she noticed that I use a salon-quality conditioning treatment?

My expensive moisturiser? My perfume even has a French name. The thongs, though. Giving the game away.

Her little room is at the back of the clinic, away from patients with actual problems. It has an Officeworks desk and a pot with a fake plant in it. I take note of the tissue box. The air is hot and still and it lodges in the back of my nose. I sit on a black couch. It's too low to the ground so I kind of perch there and don't ask if I can move to the chair instead, in case this is a test. I'm easygoing. I can adapt to all kinds of couches.

My new therapist folds her hands over a notepad in her lap. I think about how I chose her because the centre's website said she was a specialist in anxiety and psychosis. I am also a specialist in anxiety and psychosis, but in the other way, where they sometimes try to kill me.

'How are you?' she asks.

'I'm okay.' My head is currently attached to my body. I am not crying or screaming, not thinking about how I might die. I try to sit more upright. My shirt pulls against my stiff back.

I won't tell her this, but I dread starting over from scratch. With each new therapist, there's the Beginning Again. There is so much to say. So many scabs to pick. I wish I had prerecorded a little intro video. I try to remember every single thing at once. I want her to somehow realise both how deadly serious my mental illness is and how capable and fine I am.

She smiles. Her PhD testamur in clinical psychology beams at me from the wall. 'What can I do for you?'

I don't want to waste this one chance to get the order right. With previous therapists, I've started with the wrong thing and we have fixated on that thing and never even got to the real parts. I've spent a year talking to a therapist about How Was Work? and

What Are The Kids Up To? because they were the first things I mentioned and I couldn't ever figure out how to shift the course of the conversation.

'I'm very ... tired,' I say.

'Hm,' she says.

'So tired.'

'Have you seen a psychologist before?'

'Yes. Lots. And psychiatrists.'

'What have you seen them for?'

I want to say: misplaced optimism. But instead I just go, 'You know. Brain stuff.' Run-of-the-mill. I'm totally-fine-and-normal. Actually, I don't even need to be here, sorry for wasting your time, I'll just leave.

She says, 'Can you tell me about your family? Who do you live with?'

She does what psychologists do with new patients, which is to draw a family tree and make notes next to everyone. She underlines a few names. Those people would hate to know their names were underlined, which is one of the little joys you get from going to therapy.

'And what would you say is the main reason you're here today?'

I notice that the room is just a space partitioned off from the hallway; the top of the wall doesn't meet the ceiling. I wonder if the people in the waiting area can hear me. What will they think? *That's not a good enough reason to be anxious. That's not real trauma. First-World problems! Someone should take away your children!*

'Anxiety,' I say.

She makes a note.

I search for words to explain that it's not *just* anxiety. I mean, it *is* anxiety, but it's the kind where everything else about your life is all bound up in it. It's like a room full of mouse traps. It's like the dream about going to school in your undies and everyone looking at you, except you're also all the people looking at you, a hall of mirrors of you looking at yourself in your undies and pushing yourself into your own locker. It's like being trapped in jelly and also being allergic to jelly.

I want to say, I'm anxious, but all the time. I'm anxious, but *for reasons*.

'It's more than just anxiety,' I explain to this new therapist. I use words I've had to learn so doctors will take me seriously. 'I feel dissociated. I have intrusive thoughts.'

She makes notes.

'And my obsessive-compulsive behaviours are heightened lately. I'm, uh ...' I remember I'm wearing mascara and not the waterproof kind. A beginner's mistake. 'I'm not feeling good.' My voice cracks but I think I've got away with it.

She says, 'I understand.' Her tone is frank but empathetic and it strikes a tendon behind my ribs. Heat brews there. Don't cry in front of the new therapist. Make a joke!

'Just covering all my bases.' I wave my hands like an anxiety larrikin.

She books me in for three more sessions and I'm relieved she thinks I'm good/bad enough for her to see again. I like her. She won't let me get away with nonsense. I smile politely and thank her for her time. At the front counter I banter with the receptionist and decline a receipt. I pop a few dollars in the charity box. I step back to let an elderly patient through the door before me. The sun is out. A soft wind blows my clean hair into my face.

In the car, I flick open the vanity mirror and study myself. Make-up has collected at the corners of my eyes. Carefully selected tinted lip balm has something stuck in it. My skin aches from smiling.

I adjust my sunglasses. I reach into my chest and touch the hot stones that live there. Onwards.

Symptoms persist for a substantial period of time*

Where do mental illness stories begin?

Mine starts at three years old in the kitchen my parents had renovated, sitting on their suite of wicker furniture with those cushions every 1980s white family had, decorated in pussy willow and orange smudges. I had realised I would eventually die, which must have been shortly after my cat, Brutus, did die, and that fear just continued on with a vengeance until the present and, I assume, future. I had small fat hands that I forced into fists and plunged into the gaps between the cushions, feeling that I must, somehow, secure myself to the world in case I flew right off and into space. My body was so tense. Tiny knees locked, teeth clenched, determined to remain consciously and deliberately alive.

---

* Each chapter of this book begins with the clinical or technical definition of an aspect of life with mental illness. You'll see, I hope, what a tremendously poor job they do of offering any insight whatsoever to the lived experience.

It starts in other parts of the space-time continuum. There it is, on the afternoon my grandpa wrote that he had *absolutely reached the length of my tether* and then he was dead. And a hundred years before that, when a long-ago uncle blew his face off in a wheatfield and his little sister watched his flesh pulse until it stopped. It starts when several different long-ago uncles were admitted to the Parkside Lunatic Asylum and tried to die there. It starts when my grandmother checked and triple-checked her very first power point, knowing in her heart that if she didn't, her house would burn to the ground.

But, mostly, my mental illness story begins one night in 2001, in a California bungalow in a beachside suburb of Melbourne.

I had my first inkling of psychosis on an afternoon a few months earlier at the Adelaide UniBar. At the time I was living with my grandparents and working as a database developer, which was a job I had acquired through nepotism and did not understand. I had my own office with a big window. Because I didn't know how to be a database developer, and was generally an arsehole, I took long early lunches and walked down to Adelaide University, where my friends were all studying. We would get chips and gravy, play pool, and smoke cigarettes indoors and drink schooners of good local beer and flirt with engineering students. On this particular day a band played. As the hours ticked by, people came and went. And someone had weed. (Let's be honest: being Adelaide, someone usually had weed.)

Adelaide Uni in 2001 was like a Sally Rooney novel. Sandstone buildings by a lazy river, beautiful people touching fingertips under willow trees. I fell in love with a different person every day. I snuck into philosophy lectures and sat in quadrangles and wore low-cut shirts. One day I arrived to a circus already in full swing, with free camel rides and fairy floss. We got high, and an actual clown made us balloon animals in the sun. I think. I'm pretty sure.

The thing about a long afternoon at the uni bar, rotating through several groups of people, was you had to have a cone with each of them. Someone would swing by after a lecture and you'd pack a pipe. When they left, someone else would turn up and you'd pack another. And in Adelaide there was no nonsense about chopping your grass with tobacco; it went green into the cone and that's how it went into your blood, too.

This one afternoon I had been sitting out on the balcony for quite a few hours, pilfering snacks from the vending machine and passing the pipe around. Maybe it was three o'clock. I was, frankly, fucking baked.

I guess I decided four hours was long enough and I should probably go back to work. You must understand, I was awful. I remember I was wearing knee-high boots with heels and trying to navigate the cobbled laneways behind the Art Gallery as they swam away from me. The city was bright and mobile. Buildings moved like trees in the wind. You know the last stage of the TV show *A*mazing*? That's what getting back to the office was like: a sick, hilarious obstacle course.

When I finally arrived, I collapsed into my chair, looked around for more food and realised the floor in my office was writhing. Tiny brown bodies flexing in the fluorescent light. Hundreds of them. A living brown carpet.

I wasn't scared – just annoyed and confused. I had work to do! Database stuff!

At that moment, my boss entered. I have no idea what he said. But I stood up from my chair, pointed at his face and yelled, 'Look at these fucking rats!'

For a few days after that, rightfully unemployed, I just sat on my grandparents' porch. From there, I could see from the smokestacks at Torrens Island to the steamers coming up Gulf St Vincent. All the busy industry. People in motion. I couldn't understand them and the way they also existed out in the world. My same world. It seemed so far away.

When I managed to peel myself away from the porch and start moving again, there was a trip-wire inside me. A trap had been set. Strange, unhinged, exposed. Brain rattling, I would walk down to the bus stop and wait for the metal capsule to take me to the sandstone grounds of the uni. Other days, I sat in the death-quiet of my grandparents' kitchen and played chequers with my grandfather, whose fingers were too clumsy to pick up the pieces. I was always contending with something that wasn't there: a flash of light, movement in my peripheral vision, an invisible friend calling my name. I felt a catastrophic vulnerability.

Unfortunately, the chaos was outside, too. A September night: I was on my nanna's floral couch, tapping away on the internet (I had run a phone cord from the kitchen, down the stairs and into my laptop). My grandparents had already gone to bed. The TV was on. I don't know what I was watching except that suddenly it was something different, something inexplicable and bizarre. I remember trying to fit it into my brain, which I had cracked. I tried to wake my nanna, to explain that a plane had crashed into a building, to beg her to confirm it was real. All night I watched – we all did, of course – and the next day I went bleary-eyed back to the uni bar, where every TV played the same footage again and again. Smokestacks, only not.

At the time, I had been planning an adventure. I'd paid for a one-way ticket to Heathrow and was planning to live in the UK, writing stories and listening to bands from Sheffield and doing cocaine. On 13 September 2001, I got a refund on my flights and bought instead a ticket on the Overland, the old train that would take me cross-country to where my family now lived in Melbourne.

I was nineteen and my parents had become distant and peculiar to me. I scoured the ads and moved into a share house: a bungalow with a tree in the front garden and a bay window. My housemates were three dudes in their twenties who liked to party. I feel ancient saying it like that, but they did.

'Do you do drugs?' they asked when they interviewed me, their eyes narrowed.

I wasn't sure which answer they wanted. 'Yes?' I said, in a way that could become, 'No?'

It was a beautiful house, with its verandah and its peppercorn tree and its leadlight. I found a spot under a weeping branch and sat in a wicker chair and pretended to write in a Moleskine. I stretched out on the grass and looked at the sky and thought about what a very, very long time I had ahead of me in which to do everything.

I didn't own anything so I slept on a mattress on the floor. My room was bright and otherwise unfurnished. I found a metal clothes frame in hard rubbish, draped a few dresses over a single coathanger. I didn't have a lot of money, but the refund on my flights covered bond and the first month's rent. I was sure a job would materialise by the time the next month rocked around. I could type fast and hold a conversation, and that had always been enough.

The mattress was hard. I lay on it and rolled cigarettes and watched the way the sunlight jumped at the cornices. Each day the three guys went to their city jobs and I sat under the wooden pergola in the backyard and tried to blow smoke rings around vine fronds. I lay on the couch and watched DVDs from their small collection. I went online and ordered *Shrek*, *Empire Records* and *10 Things I Hate About You* and put them on the shelves because it was my house, too.

The lease belonged to a guy who, at the time, seemed a million years older than me but might have been twenty-six. Experienced, wise, well-lived. Let's call him Simon. He had an iconic electronica tattoo, which I recognised because my ex-boyfriend had forced me to listen to his late-night hard trance DJ sessions. Simon and I saw eye to eye on nothing at all, but sometimes he would roll a joint and drop into the Bunnings outdoor setting next to me and talk about what a great dancer he was. Simon threw a party and I met a new guy, hours into a puddle made of every mattress and blanket in the house. He seemed like a mess and I seemed like a mess, so I liked him. His eyes were pretty.

One night – a weeknight, which in that house was largely indiscernible from the weekend – some guys came around for a few drinks. Maybe there were eight of us, sitting in a circle of chairs under the pergola. Someone pulled out a bong made of red glass. When it got around to me, I pulled hard. Smoke lodged in my throat. I coughed, coughed again. Passed it along to the next person, coughing until my eyes watered. We'd all been there, though – greened out. I coughed and laughed and coughed, embarrassed.

But after a few minutes, something was different. Their voices were far away, dreamlike. Then I was. My brain was a bit to the right of my body. Then on the ceiling. I was inside and outside the house at once. When I moved my hands, bright shadows trailed behind them.

Fuck.

Fuck, fuck. Run. RUN.

Which one of me should run?

I called an ambulance. Sitting on the floor, phone cord wound around my wrist. Banging the keypad. Numbers, numbers. I remember the way all these guys were standing in the kitchen, watching me doing it. Screaming into the phone: SOMETHING IS WRONG. Howling. Shrieking. Strangers looking sideways at each other: check out the crazy chick. All their faces melting together. Six or eight or ten guys with one face, sliding into the kitchen tiles.

Then I was lucid again, briefly. 'Did I call an ambulance?' I said.

Most of them laughed nervously, but Simon was fuming.

'What the fuck did you do?' he shouted, his spit landing on my cheek. 'You fucking idiot – there are *drugs in the house*.'

One of the other guys: 'They won't send the police.'

Simon paced back and forth across the kitchen. As I watched, his body shimmered and glitched. 'They will. The police will fucking come.' He grabbed the phone from me, hands twitching, and mashed the keypad. Then I was on the floor. Brain like glue.

'Hey,' he said into the receiver. Something is wrong, something is wrong. 'My friend called an ambulance. As a joke. Yeah. Yeah, can you cancel it? Great.'

'Ha ha,' went someone.

I can't, I can't. Something is wrong.

'Get her into bed,' said someone else.

They bundled me into Simon's double. He got in with me, pressed his forehead hard against mine. 'You can't do shit like that,' he said. I felt the heartbeat under his skin against my heartbeat.

'Why is my phone ringing?' I whispered. 'Can someone get it?'

'It's not ringing,' Simon said. 'No one is calling you.'

But the sound went on. For hours, my phone. Ringing from somewhere inside my head.

I didn't think you could cancel an ambulance. I thought they had to send one, just to be sure. But no one came. My forehead melded into Simon's forehead. We were two aliens in a bed. A man cried out from the doorway on another plane of existence. At one point I might have heard sirens, but it was impossible to know whether they were real, or a tune from the mariachi band I was hallucinating.

The next weekend we took a friend's white Commodore out along the Ring Road towards Ballarat for a bush doof (which feels like 90s vernacular, but I'm told kids still go to them). I don't remember exactly where it was. I don't know what the weather was like, or who was there with us. I remember my very new boyfriend's hand in mine and the fact that he had brought with him a camping stove and the intention of making pancakes in the morning.

I remember I was nervous – of being outside of myself again, of flying off the world, of losing my grip.

When the sun went down, we sat in the back of another friend's Volvo and I unwrapped a little yellow pill from a foil packet. I thought, I'll only take half, given the situation with the weed and the ambulance. That should be safe. Just half, and I'll have a good time and won't freak out. It was the second time I had ever taken ecstasy. Outside the car, a friend twirled fire pois and another friend danced next to him in the dust.

I waited.

'Going okay?' asked my boyfriend.

'Yep.' Waiting. Still inside my body. Waiting. Around us, people laughed and danced and touched.

A pot of adrenaline collected in my belly. I breathed sharp and fast.

'Still okay?' he said. His mouth moved out of time with his voice.

The world pushed back from my eyes, grew further away. My peripheral vision clouded, then blackened. 'Oh, fuck,' I said to whoever was there, 'it's happening again.' Then I was running, fuck, it's happening again, fuck, how do I take my brain out, flip the latch, flick the switch, drain the poison. Sir, have you seen my face, please point me in the direction of my home universe, fuck. Run. Flee. Sprint. Panic. Up the hill, feet in the mud, grab the camping stove, THROW IT.

Then it was into the car. Someone shoved me. Me, my body, a combination of the two. Together and separate like skin on fruit. Blink. Who's touching me? Hands off, roll over, finger the condensation on the window, am I dying, am I dying? Okay but AM I? DYING? Take me to the first-aid tent, the tent, behind the toilets, the thick brown sludge running out down the hill through the trees into the river, take me to the – fuck FUCK you guys FUCK how do you oh Jesus fuck tranquillise me, put me down, get a brick and bang it into my skull until the bones break why is it shit oh fuck let's

sleep WAKE

take me to the first-aid tent, behind the toilets near the trance stage look behind the mouths moving and the colours the masks and the dirt, after that there's a man in a white uniform and he'll know how to FUCK FUCK JESUS stop the organs from being vomited out of my throat stop the tips of my toes shooting off stop the skin melting take me to the first-aid tent TAKE ME TO THE TENT FUCK

fuck fuck fuck fuck fuckfuckfuckfufufufuckk

get out of my way don't breathe just force the air in grab it fistfuls of it shove it drink it punch it you will suffocate TO DEATH run and fall and sprint and cry and push your body out of the walls of your other body, like take your spiritual body and mesh it into the air and leave the other one behind, why are you dancing, scuff your toes in the hard dirt and fall against it, where is the gate, where is the white car, how do I get safe now, drop your head into the back-seat mattress and someone touches your hair again, touch it, comfort me, BUT DID I? did I die?

At a guess, this went on for about twelve hours. For the last few, I dipped in and out of a kaleidoscopic blackness in the back of this station wagon; each time I woke again, I was amazed I hadn't died. The morning was crisp, I think. There were birds.

In the forest, bark peeled from the trees and crashed into the undergrowth. My boyfriend did make pancakes on his camping stove and I ate them. I touched the silk fronds of a psychedelic decoration shaped like a spider. All the portaloos had overflowed. The light was soft and grey. When I looked at my hands, they were someone else's hands.

After we had packed up the car we drove to a friend's house at the foot of the Dandenongs. He had a pool and people swam in it to take the edge off their comedowns. I couldn't stop shaking. I had a steaming hot shower, hoping to wash away the disconnection. I ate a packet of Twisties. I looked up at the mountains and worried I would shoot right into them.

Simon drove us home. Sitting in the front room of this share house where I lived, I watched my fingertips melt into the floor. The air around me vibrated and glimmered. Every part of it seemed alive and heavy, like undiluted cordial. Alive and heavy and slow and unfamiliar: a film I'd been cast in without realising.

A couple of weeks after the night in the Volvo, I had a job interview. It was in the city. I caught the tram from my place, under the St Kilda Road plane trees. Every time I looked up too quickly, parts of the world exploded. If I listened too hard, voices became visible and full of colours. Music played where there was none. People's faces contorted, grew grotesque and frightening. I had on a pencil skirt and a shirt with a collar, and I sat at the front near the tram driver. My breath was a tied balloon in my chest. Couldn't deflate it. Couldn't inflate it. I felt I was breathing carbon dioxide.

Hands trembling, I stepped off the tram into the cacophony of Collins Street and lit a cigarette. I tried to blend in. The interview was five-storeys up in a room no bigger than a toilet cubicle. The recruiter must have told me all about the job but I didn't hear a word of it; I couldn't stop watching the way a plant on the table was moving. Arms or tentacles. At the end of the conversation we shook hands, and I didn't remember anything he had said, but I got the job. For three nights, from 9 pm to 4 am, I sat in a Brunswick warehouse and typed barcode numbers into a spreadsheet. I don't know how I got there. I don't remember why I got fired except that there was an incident with a meat pie.

These breaks in conscious thought got worse. I would be doing something completely ordinary, then switch out of it. (I understand now that this is dissociation – disconnecting from a sense of identity. Being cut off from my self.)

One afternoon I was standing with my boyfriend on a street corner in Chinatown. We had been out for yum cha with his parents. It was getting into late spring, which in Melbourne means air littered with allergens and bird shit. It was hot, noisy and crowded.

'How much do you like me?' I asked him, love-struck and insecure. 'Out of ten?'

As the words left my mouth, reality caved in. In an instant, I was out of my body. A mouth that was not my mouth shouted, *I need to get out of here*, while my boyfriend pulled me into him. I will never forget the cool sharpness of his voice in that chaos: *Breathe like me. Breathe like I am.* His ribs moved against my back. Slow in, slow out. Eventually he barrelled me into a taxi and we took it back to his parents' house. It was the day George

Harrison died; we listened to 'While My Guitar Gently Weeps' until my heart beat slowed.

For a while I tried to keep doing everything more or less as normal. I went to parties at a replica medieval castle, which was a tourist attraction and wedding-reception venue by day and filthy drug den by night. I slept on the mattress on the floor in the share house where I lived. I went to clubs and bars and house parties and pubs. I caught a train then a tram to St Kilda, sitting opposite a large dog wearing a man's shirt; I am almost certain this happened.

It was exhausting to pretend to be fine. A night with friends drained every drop of energy from my body and brain; afterwards, alone, I would flicker in and out of the self I recognised. It could last all night, waiting to lock back into place.

One afternoon, perhaps a month later, I went with my boyfriend and his parents to their friends' place in the hills for a barbecue. It was far, along an unsealed road. After lunch, this boyfriend and I sat at the top of the undulating back garden. I felt quite calm, even with my brain outside of my skull. The valley might have been beautiful. Birds might have been singing. I pulled my knees to my chest.

'What are you thinking about?' he asked.

I said, 'I'm going to die soon.'

He sat up straight. 'Why?'

'I don't know; I just know that I am.'

A few days after that, he broke up with me. And fair enough. Imagine being a twenty-year-old guy who just wants to put his dick in some girl and it turns out she's 90 per cent existential delusion.

I was afraid to be on my own. I felt I needed this now-ex-boyfriend – he had been there at the doof when it all went pear-shaped, so he was the ticket to getting better again. I would catch a train and a tram to the house on the other side of town where he lived with his parents and wait for them to go out so I could knock on his window. Sex was an easy way to lower his guard. It was a way to take charge of what seemed totally out of my control. He would relent, and we'd fuck, and I'd feel a bit human again. Connected. Objectively still in existence. Then he would try to see me out and I would refuse to go. I sat in his parents' garden and yelled that if he wanted me to leave, he could call the police. When his mum returned she would try to talk me through it gently – Anna, I know you're sad, but there will be other people who care about you – and then increasingly forcefully – Anna, I know you're having a hard time but you need to go home. I had become frightening and unstable. Nowhere seemed right, least of all the space inside my head.

I felt, in the months after what I later learned was a psychotic break and before I told anyone what had happened, that I was totally unreal. A ghost. I had died without realising. I would spend a lucid minute connected to my surroundings, then switch into dissociation. My brain protected itself from itself, sliding more and more layers of glass between me and the world. I was not safe out there. I would be hurt, assaulted, abandoned, kidnapped, murdered. My only refuge was to burrow deep into my mind and watch life orbit around it.

According to the rules that must be applied rigidly

This isn't exactly where it began, of course. Like most people living with complex mental illness, hindsight locates it. Mine had been there for years, dormant and not-so-dormant, tickling the synapses it intended to ruin. But there was nothing so extraordinary about my childhood, besides the unfathomable fact of being alive.

Mental illness often runs in families. Nature versus nurture and all that. Clinically, some illnesses can be hereditary or come with genetic predisposition. Others are made more likely by the experience of being raised by someone with mental illness. Then there is a third dimension: family folklore.

My nanna – Betty, a wholly grandmotherly name – taught me all I needed to know about existing anxiously in the world. She was a maestro of magical thinking. Everything in her house had a particular assigned meaning and associated requirements. If she managed it all precisely, nothing 'bad' would happen (the 'bad' that might happen was unspecified but likely included the death of loved ones, her cats going missing and being embarrassed where her church friends could see her).

I watched her do this with both fascination and recognition. Aspects of comfort-seeking and control resonated in my still-developing brain. Nanna and I seemed to vibrate at the same natural frequency (broad panic). But while I remember her fussing, I learned my most important lessons in the back of their old Datsun, waiting and waiting and waiting for Nanna to perform her rituals of protection.

Gramps and I would sit in the carport in the red car. He was noisy like an old house; his throat groaned and his bones banged in the wind and his hearing aid screeched. Every few minutes he smacked his false teeth together, and when he had finished doing that he whistled like a tame cockatoo.

The radio was always tuned to the national broadcaster, and the footy would be on. The footy always seemed to be on when Gramps and I were in the car. Even when it wasn't, the spirit of it came through somehow.

This one day Gramps and I had been waiting in the car for forty-five minutes for Nanna to get ready.

To pass the time, I told him about the new Texta markers I was planning to buy once we made it to the shops. I had packed a wad of paper in my backpack so I could start drawing stories right away. He tried to listen to me and the footy at the same time, but it meant he couldn't understand either, so he just smiled widely instead. I told him I thought he did some good gardening earlier.

His teeth went *clack pop*.

He liked me, my gramps, I think.

The day was cold. Their house was at the top of a hill and the weather rushed in from the road and under the carport and spun around there. It darted through the gaps in the old car's windows and heating vents. I looked out the back windscreen at the garden, where lorikeets gathered in the birdbath, their feathers bristling in the wind.

I told Gramps about them – how they looked like they were laughing – and his teeth went *slurp glop*.

When we had been waiting for more than an hour, I asked him straight out: *Is Nanna coming?* It was just, the Textas were so urgent, and I wanted to go to the bookshop as well, and what could be taking so long?

He said, *She's just checking.*

I looked up to the big window at the side of the house. I could see the reflection of the birds in the glass, and Nanna behind them. She wore a pink cardigan and a bright scarf with flowers on it, and her hair was sprayed into a tight nest. She was looking at the clothes iron. She picked it up and touched her hand on the metal part, then put it down again. She flicked the switch on the wall. Then she picked up the iron and touched the metal again. Flicked the switch. Touched the iron. Flick. Touch.

Gramps's teeth went *blop gark.*

Nanna and Gramps lived in a split-level mid-century house on a corner block in the Adelaide foothills. It was exactly the way a grandparents' house was supposed to be: there was always a cake in the oven, ice creams in the freezer, a tin full of biscuits. In the sunken lounge room Nanna had a little bar heater and we played her *Keeping Up Appearances* VHS tapes until they grew indecipherably faded.

We spent perfect days there: cricket in the front garden, eating impossible pie and drinking Sno Top from Pizza Hut glassware, watching the footy on the ancient telly. My brother and I would turn over pieces of their slate wall and find a gecko and, separately, its squirming tail. At night I helped Nanna leave pieces of fruit for the possum that dined out on her garage roof, and in the mornings we fed fresh meat to a family of magpies who ate from her hand. Sometimes a koala came down from the hills and slept in the crook of their red gums. On hot summer nights, Nanna's covered pergola filled with orb weavers and all the ghostly webs strung up between them.

One time I ran away to their house for eight days. I remember how eight days seemed like the absolute limit for how long you could run away from home without being a bad guy. I brought a bag of clothes with me and told Nanna I was never going home again. It must have been the school holidays because every day we drove down the hill into town and went shopping. We had cakes for morning tea and Nanna bought me a new *The Baby-Sitters Club* book and Gramps clicked his teeth together. And each night Mum called and asked if I was coming home, and I said no. I can still feel the slim white plastic of Nanna's phone as I hung up the receiver, triumphant. Then Nanna performed the ritual of washing my feet with a warm face cloth, before giving me a plate of sliced green apples.

This is still 'home' to me: the fresh Adelaide air, the broad sky with a fingertip at every horizon. The warble of those big birds waiting on the brushed fence. Our house was only a kilometre down the road (everything in Adelaide is quite close together), but Nanna's house was a sanctuary. To get there, I literally had to walk through a national park, footsteps cracking the dry undergrowth, eyes scanning for snakes. It was deeply quiet – just rustling where rats fossicked, a blue-tongue lizard, the slap of bark stripped by parrots as it hit the ground. I would walk through the park and up the hill, and at the top I would get the spare key from under its rock and let myself in. Safety. Unreality made us comrades. My nanna taught me the language of insanity but she has never yelled at me, not once.

It makes sense, then, that she also featured in my earliest experience of sliding out of myself. I was in Mrs Gill's year two classroom. It was an ordinary day. I sat with the other kids, trying and failing to listen to whatever Mrs Gill was saying because I was thinking about how, at any moment, Mum would walk down the steps, open the door and tell me Nanna had died. I was absolutely certain this would happen.

The longer I stared and thought, the more frightened I became. Things started happening in my body. Mrs Gill's voice changed. The other kids got so loud it was like they were inside my ear canals. All this noise, a yelling-kid orchestra. I couldn't fit it all into my brain at once. I couldn't listen to the sounds the kids made and think about Nanna dying at the same time. With my actual eyes, I could see Mum in her nineties-lawyer pantsuit with a fresh perm. I could hear Mrs Gill telling me, *Anna, your mother is here to see you. Your nanna has died.* I thought of shouting to the other kids, the so-loud kids: My nanna has died, please stop talking!

'Shut up!' I yelled.

Then I thought (and I remember this very clearly, except I suppose I thought it in eight-year-old language), Holy shit, *how do* eyes *work*? It was the scariest thought I had ever had.

I leaped from my chair and ran. Out the door, around the toilets, along the corridor near the stairs, past the art classroom and into the playground. Heart pounding, legs pumping. *Why can I see? What does it mean?* I threw myself under the swings, plunged straight into the bark chips and stayed there, pushing my fists into my eye sockets until stars came.

That's where the memory ends. I assume someone came out to find me. That would become an ongoing source of embarrassment: another student being sent to fetch the crazy girl from wherever she was hiding today.

On that day, my nanna was only sixty-five and in extremely good health. She had not died. In fact, as I write this, she is ninety-seven and still has not died (Mum says she is too scared to). But I know it happened. Somewhere. Sometime. My memory of that day in Mrs Gill's classroom is a space-time echo. No one can prove otherwise.

This story begins in many places. I remember spending an afternoon in my great-grandmother's house, which was stacked with caged birds. The noise was immense. Budgerigar song clanged, notes thrown by blue and green and yellow feathers. Mice ransacked the bowls of seed and left trails of droppings across the lino. Nanna Greenslade couldn't see or hear by then, but she thrived in the cacophony of her aviaries. No one was brave enough to tell her about the mess, the smell. She had a Pekingese dog and her greatest fear was that she would die first and leave Tui behind (she did; the dog died a few months later).

Where Nanna Greenslade existed on a strict diet of narcissism and chaos, my nanna taught me to demand control. She always made sure everything was just right, lest some unspecified ill befall her. Quite often she cared for us overnight while Mum and Dad were away; before we went to sleep, she would close all the curtains and deadlock every door in the house, unlock them and deadlock them again. After Gramps died, in her grief, Nanna began to hear choirs in full voice in her empty house. One day, quite soon before she realised she could no longer live alone, she went to get the mail and just … stopped. Her legs wouldn't go another inch along the path. She pressed the button on her alert necklace and the ambulance came and took her to hospital. They scanned her brain, monitored her heart, checked her organ function, and found nothing. Fear had simply overwhelmed her.

And after her came another little girl, the best little girl. Bright, clever, pretty: my mum. These women have all been afraid, and they have passed along the fear like a baton.

The process of retaining information over time

Some of these memories are falsehoods. Not because I have set out to deceive you, but because memory is fallible and childhood is confusing. And yet the way I remember it has become the foundation of who I am as a person. Memory is unreliable, but it's also critical to forming a sense of identity.

Throughout our lives, but especially as children, we take in and store information that propels us through the rest of our existence. None of it is definitive. Memories that seem clear to us as adults are changed by many factors: the passing of years, trauma, injury, decay. Even the act of remembering distorts it; we recall and store a memory differently every time. Among our tools for developing our sense of self are fabrications, hearsay, things that happened in a dream and stuff that was actually on TV.

Here's how it works: you might be reading this book on a train or lying in bed or while making the kids' lunches or putting the cats out or, ideally, having someone else quietly read it to you. If you then imagine last night's dinner, what happens? You cast your mind back, right? You know those rissoles happened at a time before now. You *remember* (congratulations).

In 1985, Canadian psychologist Endel Tulving used the term 'mental time travel' to describe this phenomenon of being able to move back and forth in temporal memory. Humans can differentiate between an experience we're having now and one that happened in the past. Sometimes it hurts to remember, and sometimes it's joyful. Sometimes you were eating a finger bun with your nanna in a cafe, and other times your cat got run over. We use memory to sink into nostalgia, recount an old story, find understanding and look for answers.

This is a clever thing healthy brains do to keep us safe. We can use our knowledge of the past to help us plan for what might happen in the future, to predict dangers, to make decisions and to reinforce who we are. All of this is the rich tapestry of our lives and the many exciting and boring things we've done.

Mental time travel can happen in the other direction, too – most of us can imagine ourselves in a projected event. We can travel in our minds to something that hasn't happened yet. Sometimes that's helpful – we decide not to go to a crowded bar during a pandemic because we can imagine ending up on a ventilator. But it's also how we experience irrational or disordered fear, by seeing ourselves in a future in which we are in mortal danger, however unlikely it might be. That's why a kid in a perfectly normal classroom might be flung to an unknown date when she will find out her nanna has died.

If we're healthy, we slide through time, reflecting on the past and imagining the future without moving from our chair.

Our brains are designed to do this. It's a critical part of human development and a normal way to have the whole experience of a life. We take all this information and use it to create a portrait of ourselves. The narrative of us – the story of what happened and when – is how we understand who we are as people. We use these slices and pockets and crumbs of memory to form our identity. And, unlike our memories, our *identity* remains relatively fixed over the course of our lives.

Tulving says it comes from having an *autonoetic consciousness*: being 'self-knowing'. It's like a temporal sentience, the ability to mentally place ourselves at our friend Sally's eighteenth and perceive continuity. We know the person at the party was the 'same person' as our present-day self. Yesterday, today and tomorrow, I'm Anna, the person who features in all the memories I have. I went to school, had a favourite cat, stole a Snickers, bought a car, had a family, whatever. We have a built-in sense of how long ago life events happened. We know that 'now' is different from '1999'. It's how we can be sure that even though the specifics change, we're living a single life, one day at a time. We are here 'now' – everything else is before or after.

But it doesn't work like that for everyone.

The magic of mental time travel can be ruptured. The past can be forgotten, reshaped and restructured. A mother disappears from a memory and reappears in another, coming down the stairs to the classroom to deliver terrible news. In one version, she is smiling; in another, she frowns.

Or, we can become trapped in a past moment. We can mentally time travel to our greatest fears from the past and we can get lost there. Trauma draws fault lines between short- and long-term memory to the extent that it can be impossible to know when we are in time. Long-ago atrocities persist as newly created memories. As threats.

Sometimes, an illness rewires these processes. Instead of being fixed over our lifetime, our identity is formed and re-formed, inconsistent from one day to the next. It's pieced together from warped fragments, events that happened one way but were stored differently – a *dis*remembering. For some of us – for me – the tools available for creating self-identity are blunt. They manufacture misshapen building blocks and so the identity built with them is also distorted. Then we wear all of this malformed self as armour – protection from the very memories that created it. Anna, but a homebrand knock-off. Anna, but not exactly the same.

Something I think about often (along with people I miss, books I haven't yet read and names for future cats) is whether the verifiability of memory matters. Is it important that it didn't happen 'in reality', whatever that means? Our brains find it almost impossible to distinguish, at a physiological level, between what happens in our waking hours, dreams we have and lies we tell ourselves. This is the basis of many kinds of therapy: 'self-talk' – whether negative ('I'm bad at everything') or positive ('My parents did love me, actually') – can change our self-perception because our brain takes it at face value. The objectivity of an event doesn't change its impact on self-belief.

In her book *The Memory Illusion*, Dr Julia Shaw poses a thought experiment: if you woke one morning and couldn't remember anything you had ever done, thought or learned, would this person still be you? After all, memory is one of the most important tools we have for understanding our who, what, why, how. As she writes, 'if we begin to call our memory into question we are also forced to question the very foundations of who we are.'

When I started trauma therapy in my thirties, my psychologist asked me to write down the most distressing memories I had. 'How to narrow it down?' I said with a laugh (laughing about trauma is a great way to prove to your therapist how well you're doing). But, actually, it was simple. There was one that had always stuck out for me as the worst – easily the most traumatising – thing I could remember from my life.

It was a school day. I was nine, which means my brother was probably six and my sister four. She was so little, my sister. She sat on the steps that led from the hallway into the living room. My brother was holding a cup of tea he had just made. And I was shouting, shouting, shouting, because I couldn't find my shoes and so it was my fault our mother had just died on the couch.

That was the memory. Clear as anything.

I howled while I recounted this to my therapist. I felt the anguish of my dead mother deep in my psychic self like a marble.

Except, here is another version:

It was a school day. Morning. We were running late because someone couldn't find their shoes and now everything had gone tits up. My sister was wailing on the steps leading from the hallway into the living room. My brother had a cup of tea and he was holding it out to our mother and screaming: *Mum? MUM! WAKE UP!* and maybe I wasn't even there at all.

It was a school day. In the backyard, our cats were fighting and my brother was carrying a bowl of water to them. My sister was sitting on the steps leading from the hallway to the living room, talking about the costume she was supposed to wear to kindergarten in ten minutes. My mother was crying on the couch because she couldn't find her shoes and everything was hard and she had to do it all on her own, and I was melting into the floor.

It was a school day. No one had any shoes on. Every school shoe we owned had disappeared into thin air. My sister was sitting on the steps leading from the hallway to the living room, laughing because she was going to have to go to kindergarten in bare feet. My brother had a cup of tea and it rattled in its saucer when he slipped on the tiles. And I was shouting at the top of my lungs because I was going to get detention and our mother had just pretended to die on the couch.

This memory of Mum 'pretending to die' was fundamental to the way I thought about my childhood development. I had parroted it to every counsellor, psychologist and psychiatrist I had ever seen (many). Pointing to it like, *look here,* this is the singular explanation for my years of blaming myself for everything and crying when I see tiny puppies outside cafes. I have therapised myself. I am clever and cured.

But through the therapy, I realised I was a child using a child's memory to understand something immeasurably complex. My beautiful mum hadn't purposefully traumatised me out of some kind of malice. She was a woman under immense pressure, juggling her own bullshit in exactly the way I do now, which is to say one part having it under control and one part *sheer terror.* She'd lost the thread, just like I do. She had panicked, and I had understood that to mean she was dead/in danger/unable to take care of me/didn't love me.

It hadn't happened exactly the way I had remembered it. That is different from saying it had never happened, or that it was less traumatic or more traumatic. In reality, the lasting impact was as traumatic as I felt it was (and a quantifiable value for 'traumatic' is tricky – does it matter 'how traumatic' something is by someone else's measure, or only the degree of trauma we take away from it?). And it may have been this awful; the fact that I now understood the many ways it could have gone doesn't mean my first guess was untrue, either.

As the therapeutic process went on, the picture I had stored changed over and over; sometimes I wasn't even in it. By the time we finished the session, I could think about my memory and feel no emotion at all. The marble had disintegrated.

I was bereft. Not sad – I was glad to be rid of the hurt that it carried – but adrift. Without that memory, the one that had done such heavy lifting to shape my understanding of myself, how could I know I was me? What else could I blame?

When we travel through time to these moments, we reinforce things we feel we know about ourselves. That's what makes trauma such a seductive and dangerous tool for our identity. We can craft a whole self around events that a) absolutely never should have happened, or b) never *did* happen, drawing on the negative to support what we believe (we are damaged, we are broken, we are worthless). Trauma doesn't distinguish between past and present in the way other memory does; as Meera Atkinson writes in *Traumata*: 'Those who are significantly affected by it are trapped in a temporal whirl they can neither comprehend nor control.'

In my own life, it's why I fear the dangers that may lie ahead; past trauma teaches me that the future has trauma in it, too. In the most ordinary circumstances – buying cheese, watching TV, taking my kids to school – I can, in an instant, be gripped by a feeling of real danger. Proper danger, as though my life is at risk. It's not the gruyere that's attacking me but the past, reminding me to be afraid. American sociologist Kai T. Erikson writes that, during these periods of hyper-arousal, 'evidence that the world is a place of unremitting danger seems to appear everywhere'.

A person who hasn't experienced any trauma might watch TV and feel no peril whatsoever. They might know from past experience that their eyes will dry out, or that they like shows where a man dates thirty women at once, or they might recall a time they watched TV with their sister in their childhood living room. But trauma and illness are there with us on the couch. And while no one responds in exactly the same way – for some, it is closed into a lockbox and tucked away in dissociated memory – for many, those recollections become the most prominent. Certain types of mental illness cause a person to prioritise negative, upsetting memories. When this person casts her mind back, the trauma may be all she finds – even if many, many other events took place.

So, okay. My nanna did not die that day I sat in Mrs Gill's classroom, but it doesn't matter. I can still remember the sensory experience of Mum coming down the stairs to tell me about it, the great loss I had already internalised, the calcification of my fear. The self I am today has pockets for all kinds of memories. Even if I recognise the events never happened, the foundations they created for me are real. They taught me what to believe. The journey to find them on my mental time travel highway requires only the smallest of detours.

The person finds it difficult to control the worry

I was a forceps delivery. This is something psychiatrists ask you in adulthood: Did you have a traumatic birth? We are so marked before we even have consciousnesses in which to retain the memory (our bodies keep the score). Having had me yanked against my will from the safety of her womb, Mum was promptly whisked into surgery for reasons I have never fully understood, cloaked as they are by mythology. Haemorrhage? Retained placenta? Nerves? I don't know, but every year on my birthday, Dad reminds me of how he stood outside the operating theatre, holding his newly delivered daughter and waiting to see if his wife would consequently die.

He played 'A Little Ray of Sunshine' by Axiom when I was born, my dad. His enormous heart and his cognitive dissonance.

My parents named me Michal, and then a few weeks later named me Anna instead. Identity crises can sometimes be very obvious.

I had entered an extraordinarily easy existence. My parents were white-collar professionals from working-class families and we lived in a bungalow in the eastern suburbs of Adelaide, where we had a big garden and a mulberry tree, and every year a daddy-long-legs hatched a brood of baby-long-legs in the corner of my bedroom. But there was an undercurrent of something else: to put herself through law school, Mum had worked in a children's mortuary; her job was to prepare their small bodies for autopsy. I had one set of grandparents; the others were dead. Eventually I had a little brother (Jono), and then a little sister (Julia). We had a surprising number of cats (seven).

Three days a week, my brother and I went to child care. Mrs Penny was the head of our centre and she was terrifying. She had many rules, and the threat of punishment loomed large. We were expected to know the words to all the songs, remember what time it was, play outside but not too loudly. My brother was in another room with rows of hammocks attached to the wall, where 'the babies' napped like pupae on a leaf. Once a week, we were served a huge plate of stewed apple, and if you ate it all, a splat of floury custard was the reward. It was like being in a Roald Dahl novel. I worried constantly about getting into trouble with Mrs Penny; she had a knack for somehow choosing the exact moment you were doing something wrong to check in on you.

In the afternoons and on weekends, Mum and Dad walked us to the park to visit the duck pond. There was an island in the middle where the broody ones went; I remember the glossy emerald heads of drakes as they attempted to mount their smaller, duller counterparts. There were white runners and mallards and sometimes a loud grey goose. Dad showed us how to feed them bread from a bag, before we knew that it was bad for them.

My brother and I wore pixie hats Mum had sewed. Jono had a shrill little laugh and white-gold hair.

After the ducks were fed, Dad pushed me on the swing and sang about a girl on a flying trapeze.

Nearby, Mum's worry brewed. 'David, be careful,' she hissed. 'She'll fall.'

Years later, I was 'running' (walking) the school's cross-country race in that same park. I was probably fourteen. I made it to the pond, where there were still ducks, and I stopped. All the breath was pulled from my body like a clown's infinite handkerchief. I sat on the grass near the chain-link fence and I cried, and I did not understand why.

A degree of anxiety is clinically normal. Necessary, even. Our evolutionary seeds still push us to fight, flee or freeze. Is there a bear coming? Run from it. Is the food source disappearing? Kill the animal taking it. The modern-day problems we face are different, but the 'lizard brain' response still exists.

Anxiety is simply a bodily response to a threat, a feeling of worry, stress or unease in a given situation. Often – usually – it's a reasonable reaction to something external. Maybe we're not sure where our next meal is coming from. Maybe we're diving with sharks. Maybe we're meeting our internet boyfriend for the first time. All of these situations create understandable worry or fear. The anxious feelings are not clinically significant.

This is partly an issue of vocabulary. An anxiety *disorder* (or a 'condition', as some mental health organisations more palatably label them now) is a different thing altogether. Some of the feelings are the same, but their causes, intensity, duration and frequency are not. A person with generalised anxiety disorder might feel a level of nervousness all the time. *All* the time. Anxious being at work, seeing a friend, sitting on a bench, going to the bathroom. Some people live with a constant underlying dread that spikes in peak anxious times but never completely goes away.

(It's me – I'm 'some people'.)

When I was seven I went to a Remembrance Day service with my dad. The joke is, I looked so distressed that a newspaper journalist thought I must have been moved by the ceremony and asked if he could take my picture among the poppies. There was a full page in the Sunday paper, and on Monday all the kids in my class brought in the clipping for show-and-tell.

Mum's way of being anxious was different from Nanna's. She also checked the iron, and that the doors were locked, and assumed the house would burn down, but she spent a lot more of her time focusing her fear on the people she loved. Every time someone went outside, they put themselves at risk of gruesome and permanent death. I wasn't allowed to go to the shops, or catch the bus, or walk home from school. To Mum's mind, every person on the street was a would-be rapist, murderer, kidnapper, pervert or Liberal voter, and if I so much as brushed past them I would perish.

Dad ran in tandem. He tells a story of walking with my brother to the postbox up the road. Jono shot off ahead and around the corner, and when Dad rounded it himself a moment later, my brother was gone. Abducted. Except he wasn't, of course; he was hiding in a bush as a joke. But this was how our household operated: constantly jumping to the worst-case scenario, the news headline, the terrifying phone call.

And, worse, there was no sense of relief when it turned out things were fine. Nothing was ever really fine – it was just fine *for now*. Respite on the journey to inevitable devastation.

I don't remember the word 'anxiety' being used in my childhood. I have the impression it was only popularised much later, probably to sell mindfulness apps. But Mum explained it in other ways, telling me I had 'nervous energy' – my feet always wanted to move, my shoulders fizzed with bubbles. In an enclosed space, I felt a sudden need to get out. I developed specific fears, most of which involved being trapped somewhere: I refused to catch elevators, wouldn't hide in cupboards, even hated being in the shower. Whenever a door closed, I felt waves of non-specific worry about being stuck. I needed to get out; I couldn't get out.

Mum had words for her own anxiety. She is afraid of heights – she would magically appear from anywhere to pull us back from a ledge or a railing or a first-floor window. She could be hundreds of kilometres away and still know we were about to plummet to our deaths from a low step. She taught me about the bodily sensations of anxiety. Being in a high place made a sharp pain shoot up the back of her legs. I started to look for that in my own fears. Was pain shooting up the back of my legs? Was that how I'd know when I was afraid? *Was I being afraid correctly?*

On her low days, she would explain she felt 'flat', 'stressed' or 'a bit worn out'. I took all of this language and tried to apply it to my own experience. My teacher would say, 'Anna, why haven't you done your work?' and I would say, 'I'm just a bit worn out.'

My parents worked a lot. Dad had left the public service to start his own business, and Mum was billing in six-minute blocks as a lawyer. When they weren't working, they were fixated on all the terrible things that could happen to us. They must have done other things – surely they read books, saw friends, maybe caught the occasional movie – but to my child self, these felt like their only modes: absent or everywhere.

A little spring of fear opened in me. Everything would be fine – I'd be doing my phonics or reader or arithmetic at my table with the other kids – and then part of my head would explode. Flicker. Bang. Without realising I was doing it, I would be on my feet, heart in my throat, out the door. All of my feelings were new then, and I struggled, as children do, to name them. But I knew the way my body felt: full of warm milk ('happy'); like someone was pushing on my shoulders ('sad'); exploding ('anxious'). Sometimes my body told me to *RUN QUICKLY RUN GO* and I did, with words and colours colliding in my head.

I became too loud and too quiet. I disrupted the other children, picked my nose, cried, daydreamed. I fretted about trying to do the right thing but could never seem to actually do it. I was constantly distracted, drifting off and catastrophising. School reports and letters home to my parents had a common thread: *Anna could achieve great things if she just put her mind to it.*

The trouble was, my mind was full of other junk. I thought deeply about everything (which was, as a child: television, space, cats, making cakes, *The Little Mermaid* and the inevitable day my parents would be dead). I took reams of paper from Dad's home-office stash and wrote about the animals in the garden, and little girls who were afraid of things, and people going away on planes forever. I drew pictures of people with heart-shaped heads, and other pictures of people with an X for each eye. Adults sighed when they saw them. They said, 'Draw something *nice*.'

Nearly every day, I got sent out of class. I sat in the atrium on a hard chair and thought about flying off into space. I noticed the burning in my arms, and the way my heart flipped behind my ribs. A flat rage lay inside me. It was a blunt and determined fear. An impotent fury. I didn't know how to soothe it. People got angry. Teachers, parents, librarians. Why couldn't I just be normal, do normal things, act like a normal kid? I was so burdensome. Always in the way. I made my parents stressed and agitated. I felt it had to be my fault that I was *so hard to get along with*.

I let it all get inside me and grow like barnacles on my skeleton.

I tried hard to do what I thought they wanted, these abstract *live up to your potentials* and *don't waste your opportunities*. I finished all the new school year's writing exercises on the first day. I borrowed long books from the library – *Watership Down* and *The Power of One* – and opened them where I knew my teachers could see me. I read so much and so quickly that adults accused me of *pretending* to read; one day Mum took my book (*Matilda*, of course) from my hands and quizzed me, to check if I was faking it. I heard the word 'precocious' a lot (and, obviously, learned to spell it).

I did ballet, art classes, writing workshops, played piano. I was in the advanced maths class, a special principal's research group, an after-school computing club and two choirs. My parents, busy with work during school holidays, sent me to tennis camp, cricket camp, basketball camp. I wrote stories and made them into little illustrated books. I started a neighbourhood newsletter and 'designed' it in ClarisWorks. I put an ad in the paper for a penpal club – for a dollar, I would match a kid with another kid for letter-writing purposes (I kept all the best penpals for myself but lost interest before I ever wrote to them). As I got older, I aced interschool debating and maths competitions, joined three more choirs. I played basketball, cricket, netball, competed in state athletics, was the captain of my touch footy team. I read and read and read and read. When I did manage to sit quietly, I wrote, letting it flow from hand to page so it wouldn't calcify in my brain.

I did not stop.

If I was still, I would fail.

A minute wasted and I would fail.

Every time I slipped up and let the fear overwhelm me, allowed my feelings to come to the surface, they would send me back into the corridor to think about what I had done, as though I wasn't already doing that every minute of every day, trying in vain to keep my feet on the earth.

All the energy I spent masking my feelings at school meant I was a coiled spring by night-time. Once the lights were out and I was alone with my thoughts, fear came at me at full force.

Not a moment passed when I wasn't smooshed into a wad of immovable tension.

My parents stroked my body to help me sleep. Dad brushed my hand, gentle, careful. Mum played with my hair. She picked at my flaky scalp, pick pick pick, sharp nails going under the skin. Sometimes I would shake her away but her fingers always drifted back to tear off the excess parts of me.

I had a recurring dream in which I was standing on a steel beam as it groaned and glided towards the infinite expanse of space. Some nights it made me so anxious my whole body shook. *We're all going to die. I'm going to die.* I couldn't stop thinking about dying. The harder I tried, the more I thought about it. That's the kind of kid I was: existential panic in a snowfield of my own psoriasis scalp.

I remember one night, when I was about eight, looking across to the school shirt hanging on my wardrobe and realising: that shirt will take thousands of years to decay, and I won't. One day, that shirt will be here in the world without me. I will be dead. Gone. Not even a skeleton. Dust.

My body roared. Fear flowed through it, a hot panic. I could only run. I flung off the bedcovers (fitted sheet, top sheet, Merino wool blanket, quilt, tucked in like I was a patient on a gurney) and sprinted as fast as I could to my parents' room at the other end of the house. It was a marathon. I climbed mountains and swam across lakes, chased by an invisible vicious, imaginary, grotesque, irrational creature that would devour me head to toe if I stopped.

Dad woke blearily and let me climb in next to him. He asked, 'What's wrong?' I breathed enough oxygen for two people. My heart rattled like a snare drum. In the quiet room, safe in my parents' bed, I had no way to make him understand that I was in danger. I couldn't tell him my shirt was immortal or that my parallel universe Nanna had died or that one day, truly, unavoidably, actually, time itself would end.

If someone strokes my hand now, I cry. It is totally involuntary, like yelling when someone steps on you.

MAY

My new therapist thinks it would be helpful to do the Young Schema Questionnaire. This is a type of therapeutic approach that will help us identify which of my brain worms to focus on first. She gives me a pen and a clipboard and several sheets of paper. There are 110 questions. They offer suggestions like *I feel guilty if I make my needs a priority* and *I do things I don't want to do in order to avoid disappointing others*. I want to win at the questionnaire so I do it really fast. I look at her while I'm doing it. She's concentrating on her computer, but if she looks over she'll see that no one has ever been as good at the questionnaire as I am. Next to *I am good at understanding people and helping others* I circle *Strongly Agree*. When I get to *I am fearful that people will betray and hurt me* I have to gently push on my solar plexus to stop the burning sensation.

'Done,' I exclaim, 110 questions later.

'That was quick,' she says. She takes the paper. I want her to mark it right away. She tells me she's not 'marking' it and that there are 'no right answers', but I know this is something she says so people don't feel bad when they lose. It will take a week, she says. In the next session, she will give me my results.

'Okay,' I say. I try to remember what I circled next to *I often feel that my accomplishments are not good enough*.

In the next session I take off my jacket and she tells me I scored high in a number of key areas. I can tell by the way she says it that I should not replace my coat with a MISS SCHEMA THERAPY 2020 sash.

'You're self-sacrificing,' she says, going through her list. 'You have the enmeshment schema. An underdeveloped self. It means you don't have good boundaries with people in your life. Probably your parents.'

I think about how I've already called my dad twice today and it's only just gone 10 am. 'Hm,' I say.

My new therapist makes some notes on her legal pad. 'You're afraid to be on your own in the world.' She turns the paper so I can see it. 'You generally tend towards shame and negativity.'

'Oh,' I say. I tell her I think I'm pretty optimistic, under the circumstances.

She says there's a difference between *feeling* negative and *being* negative. 'You scored low on failure to achieve, though. So you're overly negative, but you feel good about what you've achieved in your life.'

I try to explain that I don't think *overly* negative is really fair, given I have to spend part of every day living outside of my body.

'And you have an anxious attachment style.'

'What's that?'

'You're afraid of abandonment.' She says this as though it's not the most terrifyingly true thing there is, as though not everyone should be frightened of it 100 per cent of the time. 'You think everyone is going to leave you.'

Requiring frequent reassurance they are loved

When I was small, my parents had a nude portrait of my Dad in their bedroom. Having a nude of your dad is a weird thing, on reflection, but it was the eighties. The painting was abstract: brown and orange lines with white space between. To the average visitor it probably looked nothing like him, but the artist knew my dad so well that he had captured him exactly. The angle of his jaw, the dark smear of his beard.

Every Sunday afternoon, Dad left. It wasn't sinister – he worked interstate during the week. But I was like a dog, with no object permanence, and each time he went to the airport, I thought he would never come back. I would take my small self and sit cross-legged in front of the painting and just cry. I stared at it on purpose, at the shapes that made him, feeling a patch of sadness bloom in my chest. I didn't want him to go. I hated it when he went.

In my memory, I did this on my own. I can remember evening sun pouring in, warm on my skin, and the wedge of light on the carpet, and the large, empty room. But as an adult I told Mum about it, the depth of my preschool-aged existential despair, and she said no, she was standing in the doorway, trying to get me to come and do something fun. I know, as an adult, that this must be true. But it's not easy to apply truth to memory.

Every week I tried to do all the right things, to be the best, to work the hardest. And every week he got on a plane and left me anyway.

When my dad was small, his mother was very sick. She was sick for a long time after that, too – she had chronic and relapsing bowel disease. When he was six years old, he was taken to hospital and told to say goodbye to her. She didn't die then, or for some years afterwards, but Dad says that he lived in constant fear that she would.

I ask him about her and he recalls how even when she was deathly ill, she helped him with his Latin homework while he cooked dinner for the family. His eyes are wet when he tells me this. He says, 'If I could have, through good works, kept her around a bit longer, I would have done whatever it took. I remember saying into the ether, *I'll do any kind of thing if you don't let her die.*'

If I'm good enough, she won't leave me. If I do things exactly right, I can control the outcome.

When my mum was small, she lived on a farm in the Adelaide Hills, in a little town called Ashton. My great-great-great-grandfather had been a farmer, and each generation of sons had worked the same land to grow the same produce. Gramps was given the Ashton farm and his brother the one down the road.

Nanna, my mum's mum, was a different kind of person. Her grandfather – who had the most glorious name: Hastings Greenslade – had made bucketloads of money on the stock market and then lost it all in the crash of 1929. Nanna lived at the beach. She liked dancing and flirting. She was used to a certain lifestyle and expected it would be maintained. Her sister married a wealthy politician and they hosted balls and dinner parties at their mansion. That was the life Nanna had anticipated – not being a farmer's wife.

She didn't help with the farming, but neither did she do much mothering. There were high-maintenance pets: a headstrong Samoyed who would break through their fences and torment the neighbours' sheep, and a lanky Siamese called Thai, whose photo Nanna still has with her. There was gossip and discontent and opinions about other people. She felt adrift and isolated. There was always fighting. On Sundays, after church, tension would build until it hung almost visible in the house, the promise of her verbal violence. She would rage and threaten and shout.

And then she would leave.

Mum recalls standing in the garage of the farmhouse, aged four, while Nanna started the car and backed into the road. Time and time again she drove away. In Mum's memory, she stood on her own. Decades later, her older brother, then in his seventies, told her he had been there with my little mum, watching Nanna leave without knowing if she would come back.

That must be true. But the memory says differently.

Fear of abandonment tends to form very early in a life – in a self. Instinct tells us that if we're vulnerable, we should seek out someone to protect us, physically and emotionally. A leopard is coming. If no one helps us, we will be torn limb from limb and have our bones licked clean. Or we'll binge-watch reality TV, or drink too much, or cry, or lash out, or go to hospital. But the sensation is the same: if we look for care and no one can provide it, we expose ourselves to huge risk. When we're small, we need other people to keep us safe.

A child might literally be abandoned, left by their parents in the care of others, or in no care. Their parents may die, or be taken from them, or they may be displaced or forced apart. Or they may simply grow up in an environment where their significant relationships are insecure. Even if a parent is physically present, they can be made unavailable by emotional distance, chronic illness, putting conditions on their love and so on – they may give the impression they will somehow only love you if you read *Matilda* correctly, for example, even if it isn't true. It need not be intentional. The parent figure might not remember it at all. (This is one of many lies told about trauma – it doesn't have to be 'big'. It can be comparatively very small and still last a lifetime.)

Many mental illnesses evolve from neglect. Caretaker relationships are significant, and when they're negative, it affects the important things, like self-worth. Fear can develop through repeated small traumas over a long period. The neglect doesn't need to be deliberate; sometimes it's unavoidable. Children can imagine they are in danger for all sorts of reasons, and there are genetic links that make them more susceptible to internalising that fear. Even when childhood experiences seem innocuous, circumstances can conspire to file them right at the core of our self-belief.

As adults, the memory of being abandoned is closely linked to the way we maintain relationships with others. We might fixate on abandonment, certain our loved ones will leave us or die, or we might reject connection, fearing that others will deliberately hurt us. We might believe we're more socially isolated than we really are or carry shame about ourselves, certain we are defective or unworthy. We might internalise several of these in combination.

One of these presentations is an 'anxious attachment style' – desperate to stop someone from leaving (even if they're not planning to), we do everything we know to get them to stay. It's not limited to romantic relationships; we can apply the anxiety to friendships and work and our local librarian and the woman who reads the news. I feel a brief but profound sadness when someone I only know on Twitter moves away, even if we've never spoken and I secretly think we're enemies.

In some cases, the fear of rejection is intensely magnified. For example, rejection sensitive dysphoria (RSD) is common in people with ADHD and ASD – high sensitivity to a belief they are being rejected, even if they're not. People with borderline personality disorder experience 'intense distress in the event of actual or perceived abandonment'. A hint of someone leaving, even temporarily, can trigger this fear. It doesn't even have to be actual abandonment; it can just be someone going to the shops or hanging up the phone. When I incorrectly anticipate the next word in a sentence I'm reading, I feel a sting of rejection (from the sentence? who knows). The tiniest whiff can spark a spiral into despair.

And it hurts. Social exclusion stimulates the same parts of the brain as physical pain.

Our memories of past insecurities become present and future insecurities. As adults, we mentally time travel to moments when we feared we had been abandoned, and those memories teach us how to act today.

Research by van IJzendoorn and Bakermans-Kranenburg hypothesises that we can learn this fear from our parents. A child can watch a parent worry about being left alone and fold it into how they act much later in life. Anxious attachment, then, may be one of the outcomes of having an 'overprotective' parent; someone who fears being abandoned or rejected (even if they only *appear* to fear it) is more likely to raise a child who also fears being abandoned, and that child is more likely to raise their own insecure child.

Living under a constant threat of losing someone – whether deliberate, involuntary, regretful, devastating or cruel – is a common basis for anxious attachment. While I was researching this book, I read a study about anxious attachment specifically in people with Crohn's disease – the illness my paternal grandmother eventually died from in her fifties. According to the Agostini et al's findings, 'patients with [Crohn's Disease] exhibit a predominantly insecure attachment' and 'perceived their parents' behaviors as characterized by low maternal care and high paternal overprotection.' I never met my grandmother, but it seems likely that she was prone to insecure attachment and also that this influenced my dad's (extremely anxious) attachment style, which in turn has influenced mine.

Mum and Dad tried to shield us kids like we were Fabergé eggs. Through their very good intentions, they made me feel as though I would perish without their protection. Cherished but smothered, always aware of being unsafe. Through their love, I learned to anticipate and resent and dread loss. Sooner or later, it would find and destroy me.

Dad is willing to talk tirelessly about my childhood. He interrogates it in the same way I do. What did it *mean* when that happened? How did we *feel*? He was an engineer and has a PhD in creative writing and a psychology degree and thirty-plus years of management consulting experience, so it is in his nature to analyse things into the ground. He and I have spent endless hours doing this. If we disagree, we become the definition of an unstoppable force meeting an immovable object. A counsellor once described the two of us as 'a verbal battering ram'.

Mum is not like this. She is not a feelings weapon. She derives no satisfaction from labouring over the past or trying to interpret the meaning of things. But I ask her what it was like to become a mother and there are so many words I recognise. She says she was 'over the moon' but 'very anxious because it was so new'. She says, 'I remember getting you to six weeks and having this huge sense of relief that, *I've got her to six weeks and she didn't die.*'

She says her mother was 'never reassuring', explaining that Nanna would come to the house and, instead of helping out, read magazines. 'Nanna never said anything to give me any confidence or even seemed to be pleased that I had this little girl.'

When I was a few months old, Mum went back to work. She says she was always torn. 'I remember feeling strongly that I wasn't doing *anything* properly.' She had a stellar career in law, and she also wanted to have a family, and those two things were in constant competition (the expectation and reality that women will take on the bulk of domestic duties, even if their husbands are very nice).

'But my preference was for you,' she says. 'I hated having to leave you.'

From my own experience I know this must be true, but my recollection is different.

Markedly diminished interest in almost all activities

Anyway, I was lonely. Obviously. The other kids weren't that thrilled to be around someone who cried when she met the class tortoise because one day it would be dead.

I tried and failed to make friends at school, and when I did make friends, I didn't realise I had made them. Other people seemed to do it effortlessly: find a person you like, invite them to your party, call them on the phone. All of this seemed impossible to me. I was the kind of girl whose best friend always had a better best friend at a different school. I remember when I was about ten, a girl from my class asked me to go to a Punch and Judy performance in her local park, and even writing it now, I wonder if her mum forced her, and why.

I was disproportionately lucky to have beautiful teachers who found ways to keep me going. That must have been such hard work, in hindsight. They let me do things like be the narrator in the school play and spend time working on my own projects during class. I was sad and angry. I blocked out the other kids' voices through stories and music.

In year four, Miss Arthur let me teach the class for a lesson. She had saintly patience. I sat at my dad's black-and-white Macintosh Classic and made worksheets for maths and English, with word searches and trivia and jokes. I wrote a groundbreaking booklet about bullying, which I miraculously (?) still have:

> **Why are bullies bullies?**
> They are trying to hide that they are cowards, and the only way to do this is to bully other people so that their friends think they are strong and special. Of course we are all special, but bullies are special to people in their own way. This is a mean way, a hurtful way, but people who have bullies as friends are willing to go with this way.
>
> **Have YOU got a bully as a friend? Say if they are fun or not below.**

(Then there are five lines where you might dob in your bully friend.) I can't remember what the other kids did. They must have laughed at me, right? I put all their 'tests' in a plastic sleeve and marked them when I got home. I was lonely to the soles of my feet.

Miss McLaughlin, my year five teacher, encouraged my love of words. She published in the school yearbook a poem I wrote about Anzacs, brought in entry forms for writing competitions she thought I should enter, convinced the school to send me to workshops and festivals. It was because of her that I met my heroes – Melina Marchetta, Gillian Rubinstein, Paul Jennings.

I still think about her all the time. She gave me a way through that I wouldn't have otherwise had. It was because of her that I found an outlet for the thoughts that had caused such a traffic jam in my head. And it's because of her that I write.

In the aloneness, new feelings started to emerge. I had always been worried, but now it was tempered with a wordless weight. It was like being afraid inside a soundproof room. When my insides shouted, a wet cloth smothered them. *That's enough. We don't have the energy for this.* It was a new feeling, different from the anxiety but somehow in the same family. I felt I was being pulled into the centre of the earth.

('Why aren't you doing your times tables, Anna?' 'I'm just a bit worn out.')

None of this is particularly unusual in isolation. Heaps of kids have a shit time in primary school when their brains aren't fully developed and other kids are mean to them. I had the enormous privilege of being sad at a private school with teachers who could afford the time to notice me. Almost all the circumstances conspired to keep me well, and the illness pushed through anyway. As for many adults with serious mental illness, there were many factors at play.

We can be born with an inclination to hold tight to anxiety. Research consistently shows genetic, hereditary predisposition to developing anxiety disorders. Generalised anxiety disorder (GAD) and post-traumatic stress disorder (PTSD) both have a heritability of about 30 per cent. GAD has a shared genetic origin with other 'internalising disorders', including major depressive disorder – *Dialogues in Clinical Neuroscience* suggests this can be partially explained by 'genetic contributions toward neuroticism'. PTSD also shows genetic overlap with GAD. In 2019, researchers found a DNA modification that 'enhances our ability to extinguish fear' – a possible step towards GMO anxiety-free humans.

Fear can be part of the building blocks that make us. The genesis of my illness wasn't singularly *being lonely at school* or *having overprotective parents* but a perfect storm of genetics, environment and an overactive imagination.

There's no universal way anxiety disorders are classified, but they're usually broken down into categories like:

Generalised anxiety disorder (GAD): a person feels anxious most days and finds it hard to stop worrying, about a variety of different things, for a prolonged period (six months or more).

Social anxiety: a person is anxious about social situations, like making small talk, having to perform in front of others and meeting new people, often because they're worried about being judged or criticised.

Phobias: an intense fear of a particular situation or object, which may pose an actual threat to them (like snakes) or not (like trypophobia, the fear of clusters of small holes).

Panic disorder: overwhelming, debilitating feelings of anxiety that usually include physical symptoms like shortness of breath, chest pain, dizziness and, often, a fear of being about to die or feelings of being disconnected from reality and time (that is: panic attacks). Often, a distinction is made between panic disorder with or without agoraphobia (which is not just being afraid of 'open spaces' but of being in situations that are hard to escape from – something about which you'll read plenty more in this book).

Sometimes this list also includes obsessive-compulsive disorder (persistent and intrusive thoughts, sometimes resulting in ritualistic behaviours to combat them) and post-traumatic stress disorder (a response to trauma that may include 'flashbacks' but not necessarily).

But anxiety is even more complex than this. A person can have multiple disorders at once – a comorbidity. In fact, it's overwhelmingly likely that they will. Over a lifetime, comorbidity of mood disorders (like other anxiety disorders and depressive disorders) occurs in more than 80 per cent of patients. Almost everyone who has an anxiety disorder will, sooner or later, live with the added complexity of one or more additional disorders.

In that sense, anxiety can seem to occupy your whole body. A panic attack starts at your feet and rushes through to punch you in the throat; now you're so afraid of panicking in front of friends that you withdraw from your social life; when you're not having a panic attack, you're waiting for one. And then your nerves are on a tightrope, poised to react. You must be alert. You must always be ready for an inarticulable danger.

It exhausts you. While this is happening, the depression weighs so heavily that you can't lift your feet off the floor. Not one step.

People expect anxious and depressed people to be a certain way. I wasn't that way. I liked to be the centre of attention (this may be obvious given the book-length story I am writing about myself). I loved debating, felt invigorated by Theatresports. I was so keen to meet new people. Every weekend, I went to basketball or cricket or football or netball or softball imagining my new best friend would be playing for the other team. I joined the junior school choir in year three. Later, I would join the middle school choir and the girls' choir and the chamber choir, the jazz singers and the senior school choir and two opera companies. I *loved* to be on stage.

(Often, when I meet people as an adult, they say they expected me to be something different. More anxious. More obvious. Quaking and sweating, maybe even screaming. Just sitting with them in a cafe, shouting my brains out. This almost never happens.)

What was going on when I was a tween was that I tried hard to connect with others – probably more like an anxious attachment than social anxiety, desperate not to be abandoned – and overwhelmed them. I was 'a lot', 'too much', 'so intense'. These are all words people use to describe people with non-specific mental illnesses. God, could you just *stop*, what is the matter with you? Why aren't you embarrassed to be like this?

I was invited to this girl Jane's party, somewhere on the other side of town. Dad drove me there. I don't remember anything about that car ride except that we pulled up in front of Jane's house and, for reasons that have been lost to history, Dad turned to me and said, 'If you keep acting like this as an adult, no one will like you.'

I am sure he said this. There's a lot of cloudiness in my mind about all kinds of things, but of this I am absolutely positive.

I can't remember how I was acting, so unfortunately I can't apply the lesson to all the friends I make and lose as an adult, but I think about it a lot.

Later, I became best friends with a girl who was new to the school. She liked reading and writing and other things I liked. Our brothers became best friends too, and still are. I felt safe with her. One day, while we were eating lunch in the quadrangle, she said to me, 'People like you.'

'They do?' I said.

She took another bite of her sandwich. 'To begin with, I mean. But then the novelty wears off.'

In early high school, butchered by pretending to be a way I wasn't, exhausted by masking my feelings, I just shut down. Where once I had been a high achiever, I now started to fail my classes. My maths and science teachers took my parents aside to let them know they would have to pull me from the advanced streams if I didn't up my game. I didn't care. I was so depressed that I stopped eating and revealed my bones. No one asked why.

Long hours went into talking to people on the internet – strangers at first, who then became friends. In those days, the primary method of communicating was internet relay chat, a text-based method where you typed your deepest thoughts into a window and someone tried to cyber with you. This doesn't seem unusual now – we date people from apps, loathe people from Facebook, marry people from Twitter – but in 1997 it was a relatively new and strange way to spend time. I met (in person) a boy named Christian, who, at fifteen, was a whole year older than me; he broke up with me because I didn't want to kiss him. I met another boy called Jason; I broke up with him because he called me 'his bitch'. Although I existed in a deep slump of sadness, my friends on the internet made me feel more normal. In one year, I met about 150 people at 'real life' meet-ups, where dozens of often-reclusive nerds barbecued at a park. They were almost all good sorts; some of them are still my friends today.

At school, I was angry and tired. I picked fights, found myself in detention most Friday afternoons and at least one Saturday. My science teacher started sending me out of class before I had even opened my mouth, so profoundly disruptive did he find me. Another teacher did something I am legally prevented from writing here, a little time slip that pops up every now and again unbidden. I rotated through strings of disappointing crushes, guys who despised me and girls I felt I could only love in secret. For six months, when I was 14, I slept on a foam mattress on my parents' floor; I could not find rest anywhere else. At least twice I woke there in the damp of my own piss, covering it before they noticed.

I existed under a heavy blanket of the most unwelcome, debilitating and all-consuming despair. It wasn't that I didn't want to come out of it, I actually just couldn't find the energy to begin to form the thought that maybe I could. Do you know what I mean? The darkness was so dark I had forgotten there could be the promise of light.

I met a boy on the internet. I'm smiling while I type this because a) I really am extremely creepy, and b) he was a genuinely nice boy.

We met in person after my choir rehearsal in the city. It was 9 December and roasting hot, but for some reason I was wearing a heavy black jumper (the depression was the reason). I had had my hair cut short. Later, he said I didn't make a great first impression on him, but he didn't say it in a mean way. Did he hold my hand? I can't recall, but I held his hand lots of times after that. On Friday afternoons I would catch the bus into the city after school and meet him at the comic store in the arcade, and then we would get McDonald's and go back to his place. I loved it there. I watched him play video games and hung out with his dogs and we took his sisters to the local shopping centre to look at Pokémon. It felt safe. I didn't recognise that sensation, at first. The people in his family trusted one another to do their best. And they sometimes shouted, but never at me.

Comforted by this feeling of stability, I was able to start engaging in school again, at least superficially. I was part of a group of International Baccalaureate students, which came with a host of extracurricular requirements. We had to do fifty hours of 'creativity' – for us, that meant heading in to the Adelaide Festival Centre to the theatre. Before then, I had seen *Cats* when I was five and a stage adaptation of Margaret Mahy's *The Man Whose Mother Was a Pirate* and nothing else. That semester I saw fifteen plays. One night I was watching the wonderful actress Ruth Cracknell not two feet from me, with these friends I truly liked, and I knew afterwards we would walk out into King William Street and it would be rigged with fairy lights, and I thought, This is pretty great. And it was. Extraordinary luck, having so much, being safe and surrounded by goodness.

The bright spark of these small joys was largely why it occurred to me something might really be wrong. I felt I was doing better:

I had a boyfriend I adored, friends who seemed genuinely glad of my company. I should have been happy. My thought process as I crossed the netball courts towards the school chaplain's office was: All this nice stuff is happening *and yet* I wake up every morning so sad I could die. I have a very clear memory of walking in the bright sunshine and realising I was so comprehensively miserable I should have perished right there in wing defence.

The chaplain had a room at the end of a row of cottages that each had a different school purpose. Years earlier I had moped and cried next door in after-school care because I had been rudely forced to eat a Vegemite sandwich. Now, at the other end of my school experience, I needed a different sort of care.

I have written these events so many times I don't know which memory is the most accurate. I do know that there was a chair and a window. The chaplain might have had grey hair and a beard or no beard. I can't remember his name, but I know it's in my brain somewhere.

'Sit down,' he said, so I did. 'How can I help?'

'I sort of want to die,' I said to him. 'I think about it all the time.'

'Mm-hm,' he went. 'Tell me more about that.'

'I don't know what else to say about it.'

I'm not sure if he had a lot of kids swinging by to share the same kinds of words. Statistics suggest I wouldn't have been the first or only one. I remember he seemed a bit stricken by the premise, like maybe he thought I would grab his pen and ceremoniously stab it into my brain. He wrote a recommendation that I see a doctor. In those days people just said 'Prozac' until you were cured. I don't remember if I ever had my script filled or took the pills; I do remember my parents did not want me to.

There are so many different ways to feel lost in your mind. The words are hard. No one says to you when you're five: Hey, if someone asks you about your existential pain, tell them it's *dissociative*. Tell them it's *detached from reality* or *complex post-traumatic stress*.

The chaplain wrote notes in his book. 'You said you're obsessed with dying.'

I nodded. A statement of fact.

'How long have you felt like this?' he asked.

I could only think to answer, 'Always.'

JUNE

'I'm just so scared,' I say to my new therapist. 'I don't want to die. I don't want the people I love to die.' This is the exciting rollercoaster of having anxiety and depression together. Waiting to find out if your brain has served up *I welcome the sweet relief of death* or *For the love of God keep me alive at all costs.*

Today, it is the restlessness of conscious thought. I have been awake all night, dwelling on the inevitability of loss.

'Of course you don't,' she says. She's wearing really nice pants. Wool, I think, and brown with a thin cream pinstripe. I'm wearing the only jeans I own that haven't had the crotch seams worn out by friction. I try to fluff up my hair a bit.

'I'm not just afraid of dying,' I say to her. 'You have to understand, I'm scared to go outside. I can't even go to the shops sometimes. How' – I pause for dramatic effect, arms akimbo – 'am I meant to enter a whole other plane of existence?'

I try to explain how I'm afraid of dying – for all the usual reasons and some extras – but that's not the only feeling I have.

What will people think of me, when I lose at this thing (staying alive)? How humiliating, to expose your shortcomings so definitively as to actually stop living. What an uncouth and self-centred thing, to die. Ha ha, you're so bad at being alive! And now you're imposing on all these people who will have to do something about it – a doctor, a paramedic, a funeral director, a cleaner. Don't publicly and spectacularly fail to function, you loser. Gross.

I wait for her to say something comforting like, *Why not go home and watch telly for a while?* The springs in her couch dig into my leg. I imagine her telling me I don't have to do any more work today, on account of the tremendous distress that comes with being a sentient creature living on bit of rock that's hurtling through space and time.

She nods. Half smiles. My new therapist puts her pen in her lap and says, 'Yeah, it's fucked, isn't it?'

We sit in the discomfort this creates. I resist the urge to rapidly deteriorate into an anxious fugue state.

Finally she says, 'How are things at home?'

'Hm.' I explain the running joke in my family which is: I am always crying. They don't notice anymore, even though my face is swollen to twice its normal size. I apologise for it. I say to them, 'Sorry for crying! I was just watching videos of soldiers coming home to their dogs! You know how I am.'

I explain how, if they hear me at all, they agree that they do know how I am, and the way I am is *always crying*. Usually they don't hear me.

My new therapist cannot believe this is true. She says, 'They just *walk past*?'

It's not her fault for not understanding. None of her other clients have ever cried as comprehensively as me. I say, Sometimes I cry so much I give myself a sinus infection.

I'm not even sad. Not every time. There are other reasons to cry. Sometimes the reason is to dislodge the leaves caught in my oesophagus. When I cry they travel down into my digestive tract, and for a period afterwards I can be normal, and the only reminder is that I occasionally rattle with the memory of the crying. I don't mind crying, I explain. Sometimes it is very comforting.

She frowns. 'Does your family ever comfort you?'

I explain that I told them to assume I'm crying unless I say otherwise, even if I am smiling, which is still something I do in spite of everything.

Then I say to her, My partner tells me I cry in my sleep.

'That's' – she looks at her notes – 'Gaz?'

'Yeah. He says, "You whimper like you're being attacked".'

Lack of stability in the view of the self

Writing from memory can never be objective. We're all a version of a person who experienced a version of an event, and the way we recall it is impacted by every other thing that's happened in our lives (all of which is also entirely subjective). But memory can be further warped by serious mental illness. And that can throw into chaos everything we understand about ourselves.

Joan Didion – my literary hero and yours – began her legendary essay collection *The White Album*: 'We tell ourselves stories in order to live.' Everybody knows this quote. 'We look for the sermon in the suicide, for the social or moral lesson in the murder of five. We interpret what we see, select the most workable of the multiple choices. We live entirely, especially if we are writers, by the imposition of a narrative line upon disparate images, by the "ideas" with which we have learned to freeze the shifting phantasmagoria which is our actual experience.'

Memory is hard to grasp. I know this from having children. When they were small, I would try to take a 'snapshot' of them at a given moment. I imagined I could remember exactly what they were like when they were two, three, four. I know from watching videos that my memory is misaligned with reality – their voices are different, the way they move is not the same; they are a version of their younger selves, told through the current-day lens. My snapshots are imperfect.

So I imagine, too, that I invent things about my past self to fit the narrative I have created as an adult. I tell people things like, I was a depressed teenager, I wanted to die. I have such clear memories of these times when I was too sad to go on, wallowing in misery music, considering throwing myself dramatically from my first-floor balcony into Mum's camellias below.

But the nature of trauma and memory makes it hard to be sure about how honest that is. Because the paragraph that follows Didion's more famous quote is: 'Or at least we do for a while. I am talking here about when I began to doubt the premises of all the stories I had ever told myself, a common condition but one I found troubling.'

In her tremendous book *Blueberries*, Ellena Savage asks: 'If memory is not a tape recorder starting at zero, then how can a self exist, truly?'

Because we're humans with temporal awareness and the ability to remember and project, we write stories about ourselves. Not always literally, like I am right now, but we hold in our minds a sense of *who we are* based on what's happened before now.

Scholars variously call this a 'self-narrative', 'narrative identity' or an 'autobiographical narrative'. It's the tale of our own self, with all its many plot points (moving cities, having a baby), twists and turns (getting divorced), red herrings (doing a business degree) and climaxes (figurative and actual). Brains can't even really tell the difference between thoughts, dreams and actual events. They're open to suggestion. It's why we see a burger on the TV and jump on UberEats without even realising, why we fixate on something when we're trying not to think about it, and why Brad Pitt always ends up looking like his fiancées.

Everything we remember – and even things we don't – contribute to the person we are today.

Everything that happens to us becomes us.

Our memories help us to create a continuous, stable (that is, mostly unchanging) identity, linking the past versions of ourselves with today's version and who we imagine we might be in the future. We need to be able to mentally time travel to maintain a strong sense of self. That's called *self-continuity.*

To explain why, I must offer a brief summary of different types of memory.

Theorists qualify and discuss memory in many different ways. For the purposes of this book, let's stick with one set of definitions. We have different types of memory: I'm going to talk about procedural, emotional, semantic and episodic. They're split into two kinds of memory: explicit and implicit. Basically, we have memories we can voluntarily call up, and memories that exist to passively help us on our daily journey.

For example, maybe, when we were a kid, a lizard visited our apartment. It had soft toes that stuck to the window, and its tail fell off and wriggled across the floor. From this event, we access different memories, and we make new ones and store them in different ways.

Procedural memory is implicit. We use it to perform functions without thinking about them – our motor skills. When we saw the lizard and yelled 'A lizard!', our procedural memory is how we knew to speak, and the reason we didn't have to actively think about how to do it.

Emotional memory is also implicit, defined as 'retention of classically conditioned emotional relationships that cannot be voluntarily recollected or reported'. This describes the kind of memory that means we might see a lizard and feel a sharp shock of anguish or fear, without knowing why. Trauma (but not only trauma) can create these memories – hidden, unable to be recalled, but still eliciting a powerful emotional response.

Semantic memory is explicit and incorporates our general knowledge and facts we've learned. When we look at a lizard, our semantic memory is how we know it's not just a lizard but a velvet gecko, and that velvet geckos are endemic to Australia. *But* we don't have to explicitly call up the memory of how or when we learned this information; actively remembering lizard facts doesn't require also remembering the classroom where we heard those facts.

Episodic memory comprises events we can recall voluntarily. These are the tiny movies in our minds. When we saw the velvet gecko on the balcony, maybe we also remembered the time we went to the snake exhibit with our dad and saw baby chameleons, because they're like lizards. Then we stored the tiny movie of meeting *this* lizard and we might keep it there to be recalled later.

Our explicit memory – the knowledge we've gained and the brain movies – comes together to form an autobiographical memory. It's how we know 'who we are' – all of the meaningful events, people, places and objects we store in our recollection. I'm Anna, and I like cats and chocolate. I don't live in the town where I was born. I once wanted to own a pet shop. I work hard at my job, cry in public, watch house-hunting shows and pretend that cooking relaxes me. From this information, we form a self-narrative – a story we know about ourselves.

Our self-narrative has value judgements attached to it: the way we're socialised tells us things about what our story should look like. I'm Anna, and I got married 'too young' and now I'm divorced. My parents 'are disappointed in me'. I have 'failed' to perform 'normal human functions'. It helps us to understand our place in the world: when I was thirteen, a man followed me home from school, so I'm part of a group called 'women'; I remember making up stories when I was in kindergarten, so I'm a 'writer'.

Explicit memory can change over time. We can forget. We can misremember. An injury or illness can damage the parts of our brain that manage these memories. Neurological and mental disorders can affect the processes and pathways to the memory bank. The information we use to 'write' our self-narrative is only as robust as the limitations of how our memory works.

And, as we know, we also use our memory to move back and forth in mental time. To understand where we exist in the vastness of temporal reality, we have to believe that our memories are accurate, even though we know they're not.

In primary school, I decided to join the choir. I'd heard that if you kept performing in it until you were in senior school, you would be invited to go on a tour of Europe. While it turned out that I really liked – and was quite good at – singing, this was the singular reason I auditioned (everyone who auditioned got in; we were eight).

I have a very clear memory of sitting in the music room that day. There were rows of plastic chairs and small children dotted around, swinging their legs. It was hot; the air conditioner was droning. It seemed to take forever to get to my turn, as was often the case for those of us with surnames at the end of the alphabet.

While I was sitting there, I was suddenly struck by this thought: Soon I will be old, and it will feel like no time has passed.

I had the thought over and over. Maybe I was sitting there for twenty minutes, and for that whole time I strung those words together in different ways in my head. I couldn't stop imagining what it would be like; I was stuck in my future projection. I felt cool panic in my body. One day I would be old. I would die. It would happen in an instant.

Many years later, I was on stage at what was then known as BMW Edge – a geometric glass theatre in Melbourne's Federation Square. I was part of a production of *La Rondine*, one of Puccini's lesser operas (a sentence only dickheads write), set in Paris and the French Riviera in the nineteenth century. I was doing my best to channel some kind of bouffant heiress when the memory of that music room struck me. *When I'm old I'll remember sitting in this chair and no time will have passed.*

I did remember. And I was right: no time had passed at all.

Knowing what's happening now is one thing (though quantum physics further contests the meaning of 'now'; learning about this is a good way to explode what's left of your mind). Doctors can diagnose a person with depression and prescribe them medicine that will treat the present-day symptom. Sometimes it works exactly as intended. For an improved outcome, many professionals suggest medicine is more effective when taken in conjunction with other forms of treatment, like therapy.

Much of modern psychology works by *getting to the root of the problem*. That is: recalling things that happened in the past and using them to understand the disordered thinking that's happening in the present. The challenge is, our brains are also designed to protect us from those traumatic and formative events. Remembering and revisiting them – even in the interests of trying to reduce their impact in the present – can be made more difficult by the subconscious knowledge that to do so might cause us harm. Our brain can suppress this information ostensibly for our own good and make it impossible to acknowledge and process it. Brains, you must understand, are jerks. As Julia Shaw wrote, '… our memories are built to forget. Forgetting is a beautiful mechanism that trims down our neuronal connections to make our brains more efficient at storing only the information that is most important to us.'

Memory disruption exists in various depressive and anxious states, delusions and paranoia. But psychosis – my brain's jam – has crucial links to both trauma and memory. It's called *identity disturbance* or *identity diffusion*: a sense of incoherence, inconsistent beliefs and behaviours, and a negative sense of self. Everything that needs to be operational in order to create a stable sense of identity.

Mental time travel is different for people in psychiatric distress. We are, according to contemporary science, worse at memory. Instead of being able to recall a precise moment or event, a patient may aggregate many, remembering bits and pieces from different times and mashing them into one. That over-negative, generalised memory becomes the foundation for our identity, even though it might never have happened. Gaslights all the way down.

The first concrete evidence I saw of this was actually on Twitter, which is where I live. There, people often ask for very narrow, specific examples of life's experiences as a kind of meme format. So, someone might ask something like, 'What is the most on-brand story from your childhood?' or 'When did you first realise you were mortal?'

I watch these come up in my feed and I think, That's a fun idea. I try to recall on-brand stories from my childhood or the first time I realised I was mortal, and just … nothing. I can't relate an abstract idea to a specific memory. I always *think* I have one, I know in my *body* that a memory is there, but I can't grab it. It's on the tip of my tongue. It's right on the boundary of what I can access.

Then, every so often, I have one already 'filed' in this way. Recently there was a tweet like, 'What's the most memorable thing that's happened to you in a movie theatre?' I already had one of those, and I knew that because at the time it happened I remember thinking, This is a memorable thing that's happening in a movie theatre.

(I was at the Greater Union cinema in Hindley Street in Adelaide, watching *Romeo + Juliet* with my friends for the fourth time. It was dramatic and sexy. Tense. Moody. We were on the edge of our seats, probably wishing the whole film could be Radiohead playing to Leo's fringe but, nevertheless, the moment came when Romeo raced to Tybalt, *Either thou or I, or both, must go with him*, took his weapon and shot him in the heart. Tybalt tumbled, dead and bloodied, into a fountain. The audience drew a collective gasp. Nobody breathed. No popcorn, no rustling bags, nothing. It was more silent than silence. And then a guy at the back of the cinema shouted: 'Suck shit!' and we all broke into laughter.)

There are other memories I can identify in this way because I have labelled them at another point in my life. I know what my earliest childhood memory is because at some point I said to another person, 'This is my earliest childhood memory.'

Here are some things I can remember: my dad's old credit card numbers; my best friend's phone number from when we were six; my first boyfriend's birthday; my Medicare number; the password GeoCities generated for me in 1997. But the important, formative stuff? A room of archive boxes that a flood has passed through.

Let's bung in a bit of beginner philosophy: the Ship of Theseus. The dilemma asks us to imagine a ship. Over time each part of it is replaced – a new porthole, a new anchor, a new hull. Eventually, every part of the ship is new. At what point does it become a different ship?

Twenty years ago I was a high school student in Adelaide. Now, I'm nearly forty, a writer and a mother of teenagers in Melbourne. It seems obvious that both of these people are 'me', but for a person with a bungled brain, *connecting them together* is really hard. Selves exist on a continuum: usually, they change incrementally from one moment to the next. Being disorientated and afraid makes it more like seeing your nephew for the first time in ages – even though the changes are small and have happened over time, the *sense of self* is wildly different from the person you had internalised.

Intellectually, I know I'm a culmination of my life's experiences, but in practice I'm just this person in this moment, without the context of clear and precise memories. I can differ from one minute to the next. People tell me I'm a certain kind of person and I feel no connection to the description. My sense of identity bends and shifts. It relies heavily on external inputs: if I'm criticised, my identity is 'bad person'; if someone cheers me on, it shifts to 'decent person'. Even minor negative feedback is a rejection – briefly, the only thing I know about who I am. That thing you hear about people with identity disorders having violent mood swings, seemingly set off by nothing at all? I reckon it's this. Constant change. Never comfortable in reality. I think it's the same process that makes me susceptible to advertising and inclined to enter and stay in bad relationships. ('Oh, *that's* who I'm meant to be.') Constantly trying to reformulate a place in the world from whatever information is available.

The famous neurologist and author Oliver Sacks put it like this: 'Instead of seeing the brain as rigid, fixed in mode, programmed like a computer, there is now a much more biological and powerful notion of "experiential selection," of experience literally shaping the connectivity and function of the brain.'

'How, if there is only transience,' he asked, 'do we achieve continuity?'

If what you understand about yourself is constantly changing, at what point are you no longer the same?

I have a friend who I met on (sorry) a camp for gifted children. It was held in a grand sandstone house built in the 1860s, with a leaf-littered circular driveway and a wide verandah that didn't catch any sun. I was there for English, she for art. We were installed in a second-floor dorm room that was absolutely, completely haunted. The fireplaces had been covered by doors, presumably for ghost reasons. All night, they banged.

Although we didn't cross paths again until we were grown up, our childhoods were very alike. We went to similar schools that took us on the same excursions. We went to the same art classes but at different times. Because we were both creative types, we went to the same places and even knew some of the same people.

This friend of mine is an incredible mental time traveller. She recalls things with perfect clarity. She can extract from her mind a person's face, a location, a name, an entire conversation. In fact, the only reason we're friends now is because she could remember my surname from the four days we spent together as primary schoolers, and she emailed me. The only memory I could dredge up was of us singing 'Candle in the Wind' together at the camp's karaoke night (sorry again).

For the most part, my memories are disjointed and generalised. I listen to people who remember entire childhoods in exquisite detail and I don't understand how it works. I feel a single moment with every sensory receptor and then nothing. There are large gaps peppered by small sections of the most vulgar technicolour.

It's not all negative. I have many tiny, beautiful memories from my childhood. Driving across town to have an ice cream with my cousins. Watching a kite shaped like a fish. Unwrapping a wooden doll's house on Christmas Day. Playing in the leaves with my cat. Eucalyptus smells at the local public pool. My dad's photocopier. Kicking a footy with Gramps. Watching *It's a Knockout* on Sunday mornings. Ballet class with my best friend. Freezing air from the Southern Ocean. My brother being chased by a pelican. Thousands of minuscule joys.

But when I think about childhood as a whole – the act of growing from an infant into an adult – I have one overriding feeling: fear.

All this is to say: this book is an imperfect portrait of my life. My memories have been skewed. They have been inserted by the power of suggestion, pieced together from myths, and hidden for my own protection.

Hypochondria of the heart

In my final year of high school, Mum got a job in Melbourne, 800 kilometres away. I remember standing in the car park of my favourite Adelaide cafe, watching my boyfriend cry, and feeling that I would never be repaired. I was terrified. I had been taught, every moment of every day, to fear being removed from the safety of home.

I had thought about staying behind, living with Nanna while I finished school. But that was just a different kind of homesickness – for my family. So there I was, in the passenger seat of Dad's car, hugging my pillow and trying to disappear into a childhood blanket.

Mum had gone on ahead by plane but Dad drove us the long way – not to prolong the pain but to delay it. We went down along the Limestone Coast of South Australia, where the water is so blue it looks like it would crack if you touched it. I remember a hot wind coming through the rope door of a fish-and-chip shop in Robe, and eating lobster and watching the boats.

I remember stopping at the Commodore on the Park motel in Mount Gambier, buying and not eating a pub meal and crying all night, and Dad apologising in the dark, and the next day standing in the wind at the Twelve Apostles and the way the salt stuck to my wet face. I remember when we got to Geelong, the last big town before Melbourne, eating Chinese food next to a minigolf course, and Dad asking if we wanted to stay one more night in a motel, or did we want to just push on for the last hour of the trip?

We pushed on. The house Mum had rented was a room short; the only spot for my bed was on the landing. I curled into the staircase and tried to make myself small enough to slide into a wormhole that would take me home again.

My new Melbourne school, which was sort of a production line for cunts, had an actual onsite psychologist. Not enough of those people went to see him, frankly. He had a funny office – almost an attic – right at the top of the building. I saw him every week. It took all the energy I had to drag myself up so many staircases; I didn't sleep and had largely stopped eating. I was skipping most of my classes, which my parents had chosen for me anyway: hard maths, harder maths, physics, Java programming and English. I had fallen into the lap of a new boyfriend so cruel that I'll allow him only two sentences in this book. A couple of times he came with me to the weird small attic and explained to the counsellor that his friends were worried I was crazy. Not *him*, but his friends.

Mid-year my family moved out of our dull townhouse directly across the road to a different dull townhouse. Not long after we moved, we were robbed. My bedroom was above the garage, and I woke when it was still dark to the familiar sound of the door opening and my dad's loud V8 grumbling. He often left early to go to the airport for work. Then it was daylight and Mum was yelling, 'My car is gone,' and then Dad was yelling, '*My* car is gone.' During the night, someone had broken in. We had all been asleep in the house at the time: my parents, sister and me upstairs, my brother metres away from where they entered. They took a laptop dock, maybe a handbag, and both cars. When the police found Dad's car, it was just a chassis. When they found Mum's, it was part of a Carlton drug deal and it had a gun in it. A fake gun, but still. In this strange new place, it felt impossible to find a pocket of safety. I missed my friends, my nanna, my quiet city. I didn't know who to be, or how.

I skipped so many classes it was simpler to make note of when I *did* go. At lunchtime I would find someone to catch a tram with me into Chapel Street and buy cigarettes from the 7-Eleven that didn't check your ID, even when you were in school uniform. Then we would head into the city to go to the CD shop and try on perfume and do anything except sit in a classroom and pretend to care about matrices and electricity and long-dead male writers.

One day I was sitting on St Kilda Road outside McDonald's. I should have been in physics class, but instead I was smoking and eating fries with my friends. I had a mobile phone, in 2000, on account of my parents' need to always know if I was in the process of being murdered. My phone rang. It was my dad.

'Hello?' I said. (Not answering my phone was never an option unless I was happy for the police to be called next.)

'Hi,' said Dad. 'How's class?'

'Fine.' I tried to dampen the traffic noise with my mind.

'Uh-huh.' *Quiet, cars. Shut up, friends.* 'Which class is it again?'

'Physics?'

He paused. 'I didn't know they did physics in McDonald's.'

Then I spotted it – his blue car parked on the other side of the six-lane road. Watching. I think it was probably a coincidence. He was surely on his way into the city for work and saw me by chance. But at the time, I burned. It was a violation of my right and need to do whatever it took to cope with my absolutely shitty year.

It's a joke in my family now, the way he busted me. *You said you were in class, but you were wagging with your dickhead mates and he sprung you! Hilarious.*

At the end of the year I was given three kinds of special consideration because of my depression and anxiety. I skipped the graduation ceremony and got drunk in a Collingwood alleyway instead. There was no continuity plan for my mental health care. No one said, *We see you've been working with the school psychologist, here's what to do next.* Spring-loaded, displaced, drowning in dread and fear, my seams finally came unstitched.

I raced to leave Melbourne. Within a month I was living north of the Sydney Harbour Bridge in a mid-century house that had been converted into apartments. It was as beautiful a spot as any in the city; if you leaned dangerously from the tiny kitchen window, you could see the edge of the water where it was clipped by the ferry.

I had never been on my own. The opposite – I had always been like good crockery, folded neatly into tissue paper.

I got a temp job working for one of the big banks, as a receptionist for their international money traders. Their whole job was to buy and sell money. I got a handover from a woman called Katrina. She was the coolest person I had ever met; she had an asymmetrical haircut and she taught me to read tarot. Once she found out my 'real' name was Michal, she started calling me Mick. Mick, this is how to answer the phone. Mick, here's how to order catering for a meeting. Every time she spoke, I felt a rich lava pour out of her and into me. For a month she taught me how to be a money-trader receptionist and, in the evenings, we walked into the hot Sydney nights and down to The Rocks, where we visited rooftop bars for salt-heavy potato wedges and beer. She had long, slender fingers. I wanted to reach over and put them in my mouth, feel them on my skin. When the handover was finished, she moved to London and I flipped tarot layouts at my desk on my own.

(Many years later I found and followed her on Twitter; she has still not followed me back and I suspect this won't help.)

Sydney was not what I had expected. Life was unreal. I felt both invigorated and bewildered. In that Sydney way, I faced an impenetrable plastic film. I was from Adelaide, where 'traffic' meant three cars were using the same road. Now I watched people run both to and from their train, always late, never patient. I felt the world spinning around, with me as its stationary eye.

On weekends I went to art galleries and book launches in suburbs I recognised from songs. I caught the train further up the North Shore to drink beer at someone's house, or someone else's house. For the first time ever, I was free to do whatever I wanted.

In an attempt to make friends, I arranged to meet up with a dude I'd known online since I was thirteen. I waited by the ticket machines at Circular Quay. We had a drink in a little restaurant. A busker played Beatles covers outside the window. This guy told me everything about himself, every tedious skerrick of information, and when I'd finally finished my drink I stood.

'It was nice to meet you,' I lied. 'I should get home.'

I didn't catch the ferry often – it was a much longer walk, through unfamiliar streets – but when I did, I felt small parts of me spring to life. That night, I sat out on the deck and let the water kiss my face. I wondered about the kind of life I was trying to make.

I noticed he was also on the ferry as we docked.

I took quick steps along the wharf. Up the road, left at the corner, right at the lights. Around beside the park, the dark between the trees. Cars rolled by. My cheap heels rubbed my skin until it wept. Every time I glanced back, he was there. He didn't seem to be trying to make up any distance; he knew that I knew he was following me.

At my building, I unlocked the door downstairs. My flat was on the first floor, on the right. I gripped the key tight in my fist and shut the door as hard as I could. The sound bounced in the stairwell.

His face appeared behind the glass. He smiled and waved, as though we were playing a game.

My voice was low. 'Fuck off.'

He bounced on his toes. 'Go on. Let me come in.'

'No.'

'You want me to come in.'

'I don't.'

'*Cock tease*,' he yelled, and walked away. I slipped through my door, took off my shoes and rubbed my feet. Turned on the

TV. Connected to the internet on my laptop. Looked out the window.

He was there. Below my window, a silhouette sitting on the communal letterboxes.

I opened the window. 'Fuck off!'

He waved, the suggestion of his hand shaped by the streetlights. I heated up some dinner. Watched TV. Talked to my friends online. Looked out the window. There he was: the rapist/murderer/kidnapper of whom my parents had been so certain. They were right to worry. Who even was I, thinking I could survive a single night in the wild?

I typed to the internet:

> That guy I met followed me home.
>
> *What?*
>
> He's been outside my building for an hour. Sitting on the letterbox.
>
> *What's he doing?*
>
> He's just sitting there.
>
> *On your letterbox?*
>
> Yeah.

Another hour went by, and another.

> He's still there. I need to sleep.
>
> *Call the police.*
>
> I can't. I think he knows the police.
>
> *Can you call someone else?*

I tried to think of one person to call. *I don't know anyone else*, I typed.

I could see him from my bedroom window, so I suppose by extension he could see me. I didn't sleep. I watched as lights in other houses went dark and the street emptied of people. Every so often, he lifted his hand in a wave.

After six hours, he stood up and left.

I still didn't sleep. Not that night, or the next, or the one after that.

I did go back to work. I took the day's mail and put it in my filing cabinet instead of distributing it to the arseholes who put work before everything. The next day, I did it again. I kept weeks of mail in the cupboards under my desk. Eventually my boss found them and asked me to explain and I just … couldn't. I didn't care about the mail. I cared about getting hammered on the company card on Thursday nights, and having noodles with my dad when he was in Sydney for work. Every morning when I woke up alone in my flat, I wondered what was the point of me. Sometimes I wondered it aloud. What am I doing here? What have I done?

On the loneliest weekends I would catch the train out to Sydney Airport and pay $39 for a stand-by plane ticket to Melbourne. Most of the time I didn't tell my family I was visiting; I would meet this guy in the car park at Crown Casino and he would graciously let me give him a blow job while he texted his girlfriend. I waited and waited for him to realise he loved me.

When I got fired from my job, I had been partially comatose on the couch for three days. I hadn't told them I wasn't coming in. I had left drawers and cupboards and boxes of mail undistributed at my desk. Hundreds of envelopes that the money traders needed to meet their ridiculous daily targets. I muted

Oprah for a second when the recruitment agency called, then I put the phone under the cushions and kept on watching.

There was only one place I could imagine going.

I don't remember what I said to Nanna when I turned up at her house. I put my bags in the spare room, the one with the thin green blankets on the bed and rows of Billy Graham books, and asked if there were any biscuits. She sliced me a green apple and arranged it on a dainty saucer. Everything was in its place, fixed and assembled in the specific order that would keep me safe.

I felt the home-ness all over me. The wide familiar streets, the clean air, bumping into old friends in the mall. I slept in the spare room and helped Nanna cook dinner, and spent my days seeing friends' bands and rediscovering my favourite places.

One day I got off the bus in the city and, at a distance, saw my dad. He was just standing there, on the footpath, waiting for someone. Me? I ran to him. He was so happy to see me, this real Anna who had come home. I felt the layers of my old self folding back into my skin.

Because we were young and the beers were cheap, my friends and I would often drink all day at the Adelaide UniBar. One night, we had sat there long enough to become the crowd at Battle of the Bands, where a singer (how old? much younger than I am now) was wearing loud pink hot pants and nothing else. He was stretched out, sinewy the way people were then, because they thought they were Radiohead, and he was making love to the microphone.

'Can I have a volunteer?' he yelled.

We had stacked fifty plastic beer cups into a pyramid. I was the kind of wasted that volunteers for anything, when your body is separate from you. I shouted, 'Me', and clambered up *what were you wearing?* and he said, 'What's your name?' There were people in the audience I had been in kindergarten with, guys I had known since their mothers had used fingernails to pick the caked-on snot from their faces.

'Anna,' I said. I was fearless, I didn't need to *you were asking for it* be anonymous. I had on a new Abercrombie skirt that zipped all the way up, so you could yank it in one motion and the whole lot would fall away in one sheet and then you'd just be your legs.

'Anna,' he drawled. 'That's a beautiful name.' The band played. The air was full of conversations and spilled drinks and whatever was sticky on the pool tables. 'Anna. I want you to do something.' His skin gleamed in its *you must have led him on* slick of sweat. 'Talk dirty to me.' He didn't say it into the microphone. He said it so close to my ear I felt the tiny bones click together.

'I'm embarrassed,' I said.

'Don'tttt beeeeee.' Speaking in a breath like a Rudyard Kipling snake, like a harmonica.

I looked out at the crowd of people, some of whom I knew, and some of those people were hooting and clapping while others were shaking their heads, and I took the microphone and shouted some obscenity lost to history.

The man in the pink hot pants *you were drunk* laughed and he *boys will be boys* took my hand and *it's just banter* shoved it into his crotch where I felt every individual pubic hair he had ever grown and *look how short your skirt is* the slack skin of his penis. Into the microphone and my ear at once he said, 'Masturbate me,' and maybe I did, just for a second, just for the show, be a good sport, don't be so uptight.

Some friends dragged me off the stage; were they more embarrassed for me or themselves? Maybe I puked in a pot plant, or cried in the toilets, or rolled a soggy joint.

A couple of weeks later, the new issue of the uni's student newspaper, *On Dit*, came out. The archives are still available on the university's website. There's a bit of a report from the Battle of the Bands competition, congrats to the winners, what a great time we all had. And then it reads: 'Other highlights from the night included … an entertainingly offensive half-time interlude … demonstrating again just what can be achieved with a glockenspiel and a ukulele.'

My hand forced around this stranger's limp dick had been reduced to an 'entertainingly offensive interlude'.

The band, whose name I had not remembered – and I had also not remembered the glockenspiel until now, but such is the nature of memory – doesn't seem to exist anymore. But when you search for it online, the first result is 'Rules to Follow to Avoid Pump Problems'. I'm not even lying for the sake of what is quite a good joke about avoiding pump problems.

A few weeks later, I flew back from Adelaide to Melbourne to stay in my parents' house for a couple of days and look after the cats. I don't know where my parents had gone, or why they needed me to cat-sit; usually they left out an ice-cream container with food in it, which is quite similar to my memories of how they fed me. But for whatever reason, I was, aged eighteen, alone in their house (which had never felt like my house, only *their* house and occasionally *the* house), and I was talking on the internet to my friend J, who I had never met. It was very late, perhaps two in the morning.

You should come down, he said. He meant to Hobart, an hour-long flight south to the beautiful island of Tasmania. *Tomorrow. It's our uni ball.*

Can you imagine, I said, imagining.

Go on.

For nefarious reasons, I had memorised my dad's frequent flyer number and password. And I knew I had, in my old bedroom, the dress I had worn to my school formal the year before. In the dark solitude of this house that wasn't mine, it seemed utterly reasonable – bold; in fact, *necessary* – to find a way to make it to Hobart for a ball the next night. I wrangled a flight using points and didn't feel bad about it at all. Do with that information what you will.

In the morning I caught a train and a bus and a plane, the latter of which came in over the oyster farms, and then, a mere eight hours after making the decision, I had landed in a different place altogether.

At the moment I stepped out of the tiny airport and into the air (it smelled of air! oh, fresh oxygen), my phone rang, and it was Dad.

'Hello?' I said.

'Where are you?' he asked. How he knew I was not where he had left me I do not know.

I hesitated, trying to decide whether or not to lie. 'Um, Hobart.'

He yelled and hung up, and I felt a twitch of freedom.

It was a gorgeous day. There was snow on the mountain so we drove up there and dived at it, danced in its powdery halo. We went to an indoor minigolf centre with ramps and vacuums and all kinds of bizarre obstacles. Before the ball, we ate with one of J's friends near the dock, then got dressed up and went in a shuttle bus to the venue. For hours we just drank and smoked, smoked and drank. His friends were nice to me, laughing at my jokes, telling me how glad they were I came. There was a pretty courtyard with vines circling it, and fairy lights, and thick heads of foam in our pints, and I felt so happy to be there, so pleased that I had taken a risk and ended up on an adventure.

J's dorm room at the university was too small for anyone to sleep on the floor. But his friend, a guy I had met at the bottom of the third or ninth jug of Tasmanian beer, had a whole house just up the road. I could stay with him. There was no spare bed, he explained, but his was big enough *you were asking for it* for both of us. It was a wooden thing with a clean red bedspread. Everything in the house was impeccable, nothing like the share houses I had been in before. I climbed into the side furthest from the window. I was still wearing the gown from the ball. My head was a globe on an axis, so sloppy with the beer. I fell asleep quickly.

I woke in the night with a start. It took a few seconds to adjust – where the fuck was I? Back through the day's events: caught a plane, went to a ball, passed out in a stranger's bed. Pitch-darkness. A body moving under the covers next to me. Arms around me, their weight heavy on my ribs. Hands on my *you must have led him on* skin, my breasts, my nipples. The hot breath on my neck and the unmistakable stab of his erection in my spine. I lay perfectly still, fear moving up me *can't you take a joke* like fire on a mountainside. I don't know what happened next. My mental time machine will not travel there.

Then I was gone – back to Adelaide to waste time in the uni bar, to smoke weed with my friends and startle the electrons in my head into paranoia and confusion. And I wonder: which of these beginnings signalled the end?

In which contact is lost with external reality

This is not an anti-drug book. Legally, I suppose it's not allowed to be a pro-drug book either, but I want to be clear that I'm not a square.

Probably it's a message to my younger self that maybe, if you're already having dissociative episodes and unexplained paranoia, avoid psychoactives. Honestly, a good warm Milo will do.

I've never written about this publicly before. For a long time it was because I knew it was something people were bad at understanding, that society vilifies and misrepresents substance use, going so far as to declare an actual war. I was afraid no one would help me, on the basis that people believe the negative outcomes of substance use are both self-inflicted and deserved.

I hadn't realised the heightened risk for me; friends would do bags of coke over the weekend, stay awake for ninety-six hours and be totally fine on Tuesday. I couldn't have had the self-awareness to recognise thought patterns as warning signs.

I was a kid, looking for community, finding it and then losing it again. But even if I wasn't, sometimes this is just how brains go. A misfire. Circumstances that may never have an impact on one life but shape the entirety of another. Do not denigrate the person who finds themselves so affected. Luck – there but for the grace of God etc.

Many schizoid and personality disorders have their first onset in teenage and early adult years. Drug use can, in some cases, hasten or cause their onset. Usually this happens in someone who's predisposed to serious mental illness. Smoking cannabis, which can also be a very fun time spent looking at your hands and eating, might as much as double the risk of developing psychosis.

If someone had told me all of this, would I still have smoked bongs with my friends? Of course I would have. This is not the complete and utter genesis of my story. I just wanted to have a laugh. Even on this side of the experience, I wouldn't warn a teenager away from it. You can't know where your brain might go until it goes there. Bad things might never happen, but I also don't know how to convey the magnitude of risk if they do. It is impossible to wholly articulate the experience of psychosis. The words do not exist.

As a middle-aged person, I sometimes walk out of my house and look at the street and I have no idea where I am. I don't mean that I couldn't point it out on Google Maps, or that I can't remember what the street is called, or that I have somehow sleepwalked to an unfamiliar suburb and taken my house along with me. I mean that right inside of me, where I keep the things I am most sure about, this street is missing. Even though I've lived here for nearly a decade, I do not recognise it. Not even a bit.

This is something people call 'dissociation'. It can be an illness in its own right, but it is also a very common symptom for people with psychosis and/or anxiety disorders. I did not realise this when I started experiencing it. It was so alarming that I thought no one else could possibly have had it before me because surely they would have spoken about it, written about it, put it on the front page of the newspaper.

People experience dissociation in different ways; this might not be a way that you recognise. Some people have a complete severance from the present moment, a 'blackout', and can't remember afterwards what happened during this lost time. Others, like me, feel disconnected from time and space, outside of their body, the present moment, their mind. Here are some things it's like:

It's like when you're reading on a long car ride or train journey, and you look up from your book and you don't know where you are.

It's like when you drive out of a back street and expect to be on East Road, but you're actually on North Road, and even though you've been there lots of times you can't make your eyes adjust from what you expected to see.

It's like when you binge-watch three seasons of a show in a weekend, and after you've finished you just have this sneaking suspicion, a hunch, that you are part of the show and the characters are your family, and you kind of expect them to come to the dinner table even though you sort of know they don't live with you.

It's like being alive but also being a bit dead. Not all the way dead. Mostly dead (slightly alive).

I remember hearing, before I had my own psychosis, that a guy I went to school with was in a mental hospital. 'He reckons he's getting married to his ex-girlfriend,' someone told me. 'He thinks the nurses are hiding the engagement ring from him.' It wasn't a joke, but it was sort of a joke, you know? It was a spectacle.

Psychosis is unimaginably complex. Back then, my idea of a psychotic person was limited to someone who thought they were the Second Coming, who paced the streets talking aloud to themselves. I had watched *Girl, Interrupted*! Delusions were grand and significant, not just stepping outside the front door and believing you had tripped through the universe to another place. I couldn't connect my sense of self with someone's delusions about the end of the world, or believing they were a hat, or violently assaulting someone on the street (which, of course, are all harmful mostly-myths perpetuated by misunderstanding). My psychosis was more quietly disruptive. It fogged my senses of clarity and connection; I felt I needed to shake my head to focus. I was just Not Quite Right. Do you know what it was like? It was like when you look at a 3D image without wearing the glasses. I had one version of myself and another version of myself, and they refused to overlap to create a whole person.

Psychosis is a life-threatening illness. Delusions and paranoia are factors in homelessness, unemployment, being a victim of domestic violence and being arrested. As many as 21 per cent of people with delusional disorders attempt suicide – about the same rate as people with schizophrenia. They are up to thirty times more likely than the general public to die this way.

In the early weeks of my psychosis, I couldn't work. I could barely breathe. Before long, I ran out of money and had to move home. I was unimaginably fortunate to have somewhere to go when so many psychotic people do not. My parents had turned my bedroom into a study, so I slept on a fold-out couch in their living room. I couldn't tell them what had happened; their disappointment would obliterate me. Detached from the world – figuratively, literally – I lashed out and tore great rifts in the fragile fabric of my family. I was so, so frightened.

It is agony to recall that girl. I want to reach through space-time and hold her. Reassure her. Comfort her. I want to tell her about us. I want to say, Spend a minute in the future. The politics is shitty and everything is on fire, but see how tough you are. Look at what you've done. Meet these people who love you.

This story begins in many places. It begins in a share house in suburban Melbourne, near a park. It begins when imagined kidnappers followed me home. It begins the first time I watched Nanna lock and unlock her security door.

But, truthfully, it begins everywhere. It is a timeless, limitless genesis. A Möbius strip. Beginning and ending both.

Part 2

NOVEMBER

On a spring afternoon, I call the crisis assessment and treatment (CAT) team at the public hospital. I call them from bed. Even though I have been taught why I have hard feelings, my hands are too depressed to hold the phone. I wedge it between my face and the mattress and stare straight ahead. On the bedside table, my laptop plays an episode of *Property Brothers* I've seen before. The husband-and-wife renovators look like they want to kill each other, a vibe that's exaggerated by the huge mallets they're holding. My call is answered by a recorded voice that tells me someone will be with me soon. It tells me this three more times before it offers the option of a call-back. I won't lose my place in the queue, it promises, and hopes I manage to stay alive until then. I whack my head against the screen until my skin connects with the hang-up button.

An hour later, someone rings back. I miss the call because I'm sitting at the kitchen table wondering if I can teach my cat to play cards with me. I return the call. A voice tells me I can ask for a call-back; I won't lose my place in the queue.

After a couple of goes of this, a triage nurse and I manage to speak directly.

'Anna?' she says.

'Yes.'

'Did you call the crisis team?'

'Yes.'

'Good, good,' she says. 'Could you tell me why?'

I'm back in bed, watching a woman on *Antiques Roadshow* pretend not to be disappointed that her stepmother's Art Deco diamonds are only worth £3000.

'I'm really tired,' I say.

'Can you tell me about that?'

'It's just been a really hard time. I don't know what feelings I have anymore.'

'What do you mean?'

I tell her about trying to manage remote school learning as well as my own work and how one of the cats peed in my bookshelf and thinking of something to make for dinner every single night Jesus Christ and that the shower drain is full of hair and my bathroom floor collapsed and the oven doesn't work anymore and part of my shoulder is really itchy but I can't reach it and also I kind of want to drive my car into a tree.

'Say that again,' she says.

'The plumbers have been here for weeks.'

'The other part. About your car.'

'Oh,' I say. 'It's just. Well. I'm disorientated and confused. I don't know if I'm extremely depressed or not at all depressed. I don't feel *anything*.'

'I see.' She tells me it sounds like I've had a hard year. I say that everyone has had a hard year, and she tells me mine sounds especially hard. I don't think that's true. I do know I wanted someone to say it to me, though, even as a lie.

She asks me if I have a plan to harm myself, or access to any weapons.

I tell her my children are with their dad.

She says again, 'Do you have any weapons?'

I say maybe my car counts as a weapon? 'I'm afraid I might steer it into oncoming traffic. Like the impulse might overwhelm me.'

'That sounds pretty scary,' she says gently.

I tell her the road near my house is a truck route. The B-doubles go roaring down there every day, clipping the trees. My little car would be alfoil under their wheels.

I can hear her keyboard clacking.

'Anna,' she says, 'how would you feel if someone from our team came to visit you tomorrow?'

My body is so horizontal it's a spirit level.

'That sounds good,' I say.

My kids will be back tomorrow. I wait. I wait and wait until tomorrow, watching the wives with mallets who hate their husbands.

An older woman and a younger guy come to the door. I ask them, Can we please do this outside? I don't want my kids to hear anything distressing.

They ask if I might send the kids into the backyard instead.

I say, I'd rather do it here, on the porch.

We stand on the porch.

We are all wearing disposable masks with the metal part pinched around our nose. The man does the talking. He asks me the same questions they always do: How are you feeling? Do you have a plan for self-harm? How long has this been going on? He wonders how my appetite has been (poor, largely chocolate), whether I'm sleeping (thinking about every terrible thing until 3 am, then waking every hour), if I'm having trouble concentrating (a bird is teaching a smaller, identical bird to turn over the soil under the tree by my bedroom window). I know all of these questions. I know which answers will slot me into which criteria and the red flags they're seeking. Depression: low energy, poor appetite, insomnia. Anxiety: racing heart, lack of focus, obsessive thoughts. Suicidality: knowing how many pills are in the packet by the bed, feeling hopeless, pointless, nothing matters anymore, making a plan.

He asks if I know how the CAT team works, that they screen patients for the public mental health hospital ward. He wonders if I know much about that system, in particular whether I realise involuntary psychiatric in-patient wards are for people who are *in a really bad way*. He looks at me very hard as he says this. He means: If you go there, you'll be around really sick people, it's serious, it's not just a bed you sleep in when you don't feel like being an adult anymore. He says: Sometimes it makes people feel worse.

Yes, I say, I know. I don't think I need to go to hospital. Or, maybe. It's just that I'm so tired I feel outside of myself, like I might be too tired and forget not to die. You know?

He does know. Then he notices my white hatchback in the driveway. It's a sports car. I bought it for myself when I no longer needed to carry around booster seats and sixteen primary school art projects.

'Is that your car?' he says.

'Yes.'

'Nice.'

The woman makes notes on her pad. I try to look at both of them at once.

'How many kilowatts does it put out?'

I know what he's doing. I know he's getting me to talk about something else so he can see if I'm lucid, see how I behave when I'm not giving rehearsed responses about how bad I feel.

'A hundred and sixty-nine,' I say.

The woman keeps writing. My focus flicks from one to the other.

'Nice. That must go fast.'

'Yep.'

'Do you like to drive fast?' He wants to know if I'm going to drive fast in the direction of a telegraph pole or building or person.

'Sometimes, on the freeway.' Then, quickly: 'I've only had one speeding fine in my whole life.'

'You're a safe driver, then.'

'Yes,' I say. 'Yes, very.'

This seems to reassure him. He tells me he thinks I'll be okay for now. I have my next therapy appointment already booked and they'll give her their notes in the meantime and she can help me figure out what to do next. 'See how you're feeling,' he says. 'Every day is different.' He heads off down the steps.

The woman, who's been quiet the whole time, hangs back for a moment. She says to me quietly, 'You're doing a good job.'

I shake my head and she says, 'No, really, you are.'

'Okay,' I say. 'Thanks.'

They're the experts.

Injuring oneself with the intent to die

Have you been to a therapist? Every time you visit someone new, they ask the same questions. Are you eating? Sleeping? Exercising? These are screening questions, the kind that identify symptoms and risk factors. Most people with depression tick at least five of these boxes: loss of appetite, loss of sex drive, reduced enthusiasm for hobbies and interests, general malaise, feeling stressed, tired, anxious, sad.

Then they ask you: 'Do you ever think about hurting yourself?'

You might say: 'Sometimes.'

They give the requisite reply: 'Do you have a plan to die?'

A few years ago I went for a drive along the foreshore south of Melbourne, alone. I parked my car in a council-run car park, slipped my two dollars into the meter, and let the engine idle. I was on a clifftop, in my stationary car. A few metres ahead was a sheer plummet into the sand, and then the cool and crushing relief of the water. I stayed in neutral but pushed the accelerator a little, to understand the feeling of it. I imagined the car heading over the cliff with me inside it. It would be the car's death, the car's fault. My own death, body crushed by the folding metal, would be a side effect.

Perhaps you share a story like this one with your new therapist. Maybe you say it with a question mark: Is this a plan?

For thousands of years, various cultures have believed a doppelgänger to be a sign of impending doom – a person's meeting their exact likeness is said to herald their imminent death. Magical thinking. Superstition. (Paranoia. Anxiety.)

My grandfather, Dean Jeffries Ryan, was born in Adelaide in 1924. He was an identical twin.

I didn't know about his suicide until I was a teenager. I had been protected by all manner of half-truths before then: he was sick, he had been sick for ages, he'd had an accident. Until I was twelve, I thought he had died variously of lung cancer, kidney failure or a heart attack. I don't know if someone told me it was one of these things, or whether they hadn't told me anything and I had filled in the gaps myself with things I thought people died of.

One Saturday morning, on our way to school sport, Dad said to me, 'You know your grandpa killed himself?' and it shot out of him the way a secret often does, all at once: a relief and a burden.

At first, I was indignant. Did they think I couldn't handle the truth? But in reality, after I knew, I wore it like a cloak. It was as though I'd found the missing link that would explain the terror and foreboding I was experiencing. I found comfort in the idea of a 'suicide gene'. It took the onus away from me. It was almost soothing to imagine I could do nothing about it.

A spiritual double is a bad omen in folklore, and maybe it is in this story, too.

In 1980 my dad sat in a room in Adelaide's Flinders Medical Centre with my grandfather, who was recovering from carbon monoxide poisoning after a suicide attempt. His first plan: a hose through the car window.

'What should we do?' Dad asked, and the doctor said, 'Prepare yourself to be back here again. Probably soon.'

Six weeks later they were, this time to identify Dean's body.

He had quit his job to care for my grandmother, who was dying. The last line in her diary reads: *Dean retired*; underneath that are clippings from her death notices. He suicided eighteen months to the day after she died.

Two things happen when I share his suicide with practitioners. First, they write it on a piece of paper and draw a big circle around it. *WARNING. FAMILY HISTORY.* Sometimes they use a highlighter, to properly indicate the magnitude of risk. Second – reluctantly – I feel grateful. I feel glad that my place in that room is justified, that they have to consider that I might have a plan. That I might die from my mental illness.

I ask my dad about this, in the best way you can ask. 'Do you think it's weird that your father killed himself and now I feel kind of cosmically energised by it?'

I can't say this to anyone else. Society is not reconciled to the idea of mental illness as being terminal. Yet half of all people in

Australia who die by suicide have previously been treated for or hospitalised with mental illness. Of people who make a serious attempt on their own life, up to 15 per cent will die by suicide within ninety days of their release from hospital.

My grandfather's second plan: ten seconds of household current in his nerves.

I once asked my dad if he thought Grandpa might have stayed alive if he had met me. Was I a good enough reason? Dad said he didn't think so, but not in a mean way. Sometimes mental illness is like that; you can't stay just because someone wants you to.

There's a line in my grandfather's suicide note that reads: *Please retain very happy memories of me.* The *very* changes it, somehow. It's not a wish but a demand. Don't retain the moderately happy ones. I wonder what he wanted people to recall. Did he mean *very happy* as in 'Christmas morning, but before the sun comes up, when the children are in their nightgowns and Grandmother is boiling the kettle on the stove and we are all together', or as in 'when *I* was happy, a certain way, successful and well-liked and had good hair'?

The suicide note, of which I have one photocopy on shiny thermal paper and another typed copy, is both dramatic and pragmatic. Grandpa says he has *absolutely reached the length of my tether* and *decided to end it all.* Then he asks the recipient to please make sure the lawns and garden are kept until the house is sold, and for my dad to arrange the funeral service.

He writes, *I am sorry to do this to you. You have all been a tower of strength for me.* His handwriting is curly and upright. In the attached papers, he lists my dad as his next of kin, and notes that he is currently on holiday.

For my sake, he writes, *please retain very happy memories of me.*

A continuation of his story. Memory is where we are immortal.

Panic is a strange sensation. There are others like it: missing the last step; the hypnic jerk before sleep; an electric shock. But as an eight-year-old, I was sure it was just plain 'dying' – the vice-gripped heart of a person in immediate mortal danger. No one had ever offered a conversation about the way brains function, and I knew nothing about what to expect. Maybe that was a missed opportunity. Perhaps, knowing my grandfather had perched at the edge of the existential void and peered inside, they – my parents? teachers? – might have given me a heads-up.

Early on in its manifestation, mental illness is utterly solitary. You do it entirely alone. The first time you crawl into the dark belly of the black dog, the first time you see the world sliding away from you. You have to learn to live with this kind of illness as you go, to identify the signs and work through the outcomes. I think about the young girl who was me and I am heartbroken for her. Looking for the tiny box of comfort, her primitive instinct to hide. Even now, on a really hard day, I will curl into a ball under the table, as though waiting for an earthquake to pass. I think about that girl who was me, screaming in the schoolyard, and wonder if it might have been better to know what was coming.

In photos from their childhood, my grandfather and his brother are so similar even they couldn't tell themselves apart. Both have blond curls and nautical-themed pyjamas and lamb's wool blankets. Both have an eerie thousand-yard stare – the crystal-eyed gaze into infinity meant for men much older.

Some of the photos have inscriptions on the back: *John (left) and Dean (right), 8 months*. In these, their identity is easily defined. But compare them with the non-inscribed versions and there's nothing to distinguish them, nothing to find in the first photo and pick up in the second, nothing to offer a definitive: Yes, this is Dean. No freckle, no weird haircut, no initialled sweater. My grandfather is both boys, and neither boy. Dad says they were so alike as to be 'interchangeable'.

But though they were monozygotic, they weren't completely identical. They were mirror twins – they looked the same but were actually opposites. One left-handed, one right. And one killed himself, while the other didn't.

Sometimes I look for them in my own mirror. I have their eyes, a gloomy blue-grey; my dad's eyes and now my daughter's eyes. Neither of my siblings has them – only me. I look at these eyes that are also my grandfather's eyes and I wonder: Is he in there?

Men over eighty-five have the highest rate of suicide of any group. I watched my great-uncle John, after that morbid milestone birthday, for the genetic inevitability. Maybe it would, somehow, release me from my own predisposition. Not the granddaughter of the man who killed himself but of the man whose specific double helix of data included death this way. Uninheritable.

There are a small number of available statistics. Studies generally show that a monozygotic (identical) twin is more likely to attempt suicide if their twin has attempted or completed suicide. For example, a 1995 study found that of twenty-six surviving identical twins, ten had attempted suicide, while none of the nine non-identical surviving twins surveyed had a history of suicide attempts. A 2010 study by the American Academy of Pediatrics showed children of paternal suicide have no increased risk of suicide-attempt hospitalisation themselves. Earlier research shows no significant association for second-degree relatives, like granddaughters.

But statistics are not stories. My dad is an optimistic man, a kind and spiritually generous man. As a teenager, after I knew, I worried so much that he would meet the same end. Every time he was sad, I imagined this outcome for him. But he is not depressed, and even in his worst moments he has never been suicidal.

'Maybe it's the mythology of it,' he offers. 'Maybe when you're the grandchild and not the child, you're left only with the legend.'

My grandfather was fifty-six when he died. His twin brother died decades years later, of natural causes and in a nursing home, aged ninety-one.

People have told me about my grandpa. He was serious, devoutly religious, dedicated to providing for his family, sometimes mean. But there are things I know about him that no one else did, not even his genetic duplicate; things no one could have proffered to me as a heads-up. The great dark edges of the ravine. The near-unnoticeable moments when the light breaks through. The tremendous, overwhelming nothingness.

I was lucky to know the twin who lived. This man had a cuckoo clock in his living room and a singsong doorbell, and he wore slippers and had a great, deep laugh. Out the back of his house was a spare fridge just for ice cream. He grew vegetables in his garden and there was a dog buried under the pumpkins. He drove a maroon car. Both of his sons were church ministers. He had a little round table with a tea cosy on it and his voice was as familiar to me as my own. He had a very long – and by all accounts happy – life.

He had nine grandchildren and none of them were me. But in my memory, this is my grandfather. After all, they had the same DNA. What difference does it make, to look into a different mirror?

In my thirties, I wrote to the National Archives of Australia (NAA) to ask for records of times my grandfather spent at the Daw Park Repatriation Hospital after the war. He had been in the air force in Borneo but was discharged as a casualty in 1944 with appendicitis. His real injury was much harder to operate on. Combat stress. Battle fatigue. A condition close to what we now call PTSD.

The NAA refused even redacted access to his records.

In their rationale statement to me, they wrote, 'The information is of a kind that most members of the community would not want disclosed about themselves.'

Separation of normally related mental processes

Early in my psychotic experience, I went to the doctor for help. My family GP was a woman I hadn't been seeing long – maybe a year or so. Because I was only nineteen, I assumed she would know what to do. I didn't know yet that doctors do not understand mental health. I didn't know that they would create a version of me in their minds and make dangerous assumptions, that they would wilfully misrepresent and deny me, demand answers they didn't ask of others, and define me by my behaviour.

I did not realise yet that they would work against my recovery.

I took a seat by her desk. The day was sunny, swaying with the late summer, strobes of sunlight in Melbourne's elm trees. She said, 'How are you?'

I said, 'Good, thanks,' which is part of getting by in society.

Then she said, 'What can I help you with today?'

I hadn't learned any of the vocabulary for this either, so I used what little I had. 'It's like there's a layer of cling film over everything,' I said. When she showed no sign of recognition, I said, 'It's like being on a movie set. I feel like the buildings are just facades, with nothing behind them.'

'Mm-hm,' she said, typing.

'When I go outside, I don't recognise the streets I'm in. I know they're streets, but they look like …' I fumbled with language, trying to create the images with words we had in common. 'They look like anything *except* streets. They're *anti*-streets.' This felt revelatory. I had explained it perfectly.

'I see.'

She wrote a prescription for Aropax, the brand name of a common selective serotonin reuptake inhibitor (SSRI) called paroxetine. I took it for three months. At first, it did nothing. Other people described brain zaps, sparks of electricity, nausea and headaches, a dullness, emptiness. I didn't feel any of these. I felt the same as before. Every day I took the tablet and waited for it to scoop my brain back in. A while later, I realised I couldn't orgasm anymore. This was devastating. So, I did what you are absolutely not supposed to do: I put the pills in the bin, went off them cold turkey, and hid in my room with my vibrator. The dramatic part of me thought, This is how I know I'm alive.

I moved from my parents' sofa bed to a big old house on the other side of town, with my friends Stacy and Alex and some random guys we found in the classifieds. I took with me a small brown cat and a small grey cat. On the first night, I was alone. The electricity hadn't been connected yet, and there was no furniture. I rolled out a sleeping bag in front of the unlit fireplace and looked at my phone until it was flat, then I just lay there in the dark and listened to the people in other houses having domestics and talking about share portfolios, and my eyes swam with lights that weren't there.

The house was at the top of a slope in the eastern suburbs, and if you sat on the windowsill and let the night wrap around you, you could see the blinking city lights and people riding their bikes along the river in the dark. I sat on the windowsill for a month. My brown cat caught possums and left their meatless spines on my bedroom floor, and the grey cat sat with me while I rolled lopsided cigarettes from a packet of Champion Ruby. I understood this as one way to form a personality: to become someone who sat in a window with a cat and smoked, but in an interesting way. There were always people in the house; they came in through the window and stayed for the whole weekend, sharing our beds and food and TV. Sometimes it wasn't entirely clear who lived in the house and who was only visiting.

My fear kept me indoors. I looked from the windowsill to the letterbox and wondered if I would ever be able to explore so far again. In the privacy of my bedroom I wore a tiny skirt and men on the internet paid me by the minute to look under it; this, and fifty dollars a week from my parents, was how I could afford my rent.

On a day when I was briefly courageous, I went to a new doctor.

'How can I help you today?' she said.

At this stage, I was still certain someone would be able to help, that there was a cure they could pull from a drawer. 'Everything feels unreal,' I said. Again I struggled to find the right words. 'It's like I've put in too many eyedrops and now it's all cloudy. It's like my soul is a few inches to the right of my body.'

'Mm-hm,' she said.

She pulled out a collection of samples.

'I've already taken Aropax.' I tried to mime the way it stole my sex drive. 'It did nothing.'

She nodded, picking up different boxes. 'I think you're psychotic.' The right one fell into her hand. 'I'm prescribing Risperdal.'

I spent my last twenty dollars filling the script and buying a pizza. I didn't know what *psychotic* was and the doctor hadn't explained it. Because I believed her, I didn't look for more information about the medicine. I didn't find out it was risperidone, an atypical antipsychotic. After two weeks of taking it, I started lactating. I shot an arc of breastmilk to the other side of the room.

My anxiety ate me alive. For a few days I had a job as a receptionist for a couple of engineers in a nearby suburb, which mostly involved spinning around on an office chair. Most days, I went to the bus stop and turned around and came home again. When I got the call firing me from the job, I was cooking pasta from a packet in my kitchen at 10.30 am on a weekday. My brown cat brought a blue-tongue lizard inside and it disappeared somewhere in the house.

I knew if I stopped moving, my hands would fly off. I spent my days writing long letters, smoking, writing, smoking. I burned a hole in my housemate's curtains; I wasn't sure if it was an accident.

After three months, my housemates – I had six by then – called the crisis assessment and treatment team about my erratic behaviour. My ex-boyfriend had told me I was 'too mental' so I was proving him wrong by stalking him. Three nurses came to our house late at night, one of them a gigantic man who stood behind the others as a vague threat. They asked me questions like, Do you have a plan to kill yourself? and, Do you know who the prime minister is? I sat on my windowsill and blew grey smoke towards the stars. In the hallway, one of the nurses said, 'I don't think she's schizophrenic,' as though that was the worst and most terrifying thing a person could be.

I was ordered to go to a psychiatrist.

I no longer believed they would know how to help me.

Before I went I decided to look online for new vocabulary. I found a website called DPhelp.com, which to my disappointment was not a sexual deviancy advice line. An online forum of people – mostly women – described the symptoms they experienced, and I finally recognised myself in something: people who were outside of themselves; who felt disconnected from the world around them; who had slipped out of time.

I wrote down *derealisation* and *depersonalisation*.

It took three days to get an appointment with the psychiatrist. (I realise now, having at times waited months to be seen, the nurses must have considered me a medical emergency.) He had a small room on the junction above a topless bar. I had to borrow more than $400 from a friend to pay for the session.

'How are you feeling?' the psychiatrist asked.

I thought of the words I had been taught. 'I'm just a bit worn out.'

'How's that?'

'I wish I was dead.'

He sat behind his oak table. I could see his shoes underneath; they were so shiny, like they were for looking up skirts. 'What do you mean, you wish you were dead?'

What did I mean? 'I want to die,' I said, but that wasn't right. I said, 'I wish I didn't exist.' Closer. 'I don't want to *be* dying.' The distinction was confounding. 'I want to *have died*.'

He prescribed Effexor, a serotonin-norepinephrine reuptake inhibitor (SNRI) with the common name venlafaxine, and five Xanax (alprazolam), and said I must only take them when extremely anxious – which was always. He told me to come back when I ran out. For another $400, he would decide if I could have any more. Any more than five tablets, he explained, would be enough to kill me – something I now know is wildly false. I paused to recognise a plan.

Afterwards, I filled the script. I took a Xanax.

Nothing happened.

In writing this down, it's clear that I have misremembered bits, and filed other parts in the wrong order. There was a night in a Brunswick pub when I definitely took a Xanax (no effect), and that was before I met my husband because I was holding hands with somebody else. The nurses came, but the leaves had turned so it must have been autumn. Someone was with me at that first psychiatric appointment and took me to buy groceries afterwards, but I don't remember who.

Sometime before or after the CAT team came, I stood out on Nicholson Street in the dark. The air bloomed with rain. Earlier that day I had gone to a friend's house in Carlton and told them I had popped every benzodiazepine in the bottle, I can't go on, no don't call an ambulance, this is the end; we all knew I was lying.

Now it was late, after midnight, and for an hour I had beaten on the door of the warehouse where my ex-boyfriend lived. His housemates shouted from the barred windows. *Fuck off, you crazy bitch! You're insane!* I went down past the Indian takeaway and the bottle shop and crouched low in the phone booth. All the streetlights beamed their reflections from the wet road into the sky. I called the police and asked them to please take me home. Please, I howled into that plastic orange receiver, take me home. Triple zero, I can't remember how to get there.

They apologised, the police, but I was outside of my usual mental health catchment area and not in their jurisdiction. They couldn't help. Out of their control. Over and over I smashed the phone against the booth, trying to crack the spray-painted tags on the glass, but it was too strong.

I don't know how it happened that my parents came to get me, but I remember the sound Dad's wipers made as they slapped against the rain.

Difficulties relating to the sense of self

People sometimes ask, 'What's wrong with you?' It seems appalling that someone would ask this question right to your face, but the thing about having an illness or disorder or disability is that other people believe it entitles them to your body/brain. They're allowed to ask whatever offensive and terrible questions they want to, on account of you having the nerve to take up space in their abled and neurotypical existence. The only reasons you're here is to be inspirational or to listen to them tell you that their aunty had something like that once and she put essential oils on her toast and was cured.

So they ask, 'What's wrong with you?'

And I say, 'Could you be more specific?'

They gesture to empty space, ceilings, other people. 'You know. What's *wrong* with you?'

What they mean is: which movie character are you like? Are you the *Here's Johnny!* guy or are you Kate Winslet in *Eternal*

Sunshine of the Spotless Mind? Do you have multiple personalities? Have you ever tried to drill your brain? Are voices talking to you right now? Have you ever been put in restraints? Are you going to try to kill yourself while I'm standing here with you in the Body Shop?

What do you *have*?

No, but seriously, what is *wrong with you*?

Borderline personality disorder is so named *because of* its relationship to psychosis – the 'borderline' was imagined to be between neurosis and psychosis. That definition has been significantly revised since, as both the associated risk of developing symptoms and the language used to describe them becomes clearer. A 2013 analysis shows about 20 to 50 per cent of patients with borderline personality disorder report psychotic symptoms. Studies variously have people with BPD reporting auditory hallucinations (54 per cent), paranoid delusions (29 per cent) and 'true psychotic thought' (14 per cent). Patients with comorbid disorders including major depression may have longer-lasting psychotic symptoms. Research seems to suggest childhood trauma may play an important role. Some studies still report patients may just be confused, possibly pretending.

At sixteen, when the school chaplain sent me to the doctor for the wonderful things my brain was doing (crying for no reason, sleeping a lot, astral-travelling), the doctor said I was 'depressed'. Back then, in the 1990s, you could still have things like nervous breakdowns and manic depression and other terms comedians use as punchlines now. This doctor didn't give me a label, as such. She gave me a word to describe the set of feelings I was having. Depressed. I had no way to differentiate my desire to run into traffic from days I wanted to stay in bed or lash out at my startled siblings. They were all part of this umbrella of Depressed, which made it meaningless. But I filed it anyway, my first clinical word.

After I had blown my mind into oblivion in my late teens, I was given other labels. Over the past twenty years, GPs, counsellors, clinical psychologists and psychiatrists have all asked me to try on different coats. Some of these don't even exist anymore, struck out of the mental illness guidebook by newer, more accurate labels. Major depressive disorder. Generalised anxiety disorder. Complex post-traumatic stress disorder. Panic disorder. Dissociative identity disorder. Bipolar I. Bipolar II. Obsessive-compulsive disorder. Postnatal depression. *Pre*natal depression. Premenstrual dysphoric disorder. Psychosis. And, most recently, borderline personality disorder.

I've also been defined by the labels I *don't* have. Sometimes, mental illness diagnosis is a process of elimination, or reassurance that you don't have one of *those* illness (the ones people think are 'bad' because they've been incorrectly – dangerously – used as synonyms for violence and inhumanity). I don't have schizophrenia. I don't have narcissistic personality disorder. You can also be given a label with qualifiers: You *only* have depression; you're *just* anxious; or, *sorry, this must be hard to hear*, please take this leaflet and go to the URL at the bottom.

Sometimes the diagnostic criteria change and you no longer fit into the dot points of your label. Sometimes the name changes or two disorders are rolled into one or researchers decide it never existed to begin with. And yet other times, we change, and the label we had becomes a confusing former self.

But most of all, mental illness labels rely on the language a patient has to articulate their experience.

'Okay,' doctors say when you turn up. 'What's *wrong* with you?' And if you can't find the words, they will find them for you.

I was diagnosed with borderline personality disorder when I was thirty-six, a label that was revised to 'borderline traits' three years later. By then, I had (spoiler alert) been married and divorced and my children were teenagers. For decades, people had ghosted me, broken up with me, lost my number, forgotten to call. Truly, everyone I had ever met had told me I was *a lot*, that I was unstable, too emotional. *Crazy*. It was a relief to understand why.

I learned about personality disorders. Their distinction from mood disorders (like depression and anxiety) is controversial and not easily explained – there are high rates of comorbidity between these different types of disorders, and there exist no laboratory markers to identify them. Some research describes personality disorders as simply 'more chronic' versions of mood disorders; sometimes they are defined by their enduring, consistent presentation.

Unless you give a mental health professional a very good reason to think otherwise, they will probably assume you have a mood disorder. Maybe they even want you to have one. These are the most common kind of mental illness; for example, in

Australia, one in three people will have anxiety in their lifetime. Mood disorders crop up for different reasons. Sometimes they are a response to something going on in the world ('situational') and sometimes they spring from nowhere. Often they are transient, but not always, and they can be recurrent. Depressed? You have major depressive disorder. Anxious for no reason? You have generalised anxiety disorder. Anxious around people? Social anxiety disorder. And so on.

Personality disorders tend to develop in childhood and be lifelong. They're separated into clusters based on symptoms: cluster A disorders are characterised by 'eccentric thinking' (e.g. schizoid personality disorder); cluster B has the dramatic and unpredictable ones (e.g. antisocial identity disorder); and cluster C includes anxious and fear-based behaviour (e.g. obsessive-compulsive personality disorder). They affect how you connect to and understand the world over your lifetime. They're 'part of you', sort of. They exist within the tools you used to develop a sense of self; they are crucial to the way you understand your identity. It's not surprising, then, that they can be very hard to untangle.

I can't remember why I started reading about these disorders, but the diagnostic criteria resonated with me so strongly I cried as I read it (this is not necessarily noteworthy: I have cried during episodes of *Everybody Loves Raymond*). Unstable relationships. Unclear sense of self. Fear of abandonment. Tick, tick, tick.

I started asking my therapist at the time: Is this me? Do I have a personality disorder?

At first, she tried to talk me out of it. I got the distinct impression I was doing myself an injury by even contemplating it – like, Why would you think that about yourself? Personality disorders have such a reputation: psychopaths have personality disorders; sociopaths have personality disorders; select US presidents have personality disorders. If you believe the media, movies, TV, books, your distant cousin on Facebook, everyone with a personality disorder will eventually commit a murder, given enough time. That can't be you. You're a normal person. You have a family and sometimes a job. You hardly ever murder. Oh no, people say, thinking it's a comfort, only *awful* people have personality disorders.

No one would talk to me about the likelihood I had something like this. No one would let me draw those connections – over and over, they directed me away from that diagnosis and told me to try mindfulness, to go for a walk.

Until then, the treatments had been cognitive behavioural therapy or its close relatives. I was always instructed to internalise both the blame for how I was feeling and the responsibility for feeling better. If I was panicked or unhappy, I was given techniques to move those feelings along and hope they didn't come back. Not guided to sit with and accept a feeling. Not to recognise it as part of me. There was no push to better understand why it happened or how to deal with the underlying causes; only layers and layers of shame.

Not one single person said to me: Anna, the nature of your symptoms makes me think you have a different kind of disorder, one that might need to be treated differently. For nearly twenty years, mental health professionals asked me what my symptoms were and then treated those symptoms. None of them said: These aren't just feelings you're having but manifestations of the way your identity was formed, the fundamental things you understand about yourself.

And they didn't say that keeping a notebook of anecdotes like *I felt scared at Pizza Hut but I breathed through it* was not going to change that. Sorry! Bit of a decades-long bum steer we gave you.

If you're quite good at masking your symptoms, as many of us are because that's how we make friends and stay employed, I suppose differentiating mood and personality disorders can be tricky. We are, after all, taught to hide our feelings or be sent out to the corridor. We have to learn a new lesson as we grow – that there's a reason for the symptoms we experience, and that there might be a way to make it easier. Even then, the stigma of mental illness makes the vocabulary secret, too. Society will tolerate a few of the broad-brush words, like depression and anxiety. The others we have to figure out on our own.

You know how doctors complain about patients who google their symptoms before they come in and think they know what's wrong with them? Mental health care requires you to do that. You have to open up a browser window and just start whacking in search terms like *my head seems bigger than normal* and *i saw a man who's not there*. How are you meant to be sure, otherwise, which words to use to help someone understand what the heck is the matter with you?

Maybe you've been asked this, too: Is there a diagnosis you identify with? Or: Have you read anything and recognised yourself in it? Some of my psychologists have wondered out loud whether a patient is better equipped to do this than they are, based on their intimate knowledge of their own experience and how hard it is to convey that to fit someone else's diagnostic criteria.

Language fell devastatingly short in getting me the appropriate help. At the same time as I was telling them I had depression (a word I had been taught to describe my feelings) I was also trying to explain that I was optimistic – hopeful, just cloudy. When I said I had anxiety, what I actually meant was that my thoughts and body weren't synchronised and it made me frightened – I was panicked, but also extremely confused. I knew it wasn't 'normal' to feel volatile and out of control. I was fully aware that my moods swung like the pendulum in a grandfather clock. But I couldn't put these experiences into words the doctors could match up with their clinical tools.

Kylie Maslen wrote about this beautifully in her book *Show Me Where it Hurts*: 'Pain is difficult to communicate, but it's not impossible. It does, however, rely on the use of more complex language than the current normative means of diagnosis and tracking.'

Let me first state: getting help for *any* kind of chronic issue is hard. I interviewed renowned disability communicator El Gibbs about her contribution to *Growing Up Disabled in Australia*, where she wrote about the social model of disability – the idea that society creates barriers, not the medical condition. She said, 'I think every doctor in Australia should read this book and weep, that so many of our experiences with their profession were deeply traumatic.' Looking for treatment, care and support is tremendously – and unnecessarily – difficult.

For some physical pain, we are taught a basic vocabulary. When it comes to everyday ailments, we can go to a doctor and say, 'It hurts when I press here,' or, 'There's pain when I move like this,' or, 'Look at this rash.' We can further clarify whether it's a sharp or dull pain, an ache or a throb or a stab.

If asked, we might even be able to measure it on a scale from one to ten. Different words trigger different outcomes: certain kinds of pain become an X-ray, an MRI, a laparoscopy. More complex physical ailments borrow language we have for other things – there is *a* level of universality to the vocabulary we use to describe blurred vision, nausea, tightness. Doctors are trained to make connections between some specific words – *which we are taught to say* – and the clinical reasons that underpin them, so that they might make further choices about a patient's concern (sometimes, that choice is to dismiss it).

Mental illness and other invisible and chronic illnesses hit the same barriers. Physical and mental health care are part of the same underfunded and ineffective medical system, and they intersect. It's not necessarily easier to get help for common physical illnesses, but it is at least sometimes (not always) more objective.

We have no choice but to work within the confines we are given. If an explanation doesn't exist, we have to find the energy to create it ourselves. All chronic illness has this in common: you can learn to self-advocate, or you can get worse. We invent new ways to describe the indescribable and offer them to a doctor who we hope won't misinterpret them. We have to give over our new language and beg them to make good use of it, to help someone else with it, to understand us better because of it. Then we take those words and tell them to another medical professional, who may or may not have heard them from someone else, who may or may not already have a definition in mind that contradicts our experience. So, we revise and review, ad infinitum.

We are still a long way from having an accepted vocabulary to describe mental health concerns. The words are so vast and so abstract. The actions we are instructed to take are non-specific. 'Speak to your GP,' say the ads. 'Talk to someone.' Or, worse, 'Check in with your work colleague,' and, 'Office morning tea.' This is why, when we go to a mental health professional for the first time, we use words from the billboard: depressed, anxious, angry. And it's why what we mean could be worlds apart from what they hear.

Twenty years ago, when I first sought help for my brain chemistry, doctors only asked about my symptoms. They used the words they had to describe something that bore little resemblance to what I was actually experiencing. They cornered me into the superficiality of my illness, and they never asked again.

Accessing good mental health care is riddled with obstacles: there aren't enough psychologists or psychiatrists to go around, so waiting lists can be months long; even fewer (or sometimes no) services exist in regional and rural areas; appointments are expensive; private in-patient care is expensive; getting a mental health care plan is expensive; having a mental illness can make it harder to work, meaning there is no money to pay for all these expensive steps. Also, you usually need to be both well enough to seek help and unwell enough to justify receiving it.

There is added complexity. Having access to care at all is not a given because being understood and being *believed* are also devastatingly different things. Getting the right chronic illness care is made even more difficult if you're not a man, not white, not straight, not cisgender, not living in a city and/or not in a body doctors understand. Low literacy is one such barrier – asking for the right help requires a person to be able to research and articulate; that is, to be able to read and analyse, and in the language in which information is provided. English is an especially complex language full of doublespeak and metaphors to describe pain. What makes an *ache* different from a *throb*? How can a *gnawing feeling* happen in your leg *and* your emotions?

For mental health care, as with other invisible illnesses, the need to be able to speak and to be heard is significant. External symptoms are as abstract as the language and frequently occur when the time for early intervention has passed. As with many invisible illnesses, professionals rely on a patient to accurately self-assess. This assumes both a level of literacy and the capacity to match an abstract feeling to a concrete diagnostic criteria. Quickly, doctors say, be clear about something impossibly speculative! Objectively describe your subjective inner world! Use the metric system to tell me how bad it is! It makes a range of other assumptions: that the patient feels safe to report honestly; that they are lucid; that masking a negative emotion isn't in fact a symptom of the illness that's brought them here today.

The words themselves carry stigma and value judgements. There is 'weakness' in the words necessary to use in a clinical setting. It's hard enough to find the courage to visit a doctor in the first place without then needing to use language we've been socialised to reject. Before asking if this help is even possible, there's an acrylic layer of shame that must be penetrated.

Finding the right care relies on undoing a lifetime of hiding from language. We're taught that if we articulate the feelings, people will treat us with suspicion, fear, doubt, resentment. We still use language that suggests we 'admit' to having mental illness, that we must 'open up'. That we are ashamed is a given. The onus is always on us. Take the first step. Admit you have a problem. Mental illness is supposed to be secret. Don't act crazy. Don't be so weird. Call the number. But NOT TOO LOUDLY, for the love of God; others might hear you.

Is it any wonder, then, that when someone has asked, we haven't had an answer? Don't worry. It's better now. I'm fine. A helicopter whirrs in our brains and we drown in the choppy waters. I'm fine.

Being diagnosed – labelled – with borderline personality disorder has helped me to better understand myself and what I need. But it isn't the best time I've ever had. This disorder is deeply misunderstood. It's still a term others wield as an insult. People with BPD are often maligned even by those who really do love them.

It's one of those disorders that makes people think they can talk *about* you, not to you (and *never* alongside you). Published stories are often told from the perspective of a patient's children, siblings, parents, spouse – people who know what it's like to live under this cruel and deliberate unpredictability.

Probably the most famous book on BPD is *Stop Walking on Eggshells*, by Paul T. Mason and Randi Kreger. Honestly, the title. It was recommended to me on social media, so I went to the book's Amazon page to see what I might learn. The first sentence is: 'I must be defective.' The author, who does not have BPD, feels defective because, to her mind, *the patient – the person with BPD – made her feel this way*.

Said one happy reviewer: 'For years I wondered what was happening to my [sic] and why was my relationship with my now ex wife such a confusing roller-coaster ride of emotions that defied logic.' Another reported: 'This is a great read for people who are living with a volatile person.' I clicked to look inside and was informed of the differences on an MRI between a 'normal' brain and a BPD brain.

I felt all those words in my shoulders. I imagined someone I loved saying them about me. I wondered how often they had hidden from my illogical, unpredictable onslaught of pain. Me, a tornado of madness, coming to senselessly compound their trauma.

The BPD patient themselves is frequently painted not as a whole person, with their own fears and aspirations, but as something to point at. Look at this person. Do you know how they hurt me? These stories often come from hindsight: It makes sense now, on reflection, that the person who ruined my life had a disorder that scrubbed out their humanity. Their flesh skeleton attacked *me*, an unsuspecting *real human being*. The rhetoric of the label tells us this: borderline personality disorder is not an illness we experience but one that we inflict on others.

Thomas Fuchs – a German psychiatrist and professor with an apt name – writes that people like me can't create a complete identity. In a 2007 paper called 'Fragmented Selves: Temporality and Identity in Borderline Personality Disorder', he wrote that people with BPD experience a 'fragmentation of the narrative self'. He goes on to say: 'There is no sense of continuity over time and across situations, no concept of self-development that could be projected into the future, but only an *endless repetition* of the same affective states, creating a *peculiar atemporal mode of existing*.' [my italics]

He claims that we have no ability to learn and grow from the past. He says we 'stumble' into the future, that we are 'unable to commit [ourselves] to a set of self-defining values', and that we 'miss the experience of agency or authorship of [our] life'. We are outside of time.

I am not a psychiatry professor, and he may be clinically correct, but this type of language strips us of autonomy, boldness and authority. It's true that my memory is dodgy, but I'm not living passively. I'm not letting the world happen around me, incapable of forging ahead through moments of clarity and lucidity, taking responsibility for my choices and understanding consequences. BPD does not make me an emotional android.

I offer my own story as evidence I can build a self. As an interrogation of the connective tissue that exists inside me somewhere. Here's an entire book of it, you Fuchs! (Ha ha, just a little German joke.)

Are labels broadly helpful? Here are some things I feel are important to say.

The nature of diagnoses is always changing. This is the label I was given, but it has already evolved, and if history is any indicator it will again. My relationship with diagnosis is a living, evolving thing.

Even in the time since I was given this label, new research has shown various relationships between BPD, ADHD and autism, for example. There are genetic overlaps for BPD and bipolar disorder (BD), and for BD and ADHD. Impulsivity and emotion regulation are often cited in relation to all of these.

Gender is a significant factor in the way both mental illness and neurodiversity are assessed and diagnosed. The way 'emotion dysregulation' looks in women – especially but not exclusively from the perspective of male practitioners – doesn't always align with clinical criteria (again, often created by men from research by men). An angry woman might be perceived to be overly aggressive or out of control; a behaviour may be misinterpreted and then mislabelled as dysfunction.

There are now whole sections of the internet dedicated to women who were previously diagnosed with BD or personality disorders, and who have been diagnosed as autistic and/or ADHD as adults.

Two reasons are commonly given. First: In the nineties, AD(H)D was a 'boy thing'. Neurodiversity in girls is a comparatively recent field of study. 'Hyper' boys are the ones who throw rocks at one another and refuse to sit still, which has, for decades, overwhelmingly been shorthand for ADHD. Women of my generation have slipped into the shadows made by rowdy boys.

Second: Women are told they are neurotic, hysterical, emotional and unstable, gendered words charged with bias and scolding. Those words are the language of personality disorder, but they are also used to persecute, attack and condemn. Our limited vocabulary still doesn't always provide the necessary nuance.

This is a work in progress.

I keep a copy of Maggie Nelson's *Bluets* behind my computer screen (in case of feelings emergencies). In it, Nelson wrote, 'But why bother with diagnoses at all, if a diagnosis is but *a restatement of the problem*?' What can a label do besides sort symptoms into groups and, later, sort them marginally differently? Perhaps my position is also in flux; I have been given labels and sometimes they have changed nothing and other times they have changed everything.

A delicate condition

A wiser person might have thought, Don't meet anyone right now. Go to a hospital. Stand at the triage desk and refuse to leave until someone helps you. But I was nineteen, delusional, horny, scared and lonely.

The boy I met was nice. That was his main personality trait – he was very nice. He had pretty hair and long black eyelashes. We had never met before, but we were loosely acquainted with one another's friends. He sat next to me on a bench at a rave, listening to Paul Oakenfold at three in the morning. I gave him two dollars to put in a massage chair. Afterwards he bought me an apple juice and we 'recovered' in that same California bungalow where I had lost my mind.

That night, he told me his friends had warned him that I was crazy. They had heard it around the traps: that I was unhinged. Absolutely batshit bonkers. He told me this, the nice man I had met. He told me his friends had heard a rumour that I was insane.

We didn't go on dates. We ate pizza and talked shit with our friends. We went to house parties and bars and watched people rack up lines on pocket mirrors. I didn't join in. Instead, I alternated between cans of Red Bull and letting a valium dissolve in my cheek. Uppers and downers, sanitised fun.

He quickly moved into my bedroom in the big house. During the day, he went to his job in a factory and I sat in the window and wrote him letters about my feelings. When he was home, he was gentle, and confused by my inexplicable panic. My housemates liked him because everyone liked him; because that's the sort of person he is. Straightforward, rosy.

I remember sitting in the window and talking to my dad on the phone. 'I think he's going to ask me to marry him,' I said. I was still a teenager. I don't know what Dad said. If I had been him, I would have said, 'Come home right now and take some medicine.'

The timing of these things eludes me. My boyfriend and I went to a shopping centre to look for an engagement ring, and ran into a friend who was there doing something normal. We saw *Men in Black II*. I had a panic attack on the escalator from the movies; to drive the fear away, I read thick wedding magazines that were mostly ads, and the world darted in and out of focus.

We had a car accident; he was driving us home from my parents' house and then we were ploughing into the rear end of an old Toyota. A family took me into their apartment and gave me a Pepsi while we waited for the police to come. I don't know how we got home. He had several more accidents after our divorce. Once, our children were in the car with him. Another time, I answered a call from a man with a shaky voice saying, 'Anna, there's been an accident …' I cry when I think of it, even though it was just his bones that were broken.

We found a tiny flat for the four of us: me and him and my two cats. It was on a train line. Not 'near' or 'adjacent to' – it was metres from the front door, on the other side of the driveway. The flat had a tiny front garden, so I put a chair there and sat on it and watched the people in the train windows go past.

I got a job as a radio transcriber. In the interview, I had to do a typing test game with cartoon sharks; if I didn't type fast enough, the sharks would eat people swimming in the ocean. I typed fast; the boss took me into the radio transcription area and told everyone how quick I was. Lunch would be provided. All I had to do was pick out tapes and type what the people said, and they would pay me an exorbitant amount like $14 an hour.

The office was right on the beach, down a cobblestone lane. I worked from 10 am to 6 pm. Each morning, I caught the train from my front garden into the city, then took a bus to Port Melbourne and walked the rest of the way. I told people about my boyfriend, typed out interviews from the radio, ate the provided lunch and smoked cigarettes in the stairwell above the car park.

One day, I was walking from the bus to the office in the sunshine and I felt an ethereal calm pass over me. I nearly tripped, it was so startling. I felt my brain click into another, more correct brain. I called my boyfriend, who was at his own new job at the supermarket. 'I think I'm better,' I said into the phone, imagining myself bathed in a warm yellow light. He was so relieved: I had turned a corner, I was on the mend. I wasn't, but it's still nice to remember.

And then, predictably, I was pregnant. I had been shopping for groceries and was suddenly overcome by the knowledge this was true, and picked up a test, which later revealed two pink lines. My boyfriend barely spoke a word for three days. I won't write down the words my family said. I remember I was happy. Terrified, as well, but there was something comforting about performing a normal biological function and, I suppose, having a reason to keep going.

Briefly, I was very sick. I watched daytime TV and vomited into a yellow bucket. The bucket had lines on it to measure volume; I vomited 1.75 litres in one day.

At work I ate my provided lunch and got in trouble for eating a second provided lunch. Then I sat in the stairwell above the car park and smoked cigarettes even though I knew I shouldn't. I watched the waves come up over the wall at high tide. The metal stairs were cold on my thighs. I took an afternoon off to have an ultrasound and find out when the baby was due. When I came back the next day, my boss took me into the boardroom; everyone could see us through the glass. She told me the other radio transcribers had been complaining about my productivity levels. I was always taking the youth radio tapes, they said, and sometimes they caught me browsing the internet. Plus, I had taken so many days off for 'appointments' (she made air quotes as she said it).

'But I'm pregnant,' I told her as she fired me.

I called my mum. It wouldn't be right to tell you what she said.

That night, Dad came around to the very small flat with my brother and sister. I felt humiliated, like I had made the gravest possible error. I didn't even want them to look at me, the idiot who had met a guy and got knocked up seconds later. My body crumpled (my body that was really two bodies). Overwhelmingly, I wanted to apologise. I'm sorry, it's my fault, his friends tried to warn him, I am completely insane.

In my memory, Dad brought a balloon. He said to my brother and sister, 'Say hello, Uncle Jono and Aunty Julia.'

We had almost no money, but I remember powdered potato bake 'meal base' sachets were 79 cents and a bag of potatoes was $2.50. I would come home from work and stand in my very small kitchen and slice the potatoes. The whole time I was doing it I was thinking, This is how you provide for a family.

The knife was a cheap one from the supermarket and it was so blunt, but when I had finished the slices were thin enough to let light through. I thought, This is me learning how to cook dinner for the family I'm growing.

To make the sauce, I mixed the powder with milk and butter in the Pyrex jug Mum had given me. Then I put it in the oven and our tiny flat smelled like white sauce from a packet and home brand cheese and I thought, This is how you make space for a child.

We had a table for four that Dad had bought us from one of those cheap furniture places, and I remember putting the tray of potato bake straight on the table and feeling like, although I was still a teenager, I could be a parent because I knew how to make this one dish. I thought, This is how you love.

Now I have a mandolin and I call it 'potato gratin' and make it with real cream and micro herbs I grew. I don't even think about this story when I put it on the table. But it was so important to me then, when I was nineteen and psychotic and trying to figure out how I was going to be somebody's mum.

Persistent, frightening thoughts of traumatic events

A confounding factor in all of this is not understanding when something is an actual threat. Therapy – which I love and would die without – can become a process of controlling and dampening anxiety, at one level assuming the illness allows only irrational fear to come to the surface. Oh, you're afraid a bus will plough into your bedroom while you sleep? Very unlikely. Being sucked into a black hole? Billions-to-one chance, and also you could just end up on the event horizon in the stretchy bubblegum of time forever.

Sometimes it doesn't feel like there is space for the real stuff. We need anxiety to alert us to imminent danger, to tell us when to run or hide, to know when to call an ambulance or perform CPR. The 'disordered' part of an anxiety disorder is the lack of rational input, not the anxiety. It means we feel anxious 'for no reason'. Except when we don't.

I remember preparing for a public appearance and feeling nervous about whether I knew what to say. To me, this was a familiar manifestation of my debilitating anxiety disorder(s), but my therapist was firm: this was 'rational' fear. It is clinically normal to feel nervous about a job interview, swimming with whale sharks, bidding at auction or appearing at a writers' festival.

The presentation is excruciatingly similar. How am I supposed to know when to use my hard-won grounding techniques to push through irrational panic, and when to worry for real?

When I was small, we spent a lot of time down on the coast south of Adelaide. The beaches there are so bright. Dad was running management consultant training courses there on the weekends, so on a Friday we would drive to Encounter Bay, land stolen from the Ngarrindjeri people so whalers could drive their harpoons into giants. In the mornings we coloured in and wrote stories, and in the afternoons we turned over rocks to find the coin-sized crabs underneath. The rough sea had beaten the pebbles smooth, and around them were the regulars of the shallows: tiny silver fish like knives and espaliered starfish and the pretty poison of blue-ringed octopuses. The sand was dense and firm underfoot but pockmarked with the froth of hidden creatures. Fishermen sat at the end of the jetty and the old wood ached with their weight. They caught yellow jackets and puffer fish, and sometimes whiting if the conditions were right. We caught a horse-drawn tram to a rocky island with no shelter from the Southern Ocean, where the violent water ran straight from the Antarctic shelf, ripped and tore at the cross-wind currents, the ice-cold wind and the blue crush of the sky.

Then my brother got sick.

He had a mozzie bite. That was the first part: he had a mozzie bite, and because he was a five-year-old he scratched it until it bled. It got infected. The skin around it grew yellow and green, and his temperature was a bit high. We were playing in the shallows, then we were waiting outside a regional medical centre. I remember the way Mum rushed him inside. There was no obvious indication it was an emergency, but that didn't stop her from panicking. I recognise it now in my own parenting: Are you okay? You're okay, please be okay.

We sat in the car: me and Dad and my little sister. Mum's worry was contagious. I was suddenly aware it was scary. But the doctors would be able to help him. Of course they would. That's what doctors did.

'It's just an infection,' Mum said when she returned. 'Antibiotics.' But she didn't seem to breathe any easier. She took us to Woolworths to get cinnamon doughnuts and new packets of Textas, but we left the beach. The air in the car had been charged with an unspoken future concern. At home, I watched them watching him. Checking his small body for damage.

Over the next few days, the strangest thing happened: my brother started turning into a lizard. First, the thing you have to know about him is that he was obsessed with finding animals and bringing them home. Trapdoor spiders were his favourite, but he had skinks, yabbies, frogs, beetles. One time, Dad asked him, 'Jono, what's in the aquarium full of dirt?' and my brother had to admit that he had carried home a baby brown snake in his pocket and had been feeding it insects for the past two months.

(They put the whole lot, aquarium and all, into a garbage bag and dumped it in the bush. Not very sustainable, but it was the 1990s.)

So, actually, my brother was quite pleased to be turning into a lizard. He lifted up his t-shirt and showed us where ripples had formed across his belly: a layer of skin that had grown hard and necrotic. Then it began to peel off in sections. He developed a high-grade fever, and we all had to get in the car and go to the Royal Children's Hospital. I remember my mum's contained hysterics. Her pinched mouth, her shaking hands but firm voice, as though she had been rehearsing for just this kind of event. (I remember as well that there was another boy in the emergency department, and he had got his penis stuck in his fly. 'They *can't* just *unzip* it,' Dad said, and left the rest to our imaginations.)

At the hospital, my brother was tested for all kinds of things. No one knew what was wrong with him. They tried different medicines. He was admitted to the burns unit. They started to talk about the risk of sepsis, pneumonia, multiple organ failure. Meanwhile, his lizard skin continued to spread; it became red and blistered, then fell away to expose the layers underneath. He was so sick. They said words like 'intensive care', but they didn't know what they would do with him when he got there.

My parents buzzed and hissed, made frantic by the lack of answers, panicked, distressed. One night they sat me down and explained that Jono was very sick, which I already knew, and that he might not get better, which made no sense. They were grown-ups. Parents. Doctors. Why didn't they want to fix it?

Mum and Dad rotated through shifts at the hospital. When they were home, their eyes were tunnels, faces pulled out of shape by fear. My brother was not better. He was only ever much, much worse.

Desperate, Mum went over the hospital's heads and took my brother to a paediatrician she had seen once before. His name was Richard Power, which feels like exactly the name you would want a doctor to have if you needed him to save your child's life. His rooms were walking distance from the hospital. By chance, Dr Power had witnessed a single case just like Jono's, a child's outer layer cracking and wasting. A one-in-a-million illness, so rarely seen that no other doctor had recognised it. It was curable, but fatal if untreated.

Finally, with his body shutting down, my brother had a diagnosis. Toxic epidermal necrolysis: Lyell's syndrome. His skin was dying, and so was he.

My family was lucky. Through a combination of steroids and probably immunoglobulins, my brother recovered. In the intervening years, I've learned that Lyell's syndrome is usually caused by the administration of certain drugs, including antibiotics, not by a brother just really wanting to become a lizard.

I hadn't thought about this for a long time, but I went to see Clare Bowditch speak about her book, *Your Own Kind of Girl*. In it, she talks about her sister Rowie, who died when she was seven and Clare five. At this event – as in her book – Clare mused on the impact of this on her mental wellbeing as an adult.

I was at this event with my friend Eleni Hale, eating petits fours and listening to the wonderful, musical way in which Clare speaks about her life. Luckily, Eleni is a beautiful writer and understands that sometimes a writer is struck by an immense, urgent question, and would not find it strange that I had been, in that moment. I (stealthily, politely) snuck a pen from my bag and wrote *JONO ILLNESS??* on a used napkin. I stared at it. I underlined it. Before then, it had somehow never occurred to me that the danger and unease might have stuck with me into adulthood. Despite all the time I'd spent in therapy, this specific instance of threat and loss and uncertainty and blame had remained uninterrogated.

It was the first time I had seen a situation that no one could fix – that my parents, especially, couldn't fix. Even though I was a child, and I believed they loved and protected me, there could be a moment that was bigger than them, and bigger than me. It didn't matter what I did. I could try to be the best and read the longest books and run the fastest and get the most certificates at assembly and still someone might die. They might. I might.

There seemed to be something inside my brother that pushed against the fabric of life in a way I could never dare. He was adventurous, maybe reckless, the kind of boy our mum needed an extra pair of eyes to watch. While I tended to cocoon myself with books and cats, he rode his BMX from our house in the foothills down into the city and then to the beach.

One day – morning? afternoon? I don't recall – our next-door neighbour called out from the front door. I don't think I was there when Dad answered, but I have heard the story so many times that it makes no difference. Our neighbour had my brother with him, an arm around his shoulder as support. Jono had come off his bike. He was barely vertical, wobbly like a baby animal. I found him, the neighbour said, on my driveway. One side of my brother's face was caked in blood, skin and flesh torn away from the bone.

'My head hurts,' he said, through a blur of concussion.

The primary memory I have from the emergency department is of eating a custard-filled croissant from the cafe up the road. The room was intensely white. A vending machine clunked metallic as it dispensed a cold KitKat. Machines measured abstractly, loudly and often. My parents took it in turns to sit by their son's bedside in the same hospital where he had almost died years earlier. The boy in the next bed had been there for some time; I remember my brother's envy at this kid's bucket of KFC.

Another day – I can't remember if it was before or after the bike accident – I was out shopping with my parents when my brother called them. He asked something like, 'How much blood is too much?' He had been jumping off the roof into the pool, but he had slipped and dived into the slate surrounds instead. He was okay, he insisted. It was just a cut. But we raced home anyway, Mum's adrenaline the kind that could lift a car off a child, outrun a lion. Inside the house, droplets of blood had dried on the tiles along the hallway, and a larger pool congealed under the seat near the phone.

How intensely brave he was, I thought, to throw his one body at the mercy of the universe.

My family really leans into this mythology of 'nearly dying'. It didn't start with Mum's mysterious stint in the operating theatre after I was born; Dad 'nearly died' when he choked on some food at a party; his mum 'nearly died' dozens of times during multiple hospitalisations; my gramps 'nearly died' in the sense that his brother died in a war in which he himself had never enlisted.

Once, when I was in kindergarten, Dad saw me running across the white sand of the Fleurieu Peninsula towards the sea. He could also see, down the beach, a four-wheel drive screaming along. It was headed right for me. He cried out, 'Anna!' and I stopped running. And where I might have been dead, I wasn't.

When I was even smaller, I climbed onto a table in my nightie, which I've just remembered was pink with teddy bears on the front and a patchwork quilt. When I stood, my foot caught the back of the gown and I fell headfirst towards the tiles. For some reason, Dad looked up at that exact moment. He lunged over and caught me before I could break my neck. And I might have died, but instead I lived.

Years later, I jumped from the back seat of our car and, without looking, started to run across the road to see a friend. Another car came rushing towards me, and Dad's arm reached through the window and, as if by magic, pulled me out of its lethal path. I remember the wind the other car made as it went past, millimetres from my body. I remember sitting afterwards in the car park at KFC, looking at my hands, which had so narrowly avoided being spread across the bitumen.

There was a day, too, when we were visiting family friends, swimming in their indoor pool. The adults were in the next room, half watching through glass doors, and I wasn't even paying attention when my dad came sprinting from the dinner table and leaped, fully clothed, into the water. The adult who was meant to be watching had wandered off and my brother, who was not yet in kindergarten, had flipped the inflatable ring he was playing in. Legs up and kicking like a duck, head submerged. Drowning. And then he was rescued.

This is what I came to understand: life is precarious. Safety is not guaranteed. I am only alive because nothing has killed me yet.

When I was in year two, we went to a family friend's house in the hills for dinner. They lived on the edge of a deep valley, the type of place that becomes a highway for summer fires. At the top of the valley was an old gum, reaching arms for branches, and attached to one of these branches was a pair of gym rings. If you were brave, you could swing out over the valley, scream a lot, then swing back to safety. I had been doing this for some time when Dad and Jono came past with a gecko they had found. 'Watch me!' I shouted, pushing off. It was a warm night. My hands were slippery. As I reached the pinnacle of the outward swing, I fell onto the rocks below.

At the hospital, the anaesthetist didn't listen when I asked him not to pin me down. He held the mask to my face. He shouted at me that if I didn't stop moving, he would use a big needle instead. The gas was strawberry-scented. I smelled it for years afterwards. When I came out of the theatre, Mum was crying. 'I was just worried,' she said. 'People go under and they don't come out again.'

Do they? Lyell's syndrome absolutely could have killed Jono, but perhaps he would have righted himself in the pool. I truly might have been run over outside my friend's house, but it seems unlikely I would have broken my neck falling from the dining room table. These confused and confusing dangers, real and imagined. How was I ever supposed to learn the difference?

DECEMBER

My new therapist stares back at me from a rectangle on my laptop. Off-camera, her puppy is destroying something. She keeps smiling because the puppy is being silly but she won't let me see it because we are here to do serious therapy.

She asks how I have been now that we're back in lockdown and I tell her I have been Bad. So Bad. I tell her there was a day when I put my head down on my desk and it became an anvil and I could not lift it again so I just didn't. I read a book and typed an email still with my head on the desk.

'I heard you called the CAT team,' she says.

I imagine psychologists and mental health nurses having Friday afternoon drinks and talking about insane everybody is.

'Yes,' I say.

'Why?'

I have learned this is what she does – makes me think of reasons so I can do self-reflection and learn from them, even though I've told her I'm much better at simply complaining until everyone in my family leaves the room.

'I don't know,' I say. 'I just feel anxious.'

'What about?'

'I don't know. Everything. Have you seen the news?'

The puppy grizzles in the background.

'Do you feel anxious about watching *Great British Bake Off*?'

'Sometimes?'

'Do you feel anxious about making dinner?'

'Well ...'

'So you don't feel anxious about everything.'

'But ...'

Her video feed distorts as she smiles.

I say, 'Sometimes I worry I have that disease where you can't sleep anymore. You know that one? One day you just stop sleeping and you never sleep again and then you die.'

'You don't have that.'

'But I might.'

We sit and look at our digital selves for a moment. I google the name of it: fatal familial insomnia.

'What would happen if you did?' she says.

I say, 'I would sell my story to a tabloid rag.' Then I laugh at myself.

'It's easy to imagine everything is terrible,' says my therapist. 'We tell ourselves it is. *I can't cope*, or, *It's all too much*. But when we break it down, we realise it might not be as bad as we think.' Her likeness pixelates and rights itself again. 'Tell me something good that's happened. Something small.'

I start to tell her nothing good has happened but I stop. 'I walked the dogs all the way to the corner of my street,' I say.

'There you go.'

I find a place to store this memory. How the sun felt on my face. The warm air. Waving to another masked dog-walker from across the street. The momentary peace in my body. I leave it there, alongside the memories of screaming, fighting, shrieking, hyperventilating, and will it to grow.

A mood disorder associated with childbirth

So, a few months passed. We went to Adelaide for Christmas, me and my boyfriend and our baby in my belly, my parents and my brother and sister. Nanna's house – my safety, my home – blinked in the hot December night. I slept on her lounge room floor, my new boyfriend next to me. I was four months pregnant. In a few days, it would be Christmas.

Something was already wrong when I woke. It was still night-time, maybe 2 am. I opened my eyes and I was not there. Nobody was inside of me. Not me or the baby. The shell of a body frightened me. *Help*, I said. *Help. HELP.* Then I was up, scrambling out of the makeshift bed. My skeleton raced to catch up with me, running, sprinting. Gotta get outside. Grab the phone, out the door. Remembering: Nanna deadlocks everything, find the key. Fingers too fat, too sweaty. How could an empty body even run around its grandmother's house? I smashed the numbers on the phone. Zero-zero-zero. *Ambulance, please. AMBULANCE.*

Everyone could hear me shout it, the whole neighbourhood, the whole city. Yelling into the receiver: *I don't know where I am. My body is running around without me in it.*

My boyfriend had my handbag. *AMBULANCE*, I shouted at him. He gave me a crumpled packet of cigarettes and a red lighter. My hands shook so hard I snapped the first cigarette in half. The man on the other end of the phone asked me where I lived. *I don't know*, I told him, and, *Who are you*?

Ambulance, he said. Where do you live?

I could remember each detail of the address separately but not all at once. *TWENTY-FOUR*, I shouted.

Twenty-four where?

Can't you triangulate me? Twenty-four something. AM-BU-LANCE.

I raced through the side gate and out to the garden. There was a ceiling on it. A ceiling on the fucking garden. I tried to push out of it, but it was bulletproof glass, an invisibility cloak, gelatine. I pushed and pushed and I broke another cigarette between my fingers, and then my dad came out and said, 'You shouldn't do that.'

Finally I remembered the name of the street and shouted it into the phone and it clicked off. I raced myself around the outside of the house. Across the lawn, kicked a birdbath, up the steps, through the gate, past the fishponds, down the steps, out the gate. My body was in the lead. It streamed ahead of me, lapped me, forgot to collect me. My eyes spun in their sockets; I watched them as my limbs went flailing by.

My boyfriend lit the cigarette. My dad forgot to bc angry about it; he could see how I would die without it. I was four months' pregnant and I was standing in my grandparents' garden, smoking, watching my body run a marathon around a house I couldn't remember. My boyfriend gave me a small white tablet. I let it sit under my tongue. I tasted the chalk of it, the sterile rancid gritty soil. It stayed there until it turned into nothing.

Paramedics came charging down the footpath. I shouted, *She's over there!* and pointed at my body as it crashed through gum trees and flowerbeds. Catch her, I thought, lasso her. I was a gaseous form, I was floating away at the edges. Retrieve her, collect her.

Dad made me Vegemite toast and cut it into soldiers. I cried as I ate it. He said, 'At least you're not screaming.' I cried while the ambos checked my pulse, my blood pressure, my oxygen saturation. They said, 'Valium isn't great in pregnancy, but on balance it's probably okay.'

Too late – I'd already dissolved it with my stomach acid. I cried about the baby I already loved. Someone helped me back to the floor.

My body and I lay together in Nanna's lounge room, watching the Christmas tree light up and go dark, light up, go dark, light, dark. I told the ambos, *You can go now, I'm okay,* because that was the language I had been taught to speak: Sorry for taking up so much space, sorry I asked for help. They talked to my dad but I didn't hear. There was a row of toast soldiers on a floral plate. I wanted to put it in the sink but everything was so heavy.

I pulled my body close to me. I said, *I'm sorry.* Its heart was racing.

One in seven people experience postnatal depression after giving birth, and about one in a thousand are affected by the even higher-risk manifestation, postnatal psychosis. Doctors aren't exactly sure why it happens, but it's likely a combination of massive waves of hormones and the shock of growing and then becoming responsible for a whole human person. The number-one cause of maternal death in the twelve months after giving birth is suicide.

The Edinburgh Postnatal Depression Scale is one tool doctors have to measure how you're going. It asks questions to determine your wellbeing: Can you see the funny side of things? Have things been getting on top of you? Do you sleep?

(It does *not* ask: Do you think about leaving your family? Have you told your baby you hate it? When you look at your infant, the one you made with your own body, do you feel anything – anything at all?)

I think I should tell you the story of how my water broke. It was nine days before my due date, and I had read that having sex could induce labour. The doctor had told me I was going to have an absolutely gigantic baby and I was a bit houseproud. I wanted that baby out before it had a chance to ruin the architecture.

So, we had the kind of clumsy sex you have when you're thirty-nine weeks pregnant. *No, can you – roll this – ugh – try doing – stop – ouch – okay, this works*. And as I threw one leg over, my water broke all over my naked boyfriend.

We raced to the hospital – he even got a speeding ticket, like it was a movie – and up to the maternity ward. What a thing!

About to give birth to a baby! They laid me out on a bed and took a swab to check for amniotic fluid.

'No,' they said. 'Your water didn't break.'

I tried to explain about the sex. I made a joke about his penis being like a needle. 'Go home,' they said. 'Come back in the morning.'

In the morning I was having short but painful contractions. We got dressed properly and drove the speed limit back to the hospital. The nurses did another swab. 'You probably peed a bit,' they said. 'Come back when you're actually in labour.'

I was disappointed, but I believed them. Because why wouldn't you? Doctors would never give improper care because of assumptions or bias! Like you know even one thing about your own body. You maniac.

We ran a bunch of pre-baby errands. Got new tyres on the car. Went to the supermarket. I stood in line at Coles and cried as my uterus cruelly contracted. ('Are you okay?' the checkout person said. 'Yep, I'm not in labour.') I was afraid to go back to the hospital. They had made me believe I knew nothing about my own experience. Instead, we went to my parents' house and played backgammon and ordered a pizza. I said to my boyfriend, 'Should I eat pizza if I'm in labour?' But no one was completely certain if I was in labour; hadn't the nurses said I was too stupid to know? I chewed and rolled dice and every four minutes my body stiffened and twisted.

Eventually I was crunched into a ball, sobbing, and I guess Mum thought I was on the verge of giving birth on her couch as she insisted we go back to the hospital. I was so afraid of being thought foolish. My water hadn't even broken, I didn't know anything, they had told me I was wrong.

We entered the maternity ward for the third time with trepidation, our excitement quashed.

'They won't believe me,' I said, racked with pain.

A different nurse got me to lie down on a different bed. She didn't bother doing another swab; by then, I could see the pain as stars in my vision.

'It looks like her water *did* break,' she said to my boyfriend and not to me. 'That means it's been twenty-four hours, so she's at risk of infection.'

'*I told you*,' I squeaked.

Their prior dismissals meant I gave birth in the worst possible position: flat on my back, birth canal bent into a rollercoaster wave, with a penicillin drip in my hand. I remember clearly the moment they shoved a nitrous oxide mask into my face, after I had asked for oxygen alone. Two breaths – in-out, in-out – and the room started moving. The familiar dissociation, the unreality. A baby was coming out. A fucking baby. Coming out. Of my body. Panic tore through me.

'I need to get out of here!' I yelled, trying to scramble up from the bed.

The midwives grabbed my feet and held them to their bodies, shouting in distorted voices that I was doing so well, I was nearly done, *you can do it*. I screamed my existential distress until it was all over.

It took forty-five minutes to push her out. A single slippery bone. An octopus slurping from its tank. Like trying to catch a bar of soap. They passed her to me and I shrieked, 'She's so pretty!' – which she was, in all of her blueness and sticky eyelashes and white vernix cloak. Georgia wasn't enormous at all: she only seemed big, they explained, because she had been crouched inside me. A human frog, arms and legs akimbo, ready to spring forth. Knees up. Fists clenched. Preparing for war.

The flesh between my legs had torn. The doctor sewed me up. I felt each stick, the pinprick going in and going out again.

'I can feel that,' I hissed, flushed with pain.

The doctor didn't even pause as he said, 'No, you can't.'

'Who is your social worker?' The midwife stared at me, waiting for my answer. 'You must have one.'

Georgia was minutes old. I had finally freed her enormous brain from my body at 11.16 pm. I had narrowly avoided a retained placenta – the doctor, elbow-deep inside me, whispered, 'It's tearing,' and I shouted, 'Stop! My mother nearly died from this when I was born!' I didn't nearly die. I pushed until the thick ooze of congealed meat slid from me, umbilical cord still attached. Even in my exhaustion I had conjured enough guilt to think, At least I haven't traumatised her right away.

It was the end of May and cold. My new infant was small and neatly proportioned – she had a round head with a soft film of blonde fluff, and eyes blue and grey like they had a storm in them. My boyfriend took photos on a disposable camera from the supermarket, in the darkness – too dark to make out later – while I held her close to my chest. I wore green pyjamas with sheep printed on them that Mum had bought for me.

I was twenty. I had known my boyfriend for just over a year.

'Who is your social worker?' the midwife asked again in the morning. An icy wind came through the door, which I had cracked open. I felt I was suffocating in the hospital room. Cries from other people's babies had rung out all through the night – help me, what am I doing here? – and a nurse had come to take them for a little while. Now I slid in and out of reality. Walls caving in, stretching out. All the voices in the ward at once. The crying (theirs) and the crying (mine).

I sat on the floor with Georgia stretched across my thighs, on a vinyl cushion I had sequestered from a waiting-room chair. I tried to make sense of her. Where had she come from? She was a strange and uncomfortable weight. I felt I could only look at her from the corner of my eye. I was afraid to have her, to touch or smell her.

'Well?' said the midwife, face crumpled into anger.

I frowned back. 'Why do you think I have a social worker?' I said.

She gestured to the three of us: a girl, a boy, an infant on a cushion.

'This is my boyfriend,' I told her. 'We live together.'

The midwife reached across and snatched the infant away. 'Your baby is cold,' she said, turning on her heel. 'Don't you realise?'

I had expected to get postnatal depression. I felt I had been practising for it my whole life. I could barely go to the supermarket without crying (why are there so many kinds of yoghurt, for the love of God!). I'd already conceded defeat, getting my black dog a new bed and a fancy ceramic bowl. Naively, I felt it almost pedestrian compared to psychosis – I was so experienced at mental illness that I would masterfully fling PND into the abyss.

While I was pregnant, I had six sessions of hypnotherapy. I wasn't even sure what I wanted help with. I worried about the pain of childbirth, of course, but there were myriad abstract things. I fixated on what I was supposed to do *afterwards*. If she was born in the daytime, was I supposed to sleep? If she was born at night, would I have to feed her right away? What if I was too tired, too sore, too frightened? The therapist counted backwards from ten, and I pushed my eyelids closed and tried to look hypnotised. 'Listen to the sound of my voice,' she said, and I felt completely removed from my body but not in the way she imagined.

As it turned out, I had got it all wrong. I did get PND, but it didn't blend into the depression I already had. I didn't just become 'more depressed'. It was a whole distinct illness and it was brand new.

I remember coming home from the hospital and plonking Georgia in the middle of our bed. She looked even smaller there, the way a kitten does when it's on the floor. I looked at my boyfriend and said, 'What do we do now?' And he said, 'I think we just wait until she needs something.'

So, I waited.

I can't remember the first time I felt PND, but I remember it was new.

Did you know there are different ways to feel sadness? Suddenly I was regular sad *and* this foreign, alarming sad. I was two kinds of anxious, two kinds of meaningless. I had my usual existential dread and another, more acute despair. I felt it like two rivers: a rushing rapid above the ground that would pummel me to death right now, today; and the quiet flow in an underwater cave that would slowly drown me.

While I tried to fight one, the other attacked. As motherhood overwhelmed me, I could 'see' the PND, totally discrete. It approached very obviously, boldly. At the time, my boyfriend started work very early in the morning. His alarm would ring out before it was even light and fill me with horror. How could the day of being stranded at home with a baby begin before the sun was up? After I had woken three times in the night to feed her? And while I had mastitis, boobs that had swollen to an H-cup? I couldn't sleep when my boyfriend wasn't home; I feared I would roll on her, crush her or, worse, forget about her. Instead, I stared and clung. I put her on a play mat with crinkly bits. I watched *Dora the Explorer*. I waited for her to need me. I waited.

Every now and then, I shouted.

Loudly.

Why are you crying?

Stood at the kitchen counter with my fingers in my eyes.

Bargaining, pleading.

Please, stop crying.

I would walk her down the road to the park and watch the other parents. What were they doing that I wasn't? I tried to absorb their tremendous sense of duty and care. Their children weren't crying. They were going on slides and throwing sand in the air and running around. I felt so distant from it, like I was watching the playground through a one-way mirror. A spectator. A spectre.

I remember one morning, after a particularly rough night, imploring my boyfriend to stay home from work. I was literally on my hands and knees. *I'm not coping*, I sobbed. *I can't do it anymore.*

He shrugged me off.

I kicked him. In the balls!

The baby was crying in the kitchen.

Please stay home with me. I don't know for whose safety I feared. *Don't go.*

The low rumble of his car taking off down the road.

The howl of the infant in the far, far distance.

The hiss of the words I was forming.

She would be better off without you.

When my daughter was six weeks old I went to the maternal and child health nurse for a regular check-up. I knew, intellectually, it should have been nice to stroll there along the canal, but I felt nothing. I walked, in the sense that one of my feet went forward and then the other. I sat in the waiting room. I picked up the pamphlets and put them down again. A little boy played with a toy box in the corner and I despised him and his levity.

The nurse put my baby on the scales (they were out by several hundred weights of the world). Georgia was small but proportionate. Her eyes moved with the light. The nurse marked her progress on a graph in a blue book.

We sat across from one another at her desk. So many pamphlets. Sleep school. KinderGym. Yoga for babies. Meet so many other mothers. Mothers for every occasion. Hundreds of mothers.

The nurse looked right at me. She put her hand on my arm.

We were together in this room and I did not know how I had got there or how I would get home again. The tendons in my chest pulled together. My rib cage filled with energy, ready to snap. Next to me, a baby stirred; my own baby, I knew, but separate from me, as though I had read about her in a book.

'Are you okay, Anna?' the nurse asked, watching my clockwork chest. 'You look like your heart hurts.'

I'll never forget the way she said it, so plainly. 'It does,' I said. Like it had been grated sliced chopped diced. And then I cried and she let me, all the crying I needed to do.

On her recommendation, I joined a new mothers' group run in the same building. I bundled Georgia into her pram, full of nerves. We walked the three kilometres along elm-lined streets, the crunch of winter underfoot. I was a mother, going to a mothers' group. That felt like the right thing to do. I was sure it was in one of those pamphlets.

I was the last to arrive. It was the way I had imagined: a group of women sitting in a circle, babies on their knees. Plates of biscuits (not to be eaten in front of other mothers; what about your baby weight?) next to a tea urn. I unfolded my wee doll from her blankets and revealed her to the group and they smiled politely. *Isn't she sweet!* Their babies were big and sweaty and peculiar.

We went around the circle, introducing ourselves like we were in a university tutorial. They were all on maternity leave from interesting jobs. Their husbands travelled for work. The next-youngest mother was thirty-four. The oldest was twice my age – the same number of years older than me as I was older than my baby. She had a high-pitched laugh. The other women flinched when she used it.

What was there to say about me? I had been let go from my admin job in a suburban business park. I wasn't married and my boyfriend worked in a supermarket. They mumbled and nodded. I had never felt so out of place, so aware of my failings. I wanted to tell them I had been smart and interesting, once. And I wanted to eat a fucking biscuit.

It surprises me to imagine it now, but I persevered. Every week I walked my growing child to the new mothers' group and tried to contribute to the conversation. I laughed lightly about men not helping out around the house. When the weather got really cold I stole money from Mum to buy a jacket I thought these women would like (they didn't), and wore it every week thereafter.

We started going for coffee as a group. They would arrange it during the session, so we were all asked; like handing out kids' party invites at school and knowing you can't leave anyone out. I was so happy to be included. I caught the bus to a cafe at the beach and ordered a hot chocolate and we sat at one long table. I tried to be part of it. I nodded and laughed when I thought I should; I offered my thoughts on parenting, nappies, bottles, when to start solid food. Even when it became obvious they wanted me to stop coming, I turned up. I was so lonely I would have accepted a sideways glance from someone who'd been hired to kill me.

One morning, after I had tried all the friendly sentences in my repertoire without success, we walked out of the cafe and they invited each other again. They did it right in front of me: see you next Thursday, ten o'clock? Each person confirmed the invite, one after another, while I waited my turn. They didn't ask me. I skipped the bus. Instead I walked home along those same elm-lined streets and I cried the whole way. I felt I had taken my heart out and put it in my pocket. It was hopeless. I was shit at all of it. While we walked, Georgia laughed at the leaves as they fell.

And, look, maybe they were a bunch of mean girls, but probably not. They were also first-time mums trying to figure out if they would ever sleep again, or get their hair cut, or have an adult conversation. They probably also had a bit of poo on them somewhere. But I began to feel that every way I tried to Be A Mother, I was unwelcome.

I started asking my boyfriend to take me to my parents' house on his way to work, before 5 am. Georgia and I would arrive in the pitch-dark and I would unlock the door so quietly, not wanting to disturb. Then I would lie down on their small shitty couch and watch NBC's *The Today Show* with Matt Lauer. Georgia would pull off her nappy and piss on the floor, and I would clean it up and lie down again. And then the Australian version of *The Today Show* would come on and that was how I knew it was time to feed her breakfast. The whole day could go by this way. *Dr. Phil*: time for lunch. *Ready Steady Cook*: afternoon nap. When the Channel 10 news came on at five, my boyfriend would pick me up again and take us home, where I'd make something for dinner and stare at it until night closed in. In the morning, I would do it again. Matt Lauer, Dr Phil, Ainsley Harriott, home.

I felt the despair as a stone in my chest. When Mum asked how I was going, I told her, 'Sad.'

Hands in the air, she sighed, 'Well, this is what you wanted.'

When Georgia was five months old, I married my boyfriend. The wedding was two weeks after my twenty-first birthday. His family was devoutly Catholic and, in my tangled-up brain, I felt it was non-negotiable. Our local church was flashy but beautiful, ostentatious in that Catholic way, and the priest who would marry us was an old friend of their family's and seemed kindly. He didn't shout at me when, on the day of our wedding rehearsal, Georgia dropped her dummy on the floor of the church and I, with eyes hanging from my skull, rinsed it in the holy water.

I chose the wedding cake (red and black cupcakes in tiers), my own meal for the reception (chicken bangers and mash) and a reading for my dad to give. The rest of the planning happened around me. I took Georgia in her pram to go shopping for bridesmaids' dresses and the boutiques were too small to get the pram in the door. The music I wanted was rejected. I fought uselessly with the church to be allowed to recite vows that didn't promise to raise my children with religion.

I sat up at the kitchen table night after night, driving tiny split pins through layers of cardboard and vellum to make invitations and programs. Mum cut my dress from a bolt of Indian silk with farmed pearls stitched into the bodice.

With a couple of days to go, I called her.

I said, 'I don't think I should get married.'

She said, 'Everyone feels like that.'

'No,' I said. 'I think this is a mistake.'

'All brides get cold feet.' She paused. 'Everything is already paid for.'

The morning of the wedding, I woke with my throat already tight. It was a beautiful November day, warm and breezy. All along the main road near the church, elm trees flashed their ribbed leaves. Georgia wore a little white dress with red poppies around the skirt; someone carried her, a human child, in a basket of rose petals.

The service was long. We spent most of it sitting in chairs to the side of the altar, listening to the conditions of the commitment we were making. Instilling a different kind of fear, of guilt. Love each other until you die *or else*. I felt people's eyes as embers on my skin.

My great-aunt Marj gave the final reading. She smiled, filled with the spirit of the day and her Lord. I shrank in my plastic chair. Her face made the sounds of 1 Corinthians 13.

Love is patient, she read. *It always protects, always trusts, always hopes, always perseveres.* She smiled again. *Love never fails.*

I tried everything in those pamphlets. As Georgia grew into a toddler I took her to playgroups, to GymbaROO, to baby singalongs. She hated to be still. It didn't matter what we were doing, she wanted to do something else. She didn't follow rules or listen to instructions the way other kids seemed to. While I sat among the other parents and their toddlers in a neat circle, Georgia got up and ran around us, shrieking as she went. A whirlwind of non-conformity. I remember the deep embarrassment of being asked, again and again, to please control my child, and having no idea how to do that or any clue whatsoever about where I was or how I had got there or who my child was.

They didn't get to see the other faces of Georgia. At home, she was smart and curious. She taught herself to read before she started kindergarten. She read books about space and told me what planets were.

Many people talk about postnatal depression manifesting in anger or hatred towards their child. I don't have a clear memory of that. I thought my baby was amazing. I didn't connect with her on a personal level; I was just sort of awe-struck by the fact that she filled this space where previously there had been no one.

Mostly, I wanted someone to take her away. I wanted them to come and rightly claim her for somebody else. I thought she was magnificent and, therefore, that there must have been some mistake in giving her to me.

I don't know how I got better. I watched the PND crush me into a dense cube and then I watched again as it slowly unfurled. The memories from that time are so foggy. I must have seen a doctor, but I don't remember being prescribed any medicine. No one suggested I spend time in a treatment centre or offered to babysit. I guess Georgia and I both got a bit older and whatever had taken me to that place eventually dissipated.

(Don't treat postnatal depression this way. It is only through luck and love and time that I'm still here to tell you this story.)

I enrolled in university, taking my baby on a train and a bus to sit in a lecture hall and try to learn and parent simultaneously. One day she threw a whole packet of Arnott's Shapes at my marketing tutor. A fellow student, younger than me, helped me pick them up. I burned with embarrassment.

When Georgia was twelve months old we decided to have another baby. It felt profoundly important to do this. One morning I sat with my family at breakfast, explaining it to my mother. *Sobbing*, in fact. 'I want to have another baby.' It is impossible to know whether this was clear-headedness or delirium. I had been so worn down, disillusioned and exhausted, but I wanted to have piles of children. Endless children. I would have had ten children. I couldn't get enough of their microscopic fingernails and the way their skin smelled and their laughter.

I got pregnant with Quinn the second month we tried, when I was twenty-one. Everything about it was different. I was hospitalised with hyperemesis twice. For three weeks I bled bright red blood and the doctors thought I would miscarry. I was so sick I often didn't make it to the bathroom; when I did, Georgia, now fully mobile, would stand next to me and scream in fear while I puked my guts into the toilet. Once, while I clutched her in an attempt to provide comfort, still vomiting, the toilet seat came crashing down on the back of my head and cracked my face against the bowl. My nose poured with blood. We sat on the floor and cried together, me still vomiting. Crying and vomiting and bleeding. It seemed both comically and impossibly hard.

The microeconomics exam was scheduled on the same day as my due date. When I asked my tutor how I could apply to do it another way, she said, 'Maybe you should have thought about this before you got pregnant.'

While I was still sick every day, my pelvis separated. Walking was agony. I couldn't get in and out of the car without using my arms to lift my legs and turn them. By the time Quinn was born, I couldn't stand up from the dinner table on my own. When I finally went into labour, I vomited until I peed.

And yet: I was happy.

Two days before my due date I ate a hot curry; labour started that night. We arrived at the hospital at six in the morning, I had a quick shower, pushed for four minutes and Quinn was born at 6.34 am. It was early April and outside there was a mist of rain. I asked my family to leave and for several hours I slept with my hand in the bassinette, my big palm resting against a small strange face until my fingers were numb. Quinn's downy head was bloodied where a hook had punctured the amniotic sac and caught their scalp. Folds at the back of the neck powder soft, mouth open milk-drunk, tiny plump hands.

No one asked for my social worker's name. No one told me I didn't know what I was doing. They took Quinn away from me only for a moment, to prick their heel with a needle.

In the maternity ward, the other new parents told me how brave I was. No medication? Surely an epidural, though. Nothing? You are my *hero*.

Twelve hours after we arrived at the hospital, I went home, emboldened.

I waited the requisite three days for the 'baby blues' (an unhelpful euphemism), but they never arrived. I lived in an exhausted bliss. I taught Georgia my favourite songs, read her my childhood books. When Quinn woke in the night, I put my baby to my breast and looked in awe at the long eyelashes flickering on a milky cheek. It was a joy to exist in those moments, brief though they were. Haunted hours when everything was dark and quiet and there was just me, the yellow glow of a lamp, my regular old depression and a newborn I felt I understood completely.

I had asked Mum to be in the delivery room. She stood behind me, my back facing her, and when Quinn's head appeared Mum went, 'Oh. Oh, wow.' I'm still so glad she was there. I'm glad she watched me do something courageous.

Having the qualities of being a mother

When the children were small, my family speculated on what kind of people they would become. Georgia was a pale, reedy thing, always serious; my mother worried so deeply about Georgia that I took her to the doctor a dozen times just to confirm she was, in fact, quite alive. Quinn, on the other hand, was bright and energetic. Always busy drawing pictures and writing stories. At age six, Quinn became preoccupied with the impending extinction event and started making pamphlets to hand out at school:

> Because bees are endangered people have to pollinate by hand! It is very hard for us, so do you want everyone including you to be like that and have no fruit and avo etc!? MY ANSER [sic]; NO THAT WOULD BE AWFUL!

So many things to concern oneself with.

I recently found the most glorious gift. For a while, when the kids were small, I had my computer out in the living room. It had a built-in webcam. Whenever I was busy doing something else, they would jump on it and record a 'news program'. They were four and six at the time. In these videos, their little heads pop up on screen and one of them reports on the weather and the other one gives a run-down of what art they've been making and the politics of kindergarten or whatever. I have almost five hours of this footage; it's my most treasured possession.

In one video, Georgia opens the news with some serious reflection on the state of the world, from her six-year-old perspective (mostly parroting political rants overheard at dinner). Then she crosses to Quinn, who takes Georgia's place in the chair, looks right into the camera and says, with an enormous smile, 'Welcome to' – they glance to Georgia for reassurance – 'the beautiful day!'

The first time I watched it, and the many hundreds of times after that, I thought my heart would crack right open.

People always said to me, 'Doesn't Georgia look sad?' They would tell me – because apparently they deemed it an appropriate thing to do – that she seemed much more likely to follow in my footsteps of being a depressed insane person. 'She's so quiet, so introspective,' they said. 'She seems lonely. She's always reading.' As if a reflective and solitary person must be a mentally ill person. When you're sort of openly unwell, like I am, people think this is an acceptable thing to say; they even expect you to be impressed by their insight.

I thought it a pointless and morally questionable exercise, but when I was alone and I spent a minute hating myself for where my dodgy brain genes might have travelled, I knew they were wrong. Not that Georgia isn't sad, because being alive is hard and she has been raised by sad people. But I knew from Quinn's constant worry, the need to fix everything, the way the beauty of things caused them pain.

I knew it would be Quinn.

The world was full of infectious disease, so Quinn, who was then fifteen, had an initial psychiatry appointment via Zoom on my laptop. Both of our faces were squished into the frame. The person on the other end specialised in adolescent psychopathy. He was calling us from a room inside a hospital; every now and then, a code was yelled across the PA. He looked kind and frazzled. His hair was white and everywhere, Einstein-like.

My kid – my sweet and bright kid – answered questions about how they were feeling out of ten.

'Five?'

The psychiatrist nodded and murmured, 'Is that the best you've felt this week?'

Quinn considered for a moment. 'About the middle.'

The psychiatrist ran through a list of the things you ask an anxious teenager: what are your interests, do you have close friends, is that your cat attacking the clothes line in the background? Quinn talked about art and movies, anime conventions, video games, pride events. The psychiatrist admitted out loud his surprise at how drama-free Quinn's social life was.

Then he said, 'Do you ever think about harming yourself?'

My kid – my *welcome to the beautiful day!* kid – went, 'Yes.'

In my pocket, nerves forced my fingers to twitch.

‘Do you ever wish you weren’t here?’

‘Yes.’

A fist closed around my windpipe.

‘How often would you say you think about wanting to die?’ he asked.

Don’t answer, I thought. Don’t say anything.

‘Very often.’

There was no air in the room. Not one molecule.

‘You think about wanting to die very often?’

Quinn’s eyes darted sideways to me, then back to the screen.

‘Yes.’

When I asked Quinn if they would mind if I wrote about them in this book, they were nervous. I had built it up, probably, telling them it was fine if they wanted me to take it out, that I wanted them to be safe, that I would never write anything about them unless they were totally cognisant and comfortable.

‘Wow,’ they said, smiling in the way you might smile when a lion approaches you. ‘What have you put in there?’

I printed off this section and gave it to them to read. They were in a voice chat on Discord at the time, an art pen in one hand, with a cat in their lap. Their eyes flicked across the page.

‘Oh, this is what you’re worried about?’ they said, handing back the pages.

‘Yes?’

‘Yeah, that’s fine.’ Someone in the chat said something and they laughed.

I thought of the effort I'd made, when I was their age, to hide my brain funk. How different it can be. And how grateful I am.

Loving someone with mental illness is like loving a basket of eggs while it sits on a wall above a brick driveway. Every day you get up and check the basket. Sometimes it rests evenly on top of the wall and you can take a breath and go to work. Sometimes it lists dangerously, all the eggs tipped into one corner. On those days you have to stay home and cup your hands underneath. You have to stay there for the whole day, holding your tired body upright beneath the basket, in case one of those eggs falls out.

At the very worst times, an egg does fall out. The basket tips too far and now some of its goo is in a puddle on the driveway. You do the only thing you can do: scoop it up and try to make it into a new egg. You reinforce the basket. You put a soft pillow on the driveway to catch other eggs. For a few days you are nothing except the guardian of the basket.

When it seems safe again, you go back to work. The eggs quiver in their basket. You walk down the driveway every morning and whisper, Please eggs, not today.

Of course it had occurred to me that my mental illness might come bundled in with the DNA I provided. And of course I worried that, even if it didn't, I might break my children's spirits by virtue of being an impossible nightmare. I felt sure they would resent me for birthing them in the first place. None of us ask for this, right? None of us get a say in the fact of our existence, and yet, once we're here, the very instant we are squeezed through one small hole or another, our most fundamental instinct is to breathe.

Although postnatal depression gave me a pretty good whack, I have always adored my children. I'm the kind of creepy parent who stands by a bed just to watch her child sleep. Every night I open their doors a crack and peer in. Usually, they're still awake and I have to pretend I'm checking that they have done their homework or packed their lunch, but actually I just want to see them.

Both of my children are thoughtful, interesting people. They care about their friends. But they're not homogenous – Quinn is arty, while Georgia is the science one; Quinn plays music, Georgia loves video games. They have made me more tired than I thought humanly possible, but they are still the best thing I have ever done.

Quinn's psychiatrist said to me – nicely, but firm – 'How do you feel about them letting go?'

'Alright,' I said. 'They're very nice about it.'

'You think you'll be okay without them?'

'Yes,' I said, defiant.

'Because they're their own people, you know.'

(It has been my experience that psychiatrists do enjoy a little side study of the parent who's responsible for the child's brain.)

I thought then of being allowed to be your own person. Encouraged to be in the world with all its risks and rewards. Its kidnappers and its confidants.

I said, 'I want them to be.' Which is true. Because look at them. Look at what they might do.

When they were nine and seven, I wrote for the ABC about what it was like to be a parent with anxiety. I lamented my inability to take them to the museum, to the zoo, on an interstate holiday. I felt these were the markers of good parenting. How could I call myself a mother if I couldn't take them to a nearby play centre without having a panic attack in the car park?

In that piece I wrote:

> Soon they will be teenagers. Their friends will ask them why I'm always a no-show and my children will say that I'm too afraid. They probably won't hate me, but they might be embarrassed by me. Maybe they will think about all the times I let them down when they were children. All the times we sat in the car on the side of the road, waiting for the adrenaline to wear off. All the times every part of me was shouting: 'Yes! I want to do all these things with you!' and I still said, 'No.'

None of this came true. I haven't said 'no' as often as I thought I would. I am a deeply imperfect parent, but I have loved them wholeheartedly. I have tried to learn from my own childhood. I have tried to give them the space to become people in their own right. Sometimes I told myself I 'couldn't' when actually I just *wouldn't*, but I have largely done the best that I could to make my kids feel loved, accepted, treasured and safe.

I talk to them about mental health. I knew from my own childhood that a mother having a panic attack was terrifying for somebody small. All the times I thought she had died in front of me, or was about to. Times I blamed *myself*, a six-year-old, for making her suddenly die. I don't think my mum did that on purpose, but in the eighties we didn't have ways of saying these things to one another. *Don't worry, child Anna, I'm not actually dying, it just looks that way*. And that hurt Mum as much as it hurt me.

Something I tried to make myself do from very early on was articulate my feelings when I looked scary. I know it's hard to watch. I know I have turned to my kids on more occasions than I can count, wild-eyed, *help me help me*. I know they have had to watch me shout at non-specific threats*: I can't, I have to get out, oh no, no no no*. And I know these visible symptoms have got worse as they have got older.

To stop from hurting them – as much as I can, which is not entirely – I have had to learn to do better. Behavioural therapies talk about it in terms like 'riding it out' and 'floating'. I have had to find ways to identify anxious thoughts and articulate them while they were happening so I could protect my children from blaming themselves. Now when I'm having a panic attack I can pull it together enough to say to them, 'This isn't your fault. You're safe. I'm not in danger, my brain just thinks I am.'

When they were about thirteen, I started letting them go out on their own. Georgia never wanted to, but Quinn would head off on the train and meet a friend for lunch, or just wander around the streets on their own to see what was what. My parents couldn't believe it. 'You're letting them do *what*?' they said. 'Aren't you *worried*?'

'I am worried,' I told them. 'But I can't let that be more important than making them feel safe in the world.'

The penny, I'm sorry to say, did not drop.

It's been a two-way learning experience – inadvertently, my kids have also learned what to look for in me. I don't want them to do this, but I suppose it is inevitable. They are both wildly empathetic. Sometimes I'll be driving along and the road will suddenly look far away, and my breath will quicken and my heart will race, and everything inside me will want to *burst out* and SCREAM *I can't do it!* and a little hand (that's really a nearly adult hand) will reach over and hold mine and I will think: What will your therapist say? And, I'm so sorry.

Mostly I think, Thank you.

Not just for bringing me back to earth in that exact moment, but for all the other joy besides.

A strong positive emotion of regard and affection

Three years had passed since I called the ambulance in Simon's kitchen. The most acute symptoms ('my consciousness is sliding out of my fingers', 'I can see everyone's skeleton') had faded, but the residual effects had settled uneasily. It manifested mostly in moments of slipping out of the present into my past and future selves, and excruciating surges of panic.

Being a young parent was hard. That feels like an obvious thing to say. It would have been hard even if my head had been in one piece. While our friends went to parties and part-time jobs, we tried to navigate this experience of being responsible for two small people. They were both rowdy in their own ways. Georgia was curious, taking in the whole grand scope of everything and trying to decipher it; Quinn was more solitary, but industrious and stubborn. Both were clever and creative, forming their own interpretations of What It All Means.

None of this changed the fact that having a pair of toddlers was like teaching whales to fly. My husband quit his job so I could freelance full-time, which sounded sexy but quickly became 'working from home with multiple children climbing on me'. The house was always in chaos. Everything was a trip hazard. My deadlines were never met. I couldn't remember what it was like to go to the toilet on my own. All common enough experiences for parents of young children, but I was operating from within a haze of increasing anxiety and confusion. I loved my children with a great, morbid, familiar fear. Kidnappers. Rapists. Murderers. In knowing I was conscripted to keep them safe, I could see more danger than ever.

You'll be surprised to learn this is not an ideal combination of factors for a happy family life. I had given up on finding medical treatment for my atrophied mental reality; as the sole breadwinner for four people, I couldn't afford (in money or time) to recover (or believe that such a thing were possible). I worked and panicked and worked and watched my husband play Xbox while I was on the phone to clients and never knew for certain whether I existed.

Some weekends we visited his parents on the other side of town. Under the weight of my fear, it was too far. I would sit in the car with the street directory open on my lap, tracing the road from our house to theirs. Planning a route, and an escape. Visualising the roads we would have to drive down so they wouldn't feel foreign when we got there.

More than once, I unbuckled my belt and tried to jump from the moving car. He started visiting on his own.

For the next two years, every Saturday, we went to the local shopping centre as a foursome and ate a doughnut and a hot dog.

After a while, I couldn't travel more than a few kilometres from the house without panicking, slipping into derealisation, doubled over on the side of the road. I was twenty-four years old and being devoured by lifelong illness. I felt the entire atmosphere forcing my depressed body into the earth, and then the phoenix of anxiety soaring out again.

I remember sitting on my kitchen floor in winter; Mum was there, and I was explaining to her that I was So Unhappy. 'I'm so unhappy,' I said. 'My life is over.' I truly believed it. Flashes of that afternoon at an old boyfriend's parents' friends' house in the hills, knowing I would die soon. I understand now that this is part of the illness: an impending sense of doom. But then, before, it was just The End.

I met Gaz on an unseasonably hot August afternoon. A guy who worked for me was in a band, and he knew I sang so he asked me to come along and record some vocals for their album. I remember I was afraid; the studio was outside of my comfort zone. But there was a part of me that went, Fuck you, Anna, you can't lose every part of yourself. So I went.

I smelled horrible. I smelled like someone you would find in your cupboard and fend off with a rake. I know because I have been that person and I know how I smelled then.

The studio was at the back of the building, down a laneway. There, I met the guy I knew and another one, their drummer. They were still waiting on the third member; he was having an afternoon nap, they explained – a habit I would come to know well.

Entering the booth felt amazing. The last time I had been in a recording studio, I was twelve, overachieving and singing the theme song for a short-lived cartoon on Channel 7.

I felt the ghost of my former self rush in. I sang a C6 and an E6.

And then this guy walked into the studio. I was transfixed. I felt whatever I was made of spinning in the direction of whatever he was made of. After I'd finished singing, he slid into the booth and did his own vocals. A metal scream – a banshee wail – a sound I loved but had never heard up so close. It took all the space in the studio. Anguish and agitation, expression and power. I watched through the glass and this sound came out of him and it just filled me right up.

I didn't know him, but I knew him immediately. From the first instant I knew what he would smell like as an old man, and how warm the skin was in the small of his back. I knew what it would be like to be hurt by him, to hate him, to leave him, to love him.

Maybe this is a symptom, I thought. Maybe I've really lost it and started falling in love with strangers.

But I tried it anyway. A couple of days later I found a reason to go to a party at his house. It was a few suburbs away; I was nervous driving there, but I don't know if it was the distance or the night-time or the blowing-up my life. He did a handstand on top of his Hills hoist. He showed me how a chainsaw worked. He was charismatic, easy to like. People flocked to him and he made them laugh and I realised I wanted to make him laugh.

Later, we were alone in his bedroom with the door open, cross-legged on a single mattress he had found in hard rubbish.

He turned over a packet of cigarettes in his hand – the same brand I smoked: a sign, a beacon. A decision.

'Sometimes I feel like shit,' he said.

I watched the smokes go round and round. I thought of all the things I had intended to be, and the way I had become trapped in the cage I had created for myself. I thought of my children at home, the husband I barely knew, the hysterical tightness in my heart. The disintegrating edges of my life. There was a rope between us. It was the very first time I had felt like someone might see my brain and not hold it against me. And so, after three years, nine months and nine days, my marriage ended.

I went, 'Sometimes I feel like shit, too.'

People say that when you meet the person you love, time stands still. But with Gaz, it came unglued. Time moved again.

It was a twenty-four-year-old's love: *You are the rest of my life.* I had opened a soundproof door and stepped into a universe in which he suddenly was, in which the two halves of *us* shot towards one another because it was molecular physics; not even love at all but just atoms from the beginning of creation finding their way back to one another.

We existed outside of time, spending days on our backs in the park watching the sky move. We drove his old Honda to the beach and stood on the cliffs, salt-smacked. He was an arborist; he could climb a rope with only his body and hang from it with a chainsaw running. He had clear blue eyes like underwater lakes, and he wrote with his left hand, and when he smiled (which was often) his faced cracked into three dimples. His hands were huge and rough and warm. Late at night I traced the milky, freckled skin between his shoulder blades, the curves and crevasses of his body, until it was as though I had written them myself.

Being near him gave me courage. Gaz didn't know the frightened, shrunken-down version of me, and so, for a while, I could pretend she didn't exist.

My parents were raw with rage at my leaving. First, they threatened to somehow stop me from seeing my kids. Eventually they stopped calling altogether, instead spitting text messages like barbs. ***Beep****. Your children will always resent you.* ***Beep****. If Gaz goes to the house, we will call the police.* They have no memory of this.

The first job I got after leaving my husband and realising I couldn't sustain a freelance career was as a contract desktop publisher for the fire brigade. I worked out of the old headquarters in Fitzroy, way across the other side of town. It was further than I'd been in years. The night before I started, I had a wonderful dream in which I'd misheard the location and the job was actually just down the street. But I went, diligently, along Punt Road in the traffic, and sat at my desk an hour from home. I couldn't believe I was doing it.

Most of the people who worked there were ex-firefighters, these no-nonsense older folk (mostly men) who were outspoken, funny and intolerant. They had a bird call that let everyone know it was time for a smoke break; thirty minutes of every hour were spent crouched together in the long driveway, dodging trucks and managers. We laughed a lot. I liked being around people again. I liked the feeling of participating in the world at large.

Gaz often worked around the corner from me, at the university. At lunchtime I would lie to security about bringing him some forgotten paperwork, then sit in the shade and watch the way he assessed the trees, the patient care he gave them. He knew all their botanical names by heart, and how old they were, and how big they would grow. He knew if they had been infested with disease, if they had borne trauma, if their branch unions were stressed. He knew where they would fall apart.

Beep*. If you were a real mother, you would go home to your children.*

When my contract ended, I started a new job working for the state government in the city. Some days, I got a lift in with Gaz, just to spend a few extra minutes with him, to let my hand rest on his thigh. He smiled when I did it, eyes still on the road.

I moved out of my marital home and into a house with a New Zealand couple and their rottweiler. I have no memory of leaving. I don't know what I told my children or whether they understood that their parents' separation was not about them. They were so little.

The new place was a sweet cottage dripping in wisteria, with a return verandah and an actual picket fence next to which rows of dark purple roses grew. I went to work. I came home. I sat on the wall of the verandah and wrote in a hardcover notebook. When no one was looking, I felt zaps in my brain, anxiety pathways I had forced into hiatus trying to reconnect.

I worked in a library, something I didn't realise government departments had. It was deathly quiet. Five floors above a busy city corner and I could hear the blood flowing in my organs. Each morning I chain-smoked my way through the suburbs, over the Yarra River and into the Paris end of Melbourne, hardly breathing but trying to imitate 'fine'. Listening to the radio. Waving someone into a gap in the traffic. Drinking a high-fibre liquid breakfast substitute. All these indicators of my normal functioning.

When I arrived at work, I sat at my desk and Did Not Move. For 7.38 hours, I pinned myself to the relative safety of a cubicle and tried, as I had since I was small, to consciously and actively stay alive. If I went downstairs or to the toilet or the charity chocolate box, I would exist in another part of space-time and the fabric of reality as I knew it would unravel.

Some days my boss's arms moved like they weren't attached to her body. On those days, it was even more important that I stayed at my desk. It took physical exertion not to give in to rising panic. Breathe. In, then out. A sip of water. Don't look outside. People can hear your lungs expanding. Breathe.

One day the sensation overwhelmed me. I was updating pages on the intranet and then I was away from my desk with no memory of the time between. It rushed through like a dam bursting. Spikes of panic. Waves of disorientation. I leaped from my chair, in this soundless library, in this mausoleum workplace where I had tried and failed to stay in my body, and I *shrieked* my boss's name. 'Jennifer!' I yelled into the vacuum-tight silence. Everyone turned to look at me. Surging terror throbbed in my skull, pushed forward into my face. My colleagues paused for my explanation. Then the feeling trickled away, down my arms and into my legs and off across the floor. The moment was over. I stood there, stupidly, in the echo of shouting for my boss like a lost child.

'Are you okay?' she asked.

'Sorry,' I said. 'I'm sorry.' Sat in my chair. Eyes forward. Lost in the halls of this moment in time, which bore no resemblance to the one before.

Beep. *Gramps died.*

My children didn't live in the wisteria cottage with me. I couldn't afford a place with room for all of us, but I hoped I was on a path towards it. Every day I visited them, held them while my ex-husband yelled at me. It was incomprehensible that I would leave them there. I reasoned with myself – it's not for long, just until I find my feet, at least they're with their dad – but nothing stuck. I had abandoned them. I was so afraid of being left and here I was, showing them they couldn't rely on me.

Once, Gaz told me about a tree he had climbed and pruned that day. When he took off the branch, metres above the ground, he found a hollow that was home to a pair of bright parrots and their featherless offspring. He knew what to do. He took a length of canvas and rebuilt their nest, roping it together to be strong. Repaired their home. Made them safe. A metaphor almost too saccharine to even commit to memory.

In the night, the couple I lived with fought. He was always furious with her about something, though I could never understand what. Sometimes he shouted about how he liked the dog more than he liked her. I would lie awake and listen to them, vibrating with the past. The shouting, the banging. The bedframe against our common wall when they eventually made up. On the nights Gaz visited he wrapped himself around me like a python. I didn't tell him about shouting for my boss, or skipping time beats, or the way every morning I imagined making a sharp left turn on the bridge, over the railings and into the river. But he knew.

The tough exterior I had painted on was cracking. Gaz had seen me panic at the supermarket. He had watched me attempt to do something, pause, look around, breathe, try again. He had been there in the ER, waiting to see if anything was broken, hyperventilating. *I can't have the operation.* Yes you can, you'll be fine. *No, people have a general anaesthetic and they* die.

We found our first place together: a ground-floor apartment with a sun-soaked courtyard and a dishwasher. It was small but we set up bunk beds for the kids and then they were there, too, some of the time. I bought an umbrella and an outdoor furniture setting and learned which of the local bakeries made the best pizza rolls.

He didn't want to move there. Not really. I simply couldn't afford to do it without him.

We lived there for a bit more than a year. When we were more settled in our relationship, we found a real house with a big garden where the kids could run around. We got a puppy, and then another puppy.

We were held together by a symbiotic mess of love, convenience and fear.

Telling someone about your mental illness is rarely just that first step. It's hardly ever just: 'I have depression, or anxiety, or bipolar, or schizophrenia, or PTSD, or any number of other illnesses, and that's all there is to know.' Mental illness unfurls. It is a culmination of so many symptoms and feelings and words. How is one person even supposed to remember all of them?

So when Gaz said to me, 'Sometimes I feel like shit,' and I said, 'So do I,' that had been an opener, the catalyst of a conversation with no end.

Telling someone about your mental illness feels like a lot of things. It's partly confessional: You don't know the whole truth. It's partly catharsis: It feels good to tell you, I need you to know. It's partly apology: I tricked you into loving me. It is a discovery process, learning that *your* depression is staying in bed all week and *my* depression is hiding in a car park, and isn't it funny that when I told you I was depressed I thought I knew what that meant, and you thought you knew what that meant, but actually it's all of these other things?

Telling Gaz everything at once was impossible, not only because there was so much to say but also because I didn't know the words. There were things I hadn't yet learned about it back then. About how I would feel eating biscuits in a recovery room. About how I would know he was home just by the earthy smell. About how the shape of his back could quell my anxiety, even when I was alone in the dark.

FEBRUARY

My new therapist's couch is gone. I sit on the chair. On the side table there is a small pot plant and a pump bottle of hand sanitiser and the box of tissues.

'Where are people going to lie down?' I say. I have a polite chuckle to myself. The most recent lockdown was so long I have forgotten how to interact with people in person.

She smiles. 'They really do lie down, though. Sometimes it's hard to say what you mean while you're looking right at me.'

I think about this while we talk about how stressed I am with work, and how my relationships are under so much strain, and how nineteen years of parenting has turned me into a pile of sand that people kick when they go past. I tell her about my book and how I'm trying to write my life story but there are so many pieces missing. I realise how often my eyes drift upwards to the tiny gap between the partition wall and the asbestos ceiling, like my memories are hiding there.

I make a point of meeting her gaze. Eyes straight ahead. I focus so hard on it that I can't remember if you're meant to make eye contact with both eyes or just one at a time. I've never had to lie down on the couch so I give myself a little pat on the back.

At the end of the session she says, 'I have something you might find interesting. I'll email it to you.'

It's a chapter from a textbook on Schemas. Maladaptive behaviours. Self-defeating patterns. Childhood history. I read it and then I read it again. There are so many familiar words. *A pervasive, lifelong focus on the negative aspects of life (death). Excessive emotional involvement and closeness with one or more significant others (often parents), at the expense of full individuation or normal social development.*

I decide I will impress my therapist by enrolling in a psychology degree. Then I remember my Unrelenting Standards Schema (*the underlying belief that one must strive to meet very high internalized standards of behavior and performance, usually to avoid criticism*) and decide, with new emotional maturity, that maybe I will leave my HECS debt the way it is and just do a bunch of reading before our next session.

I find journal articles and case studies on anxiety and personality. I read about the impact on memory, how the cloudy, faded photos in my mind have these links to fear, to trauma. I make notes for my book. I call my dad and tell him there are medical reasons why we don't remember things in exactly the same way, then I call him another time to tell him about the Enmeshment Schema, and then a third time to tell him about the strawberries I bought at the market.

In my next therapy session I sit on the black chair next to the hand sanitiser.

'How are you?' asks my therapist.

'Good,' I say. I am full of knowledge. I'm like a coconut and the new information I have is all the milk inside me.

'You like knowing everything,' she says.

I hear the childhood insult in her words but I fall into the pillow of ego boost anyway, the way I always have. Trying to be the best, the smartest. No other therapist has let me believe there could be value in this. In exploiting my love of winning. In making me feel special for reading a bit of academic research that's freely available on the internet.

'It just made so much sense.' I look at the gap near the ceiling. I patient-splain basic psychology to my therapist. I use words that sound like a terrible play someone wrote when they were a first-year English literature student. 'My feelings aren't a deficiency. They're not a failing. They're normal.'

She is smiling. 'Your thinking is disordered,' she says, 'but in exactly the way science would expect.'

Temporarily unable to function normally in day-to-day life

At 5 am by the Formula One pits, Albert Park Lake is quiet. A swan slides by. Lights from the city skyscrapers glint back from the glassy water. Then morning sounds begin: the metal clang of garages opening, the screech of hydraulic tools, the clatter of catering trolleys rolling across uneven ground.

This is where my nervous breakdown began.

I have long loved Formula One. When I was a little girl, Dad had helped bring the Grand Prix to Adelaide, and the race was run in the same week as my birthday. Every year, we watched the cars tear down Brabham straight, sometimes because we had a ticket and other times through a hole in the fence. I will never forget the 1991 race, struck by torrential rain – the yellow flags and the aquaplaning and Nigel Mansell's Renault being winched from the track.

After I had yelled in the state government library, I had spent a year working in the worst possible web developer mines –

managing the intranet at a local council. If you've ever wanted to feel meaninglessness to the point of atrophy, that's the way to do it. I sat between a sweaty misogynist and a literal Russian rocket scientist. Every day, the first guy rated the women in the office out of ten. When I complained to HR, they told me it was in my best interests to pretend I hadn't.

Late in the year I interviewed for a job I never expected to get, and a few weeks later became the first social media marketer for the Australian Grand Prix Corporation.

Our offices overlooked the lake, which would soon be engulfed by motoring chaos. When race time came, I was set up in a makeshift room on pit straight, between the media centre and the paddock – the glamorous VIP area where the teams hung out. From my window, I watched Richard Branson pace back and forth. I met models and musicians and actors and athletes. I shook hands with drivers who had been heroes in my house for years – Michael Schumacher and Rubens Barrichello and Kimi 'The Iceman' Räikkönen. Each time a celebrity manifested in real life, I felt my hold on sanity slipping. I remember one morning interviewing McLaren driver Jenson Button under the starting gantry, willing and willing my brain to stay in place long enough to get the recording.

Race day was hectic. I had been on the track until one in the morning and returned again at five, already smashing free chocolate from a corporate sponsor as the sun rose over the lake. Now I had to orchestrate a meet-up with a bunch of race fans, people who had become friends via the Facebook page. I gathered my phone, wallet, passes, told the guy I worked with I was heading out for a bit.

A familiar voice was whispering in the lobby. A small crowd had gathered, and this gentle American drawl folded around me. The man I saw was taller than I imagined, and more softly spoken, but otherwise as though he had stepped right out of the TV. I gaped – for much longer than I should have – mouth hanging open in my work uniform.

There are times in a psychotic illness when absolute nonsense is happening and part of you knows it's not real. And then there are other times when reality itself seems like a card trick.

I looked at John Travolta standing in my doorway and I thought, That doesn't seem right.

Later in the year, we were due back on track for MotoGP. The Melbourne event is on Phillip Island, a salt-whipped outcrop famous for penguins, a stretch of headland called the Nobbies, and the annual pilgrimage of motorsport enthusiasts from the mainland. The website says it's ninety minutes from Melbourne, but to my mind it may as well be years. It's far. You have to drive past paddocks and country bakeries and signs to buy eggs.

I would need to spend four nights on the island. My task was literally to take photos of riders and grid girls and seagulls and post them on Facebook, but I was afraid. I didn't know how to tell my boss I had been deceiving her into believing I could do my job properly. A few weeks before race weekend, I made an appointment with the HR manager and said the words out loud to an employer for the first time: 'Can we find another way?' I would have to get there somehow, she said, but I could come home at night. Four hours of travel every day, back and forth. It was better than nothing, and nothing was what I had expected. 'Please don't tell my boss,' I said as I left.

On the day the gates opened, Gaz and I got in my car and made an attempt. We drove down the freeway and my heart drummed in my ears. It was hot and dry. I felt exposed among the paddocks, this flat land offering nowhere to hide from the indeterminate threats. Gaz told me stories to drown out the fear. His voice was a quiet comfort for a while, a distraction, but I felt the panic building in my feet, shins, knees. Making its journey upwards to suffocate and kill me. The road shimmied. Breathe. Breathe. Breathe.

I stopped the car. Flung open the door and dropped my head out of it. Breathe. Please. In. In. *In*.

'I can't do it,' I told him. 'I can't find myself.'

'It's okay,' he said. 'You're okay. You made a really good effort.'

I thought about the lies I could tell my boss. A donkey wandered onto the highway and I hit it! A tornado came and swept us away! A paraglider fell on us! Instead, Gaz made the call. He told her everything while I leaned against the car and listened to her voice on loudspeaker and cried.

'She's really trying,' I heard him say. 'It's hard for her.'

My boss said to him, 'I wish she'd told me.'

How could I? Risk my job, her opinion of me, my reputation as a functioning human being? I would sooner have shot myself into the sun.

On Saturday morning we tried again. Gaz was so sick that day, running a fever and struggling to stay awake. I wanted him not to come. I wanted me not to go either. But he propped himself up with our good pillows and a Gatorade and we set out. I felt tougher, less resigned to my doom. We stopped off in Cranbourne, where I bought fresh drinks. My body yearned to flee. I felt it in my elbows and my shoulders and my feet. Get out, get out. It's too far.

Breathe. Breathe.

At San Remo, the last town before the bridge to Phillip Island, I knew I couldn't make it any further. I was ridiculous for thinking I could do it. I needed to turn around *right now*, needed to get out of there, who did I think I was just driving all over the countryside? What next – *holidays*? I'd pushed my luck. And poor Gaz, bundled up with his flu in my small car. 'You can do it,' he croaked. 'Just a bit further.'

I forced my foot to press the accelerator. Just a bit further.

At the track I pulled into the camping area, where hundreds of MotoGP fans had gathered. I hauled myself out of the car. Tapped a cigarette into my hand. Gripped my staff pass tight enough to keep me on the earth. I did not draw a single breath. I found my way into my portable office and said hello to my colleagues. We took a golf buggy out to the paddock, under a bridge, behind some tents. Still I did not breathe. I choked on my terror. My organs wrapped around my bones, squeezing and bleeding. I hoped no one could see me.

I loved my job. The track, the squeal of the bikes on the tarmac. I loved the collision of languages in the press room and getting paid to record it all for the internet. I loved wearing a lanyard and saying '*mi scusi*' to Marco Simoncelli (RIP). But that day I stood in the sunlight with my breath stuck in my rib cage and my brain outside of my body, and I knew I couldn't do it anymore.

Dissociation is your brain trying to protect you from a threat. It's a way to take control of a situation that's out of your control, essentially by removing you from it. The Dissociative Experiences Scale (DES-II) is an oft-criticised screening tool, but the wording of its criteria offers insight into the dissociated mind:

> Some people find that they have no memory for some important events in their lives (for example, a wedding or graduation).
>
> Some people have the experience of not being sure whether things that they remember happening really did happen or whether they just dreamed them.
>
> Some people have the experience of being in a familiar place but finding it strange and unfamiliar.

Stress-related dissociation is a hallmark of borderline personality disorder. In my own experience, familiar places, people and items often lose their inherent familiarity. I understand the literal interpretation of a place, but it no longer looks or feels like somewhere I know; or, I recognise the place, but the body that's in it (mine) has crackled out of reality. Those are the feelings medicine calls respectively 'derealisation' and 'depersonalisation'. This type of perception uses both semantic memory – 'a motorbike race' – and episodic memory – 'being in my car on the way to the motorbike race' – without successfully combining them into a clear self-narrative. The pages of the story are there, but someone has flung all the loose sheets into the air.

I met Susan Kennedy, Australia's mother from the telly, in mid-2011. She stopped by my new office to introduce herself, in Jackie Woodburne's unexpected and delightful Irish lilt.

Working at *Neighbours* was my dream job in that I had, some years earlier, taken out a piece of paper and written 'Work at *Neighbours*' on it (manifesting!!!). I was a lifelong fan, from Kylie and Jason to Billy and Anne and Mark and Kate. I had imagined the great contribution I might make, telling stories and embodying characters and sneaking onto the set of Harold's Cafe set to see if the food is real (it is).

Of course, the trouble with dreams is that they can be hard to separate from reality, and I already had one foot out that door.

I had the presence of mind to wonder about this when I started. I might have even said it to someone out loud: 'Is working on TV going to make me dissociate?' What might happen when I watched characters who later became totally different people? When my whole life felt like a set, how would I react to being on one?

Being the social media manager on a beloved TV show was the jolly time you'd expect. I spent my days taking a camera to the green room and asking familiar actors to give a shout-out to the fans. I ran livestreamed chats with iconic characters and wrote funny episode recaps and fought with *Neighbours* conspiracy theorists on Twitter. The people I worked with were (are) wonderful; we spent our breaks sitting in a palm-fronded courtyard, discussing the future of Lou's galah over a catered lunch.

It was also the beginning of realising a person could be a writer. On Friday afternoons I was invited into the writers' room where the story magic happened. We watched the episodes from the week before and conspired about what came next. That was the room where characters came back from the dead, or discovered long-lost triplets, or married Paul Robinson. I had never known real writers before. Being around them was invigorating; I imagined I, too, could be a writer. I could create a character from nothing and make it do incredible things. I started a new file on my computer called 'DRAFT.doc', opened it and closed it again. When I wasn't at work, I tapped away at a story about a woman who'd been knocked up by her married best friend (thankfully, I have now lost said story). The days came in waves of creative energy. Too much of it, almost. A constant barrage of make-believe.

My mind was in a death spiral.

I remember being at a shopping centre and seeing one of the actors I knew from work, and putting up my hand to wave. 'You don't know her!' went my brain. 'She's from the TV!'

We had an argument then, possibly out loud. 'I do know her, I work on the TV.'

'You only think you know her! Like the time you said hello to Steffi Graf at the airport!'

'This is different,' I insisted. 'I do know her.'

'You're delusional.'

'I'm going to say hello.'

'You'll embarrass yourself.'

I had these conversations often. Even in the studio, sitting in my office, where actors were meant to be. Ryan Moloney (Toadie) would walk past and I would think, What the fuck? Every time: Should I go to hospital?

Everything seemed like a trick. Even the nature of the sets (half-rooms, facades, backyards only) fed my sensation that someone was trying to deceive me. It seeped into other parts of my life – if my work day was an illusion, what else was unreal? I would walk into the shops to buy dinner and freeze in the doorway, seeing every smell and tasting every sound. People were watching me, judging me, filming me. I became caught in a *Truman Show* within a *Truman Show*.

The studio was closed over Christmas, so I had no option but to work from home. Without structure or external validation, I went to pieces. In a matter of days I became a total recluse, hiding under the desk in my study, waiting for the day to pass and then the night to pass and then another day to pass. The 'safe' time to go outside became shorter and shorter. Every morning I was jolted awake by the terrifying unreality of having been absorbed into someone's sick game.

When the holidays ended and I tried to go back to work, I couldn't. I drove and cried, and turned around and cried. I worked in a nearby cafe, promising myself I would be able to do it the next day. I tried again. I crested the hill and could see the studio in the distance, and then I stopped. For three weeks, I drove and I stopped and I turned and I drove and I knew, then, that I would have to tell my boss about the trick. About how everything was an illusion and my family wanted me to die and I was a paper cut-out of my former self. And I knew that he would understand and try to accommodate me, and that it would make no difference.

After almost two years in the *Neighbours* studio, I was as unwell as I had ever been. I had created such strict rules to keep me safe that I could only resign from my dream job between 1 pm and 2 pm. Everything had become ultra-specific and tightly controlled. A machine so well-oiled that it was sliding right off the road.

Part 3

APRIL

To help me write this book, I take my parents out for dinner. Mum is having a sausage pizza and Dad is having a seafood pizza. The restaurant, my favourite local Italian place, is crowded. It's so noisy I can't quite tell if I'm chewing properly. It's Sunday night and I've had a good weekend; I've been to a sewing shop three times, imagining I will start this hobby as a way to relax. Mum has showed me how to cut a t-shirt pattern from fabric covered in galahs.

'This is nice,' she says now, around her pizza.

I have fettucine with chicken and cherry tomatoes. Gaz picks out the tomatoes and eats them, and I take some of his chips. I feel relaxed and calm, even in the chaos of this dinner crowd. The people at the next table are talking about investment properties and laughing at their own success. The restaurant smells like burning wood and too-full glasses of red wine.

My dad, who is a workaholic and a legend, asks how my book is going.

I say, 'It's okay,' which is partially true. 'I'm trying to write about me as a kid.' In my memory, I was a worried child, fixated on everything that might go wrong. But I have learned about memory. I know it can be a liar. Also, I am ready to hear otherwise.

'What kind of child was I?' I ask.

Dad, a man who doesn't always think before talking, says, 'You made me realise what it meant to love your child but not their *behaviour*.'

Mum nearly chokes on her *salsiccia*; she is much more inclined to tell you what you want to hear, in the best way. She tells Dad he used to say that to us a lot, and it's true. Every time I did something terrible – which was more often than I should have, but not as often as I was led to believe – he would tell me: *I love you, but I don't like your behaviour sometimes*. That's who he's always been: measured and direct, with consideration of our feelings. But, then, he has a psychology degree.

It was from him that I came to understand you can be one way and act another way. That you can really stuff up and someone can tell you it's not your fault, the shitty behaviour; you didn't mean to; they know you can do better. From Dad's desire to reassure us, I learned I could be both reckless and blameless.

Mum puts down her cutlery and says, 'You were so bright. I put you in those blue pinafore dresses and you would run around and chat away about things.'

'You were single-minded,' Dad tries.

'That's true,' Mum says. 'Not stubborn. You just liked things to be a certain way.' I think of Nanna and her iron.

They tell me I was creative. When I ask what they thought I would be when I grew up, they struggle to come up with anything. 'An artist,' Mum says. 'Some kind of artist.'

'I knew you would be good at whatever you tried,' says Dad. 'You were always the smartest.' Again, this is meant as a compliment and I am quietly pleased to take it as one, but it also reveals a threat. Don't waste your potential. We're so proud of you. Live up to expectation. We want you to be happy.

They tell me I was always busy. I would write stories and draw pictures. I ran little businesses, hand-delivering flyers, producing my weekly newspaper for the street. Mum says I was 'fearless' and 'confident'. The girl in my memory starts to fade a bit. I wonder if they have confused me with somebody else.

I wonder if *I* have confused me with somebody else.

'Was I worried?' I ask.

They both shake their heads at this. I tell them about how I thought Nanna would die at any moment.

'I knew that,' Dad says. 'You told me you worried about that.'

Mum thinks on this. 'You didn't seem worried, but you told us about your worries.' She takes a sip of her Aperol Spritz. 'The actual worriedness came later.'

I wonder if a person can describe their worries without being worried.

When dinner is over and we're walking back to the car, Mum puts her arm around me. This is something she does a lot these days, grabbing at me, pulling me into her.

'I adored you,' she says forcefully. 'I just adored you.'

My memory is exploding. I close my eyes and make myself believe her.

The fear is out of proportion to the actual danger

Everything came to a head on a Sunday morning, when I was thirty-four, fifteen years after the night in Simon's bungalow.

That morning, a possum came down my chimney.

I had put flowers on the mantelpiece. That's a thing I do when I feel like I'm made of skin and ash. I do these extremely normal things: go to the flower shop, investigate their different smells, cradle the bouquet like a baby, and say, 'Aren't they pretty?' to the person at the counter. I do all of those normal, flower-buying activities, and no one knows that inside my body my nerves and organs have grown teeth and are eating each other.

On this occasion I had spring blossoms, soft and frothy. I had put them in brushed aluminium tins, a pair, one at either end of the mantel. The rest of the house was chaos, and I had a great dark hole where my spirit usually was, but the flowers were just right.

Gaz had gone away for the weekend. He was an hour down the road, breathing fresh air on the Bellarine Peninsula. I was nervous, because that's how I am when I'm conscious or semi-conscious or unconscious. The kids and I watched a movie together and went to bed.

Around 4 am I was woken by the dogs barking. My dogs love to bark. They are like me in that way, constantly panicked: DANGER EVERYWHERE! THREATS! PAY ATTENTION! Obviously, my first thought was that there was a ghost in my house. I sprang from the bed. It was dark. I was naked. And there was a ghost in my hallway.

Do you know what anxiety does that's occasionally extremely useful? It prepares you for emergencies. When Georgia was very small, she fell over and cracked her head open on a table leg. There was blood everywhere. I could see the bone of her skull through the flesh. I used a towel to stem the bleeding and sat with her in the emergency room and held her whole small body while they put her to sleep and stitched her back up. She was not even two. When she woke from the anaesthetic, she screamed for me, and I held her hand until she was only whimpering and then pointing at biscuits, and I didn't tell her people die from general anaesthetic. Afterwards, my then-husband said to me, 'You coped really well.' But he sold me short; I was amazing, because I'm constantly in training for the worst-case scenario.

So I walked, naked, into my hallway. *Shhh!* I said to my dogs. *There's a fucking ghost.* Would the ghost attack me? Was it a friendly ghost? Would I need to do an exorcism? Noises came from the bathroom, scratching and hissing. A *toilet* ghost?

I moved closer to the bathroom. The dogs thrashed and snarled. I took a deep breath and flicked a switch to illuminate the second-worst thing you can see in the middle of the night (besides ghosts): a *tail*. Hanging over the top of my bathroom door.

SNAKE, I thought. And then, GHOST SNAKE.

And then: po— … possum? When you're very anxious, sometimes change is confusing, even if it's a good change, like when the thing you thought was a ghost is actually a marsupial. Sitting on top of the door was the biggest brush-tailed possum I had ever seen in my life. It was like a large Maltese terrier. And it was angry.

For a minute, I just ran on the spot. *shitshitshitshitshit.*

Because, wait.

The thing I was scared of was not ghosts. I was not scared of snakes, or possums, or the ghosts of snakes or possums.

I was afraid of Sundays.

Fear is funny. It remembers things so much more clearly than we do. When I was a little girl, I would always get in trouble on weekends. We were never allowed to be *still* then. Saturday sport, visit Nanna, swimming lessons, go to ballet, clean your room, go for a walk, see friends, potter in the garden, do the shopping, open a restaurant, run a marathon, make a movie. Busy, busy.

Then, when I was twenty-nine, I had a panic attack on my couch on a Sunday afternoon. I had had many panic attacks by then, but the thing about panic attacks is that they are new every single time. The fear rises in your throat and it isn't like the thousand other occasions on which panic has risen in your throat. Each panic attack is the one where you finally die for real.

Anyway, the couch was one we had found in a park or something, and I was watching the *Neighbours* omnibus on TV because I had to tweet about it for my job. On the screen, a hot doctor was having an argument with Karl Kennedy. We had a friend over, and I could hear my children's laughter coming from the backyard.

And then, for no apparent reason, my throat closed. One moment I was pushing oxygen through it and the next: cement. The couch became small and rough. My skin began to peel away from my flesh. I sprinted from the living room, through the kitchen, out the back door and threw myself into an office chair we had in the garage. I sat and sat. I tried to sit so hard that the world would swallow me in a safe magma hug. I used my hands to try to pull my throat open. The hot air pounded me with bright fists. My heart rammed and slammed against the cornices of my ribs and I screamed with my entire voice, *Why is this happening? This doesn't make any sense.*

But the fear remembered. I wasn't supposed to sit on a couch. I was supposed to be *busy.*

The next weekend, the fear reminded me about Sunday afternoon on the couch. It said, Sunday afternoons are dangerous. You should be prepared for something terrible to happen. I sat down with my *Neighbours* omnibus, in which Susan Kennedy was rescuing some teenage waif from himself. I would not panic. I would keep my throat open. It was okay to watch TV on a Sunday afternoon.

But it wasn't. It happened again – and it was worse.

Human brains are designed to find patterns and make connections. They're really, really good at it. Anxiety disorders nourish this part of us. And when I started panicking on Sunday afternoons, the pattern I found wasn't *Maybe I'm a bit overworked* or *I feel bad about watching TV*; it was *Sundays are dangerous.* I did it over and over. Every week, on my day of rest. The fear began to creep into Sunday mornings, in preparation, then Saturday night and Saturday morning and Friday night.

After six months, I lost my weekend altogether. At its worst, I couldn't even make eye contact with other humans from Friday night to Monday morning.

I was hoping I wouldn't tell you that story. How can you be afraid of Sundays?! They're just another day and, besides, they're the *good* day. Sundays have brunch and crosswords and strolling in parks.

I wanted, by the time I was as old as I am now, to have been miraculously 'cured'. Surely, I reasoned, no one would be in her mid-late-mid-thirties and still have irrational fears. Women of my age have work-life balance and friends they meet for lunch and so many blazers. I know that's not true, but still, it's a bit true. More true than being pinned to your kitchen table because if you go to the bathroom on a Sunday afternoon, the existential dread will eat you.

In the beginning, during the week I was as well as I had ever been. I went to work and did my job, where I wrote TV episode recaps and shot videos for social media. One day I drove out to a place called Kangaroo Ground, at the edge of the Yarra Valley, and made behind-the-scenes content for a special TV wedding event. Afterwards, I took the long way home, out to the Dandenong Ranges and past fields of black-and-white cows. In the evenings I cooked meals for my family, or went out for dinner, or saw friends in bars. I was happy and fulfilled.

Then, at around four o'clock on Friday afternoon, I felt my body twist with nerves. Flooding with dread, I would try to stretch out the time before Saturday by taking the kids for drives or late-night shopping or to see a movie. I watched the clock tick down. On the really bad nights, I curled into a literal brace position on the couch. I felt if I could push back, physically, I would be safe.

For five days out of seven I was a real person, and on the other two I was a ghost in a bag.

I did try to do things, even though I was scared. A couple of times I was brave enough to put lunch in the oven. Once I even took the kids to a farmers' market for a pie. Occasionally, in the early days, I would sit on my front step for as long as I could bear it – usually ten minutes.

A year into this nightmare, I missed Georgia's choir performance. She was ten at the time. She had her embroidered choir t-shirt and her sheet music and the yellow ribbon I had tied into her hair. I armed myself with every kind of anxiety-fighting tool I had: essential oils, massage bars, chocolate, sleep, sunglasses. When it came time to leave, I buckled and cried. I drove down the street and cried. I drove around the block and cried. I drove and drove and drove and did not make it. Gaz called me during the concert so I could listen, even though I wasn't there.

When I was sixteen I was part of a performance of Handel's *Messiah*. We had been rehearsing for months, holed up in a chapel across town, learning our parts and eating pizza and singing late into the night. I was so proud of my hard work. On Easter Sunday I took to the stage for the Hallelujah Chorus and scanned the crowd for the people I knew. My boyfriend from the internet. My dad. And next to him: an empty seat.

I didn't think I would ever forgive her for that, and yet there I was. My retrospective lack of empathy burned.

Missing Georgia's performance became my low point. An irredeemable moment. I felt sure that I would have to get better then, given no alternative. But it didn't matter. Low points aren't trampolines. Hitting rock bottom didn't mean I bounced back up again; I just floundered there.

I wanted it to be different. More than anything, I wanted to step out into the street and fearlessly drive my stupid car. I started writing notes to myself and leaving them around the house. *You're braver than you think. Sit with your fear. It will be okay.* I figured I could sort of charge at the weekend, surrounded by positive affirmations and family reinforcements and just a really, really strong desire. Every Friday night I looked at a sticky note with *I CAN* written on it in pink highlighter, and every Saturday morning I woke up and I couldn't.

I remember telling my then-therapist about this for the first time. By the time I did, I had already been afraid of weekends for several years. I don't know why I thought it warranted no urgent action. Inexplicably, I had let the fear build up and build up and not ever thought: I should speak to someone about this.

Gaz later said to me, 'I wish I had made you go out sooner.' There was a period when we lived in a brick house near a sports centre and took the kids there for basketball on Saturdays. Over a couple of months, taking them got harder. I started bringing distractions with me – the newspaper, or a book. Sometimes I could go there but not leave again, so I would stay and read until night-time, which was 'safe'. One Saturday morning I got up and I couldn't put pants on. I recall this feeling of pulling on one leg but not the other, and standing in my bedroom ridiculously half-panted, blocked by something invisible. I never went to basketball again. This is the day Gaz referred to – he wished he had seen me not wearing pants and not let me go back to bed, and instead asked me to please wear pants and come to basketball.

So, maybe four years after that day (the time is a bit muddled, as time is), I went to my therapist and tried to explain it to her. I was too anxious to go all the way to her treatment rooms so she let me have sessions in her home, a bright, modern space with an internal courtyard. I could see her big old dog through the window, asleep on the couch. I had been seeing this same therapist for a long, long time. She allowed me to get away with all kinds of nonsense, but I did not want her to go easy on me with this.

I sat on a chair near her dining table and she sat on one opposite. It felt ridiculous to say it, but I had to. I said, 'I can't go out on weekends.'

She nodded in her therapeutic way. 'You mean you're *afraid* to.'

'No,' I said. 'I mean, yes, I am. But it's like … I don't exist on Saturdays or Sundays. I can't exist. The world happens without me.'

She wrote some notes in my (thick) folder. 'Why don't you try making a plan?' she suggested. 'You could meet a friend for a cake on Saturday afternoon. It would be something to look forward to.'

'I can't,' I said, trying to find a way to explain how serious it was. 'I can't even go to the next room. I can't speak to people on the phone or make eye contact.'

She frowned at me and tried again: 'You could quickly drop in on your parents. Have a cup of tea.'

'I can't even stick my head out the window.' I felt the agony of past conversations, times I had sat in other chairs and tried to communicate something inexplicable. 'I can't get up from my chair.'

We seemed to be having two separate conversations. Even now, my body bristles with the frustration of not being able to explain it sufficiently. Years of creating language for myself that then failed to convey exactly how sick I had become without realising.

'What if you just take a walk around the block?'

My body collapsed. 'I can't open the front door.' I cried into my hands. 'I can't hug my children.' She gave me a tissue and I saturated it, folded it, folded it again, folded and folded to make my sadness small. From the couch, the dog whined.

'What's one thing you love doing on Sundays?' my therapist said finally.

I let my breath rattle with residual tears. 'I just want to go to the park. I want to take my kids to the park.'

Maybe she put her hand on my knee, then. 'You will,' she said. But I didn't believe her.

That day, I knew I would spend the rest of my life going to bed on Friday and being gripped by panic until Monday. Every week until I was dead.

A pattern of distrust and suspicion

I became convinced my family was spiking the water in our house. I didn't trust any of them to get me a drink in case they put some anti-anxiety medication in there. In case they had their own stash of some soluble, tasteless sedative and were wasting it by tricking me into taking it. I realised this was totally irrational, but somehow that wasn't the same as it being wrong. I understood the basis of it, too. My illness had become so tiresome and I was not helping myself fast enough. Their options were to spike my drink or leave me forever.

I told my therapist this. 'I think my family is spiking my drinks.'

She said, 'Would that be so bad?'

'Yes?' I said.

'But anti-anxiety medication might' – she took a cautious pause – 'help you.'

I only got my own drinks after that. If I left my glass unattended, even to go to the bathroom, I tipped it out like I was prey in a nightclub.

The term 'nervous breakdown' is kitsch. It's something *New Idea* headlined next to celebrities in neon aerobics gear. The only person I had ever known to have a nervous breakdown was the actor Garry McDonald, and I only knew that because a magazine had yelled it at me in the nineties. I remember it on the cover: NORMAN GUNSTON—MY NERVOUS BREAKDOWN. A nervous breakdown is something you have in a lounge suit, drinking a brandy-and-dry from a Waterford tumbler.

But I had no other words for it. I had dissolved.

I was not a person. I passed the time with droll thoughts about how terrible everything had become. Sunsets? Rubbish. Seaside? Disgusting. Chocolate? Tolerable.

I had stopped functioning at a very basic level: I didn't even go to the supermarket.

(I started writing, 'I couldn't even go to the supermarket,' but of course I could; I just didn't. That's how it feels. Sometimes I was so determinedly not going to the supermarket that I could see the obstacles in the road. I can't. I can't. I want to, but look at the size of those penguins at the end of the street. If I try to drive through them, they will kill us all. It's safer to go home.)

A nervous breakdown is something you notice from the middle (or, if you're lucky, from the end). One day things seem a bit more difficult than they did the day before. And the day after that, they're even more difficult. By the end of the week, you have to physically pick up your legs and move them in a way that imitates 'walking'. You feel tired and you don't want to eat and you're stuck in your bed, but it's just an episode, right? It'll just be a moment before you're back to normal. If you just wait a second, I'll be me again. Just wait. Just a second.

Having a nervous breakdown is a bit like getting some tree sap on you. At first, it's just a bit of tree sap that's on you. Then you realise it's stuck there. It's stuck in your arm hairs, and every time you rub it, it just gets more stuck. But then it's tangled in your arm hairs and that hurts quite a bit, so you rub it and rub it because you don't know what else to do, and then your whole arm is covered in sap and you cannot see how you will ever get it off. You're sure you just had one bad hour, and now you can't remember your own name.

I had fear in my heart every day. I woke up with it, and it stayed there into the night and in my dreams. I sobbed in my sleep. I dreaded 8 am, 9 am, 10 am, 11 am, 12 noon, 1 pm, 2 pm, 3 pm, 4 pm, 5 pm, 6 pm, 7 pm, 8 pm and 9 pm. I was a person for brief grabs as the sun came up and again when watching *Late Show with David Letterman*. But that wasn't right either, because I had started to believe Letterman was trying to convey some secret message to me and I was letting him down by failing to understand.

Having a nervous breakdown is a bit like being both the lifeguard and the kid flailing in the ocean. You think you're rescuing yourself through self-care: staying indoors, cancelling plans, wearing pyjamas all day. It feels like healing. OUT OF THE WATER! you shout to yourself. THE JELLYFISH ARE EVERYWHERE! And you think, Yes, this can only be helping me. The world was dangerous. It seemed absolutely logical to shut myself off from it as comprehensively as possible.

There I was, sitting with my nervous breakdown, and even then I was certain it wasn't a nervous breakdown. It was probably just Sadness. I was just Despondent. I was just sitting with my old friends Terror and Overwhelm. Eventually we would float close enough to shore for someone to reach in and pull us out.

Sometimes Gaz was angry. My illness was draining all the energy he had for himself, which wasn't my fault or his fault but a thing that can happen when two people are sick. This is another thing I learned about him: sometimes his soft interior would be suffocated by hard knots. That he would get a bit worn out, too, and he would leave.

The clues were obvious, of course. People around me watched as I became a shaking recluse, a quivering shadow beaten into silence by the normal passage of time.

I couldn't drive my kids 6.9 kilometres to school. They were eight and ten at the time. Every day, every single damn school day for six months, I called on a family member to please help me. I would meet them – often my parents, sometimes my brother – halfway, at a cafe, and we would pretend that what we were actually doing was having a nice breakfast, and they would take the kids on to do their learning and socialising.

It is inconceivable to me now that this happened. At least twice I kept both kids home because no one was around to do this second leg. My family rarely complained. They are kind people, but I think they could also see I was a disintegrating cotton ball.

(Their dad, my ex-husband, did not do this school run. Ever. This was one of many times I reflected on being divorced and high-fived myself.)

In all that time, I made it to school once. I negotiated with my dad to come with me and not let me fail. I remember how it felt absolutely insurmountable, that I may as well have been asking him to please accompany me to the moon. We drove the one straight road, over various intersections, past shops, alongside parks. I gripped the wheel vice-tight. I chattered at Dad, ferocious, sped-up. What are you doing today? What's for lunch? Do you have meetings? What do you think about sport? What are some good places to buy socks? And he talked back, letting me believe we were going to make it, that for a moment I would be a real parent.

Centuries later, I pulled up outside the school. My little kids jumped out, fumbled for their hats and bags. I tapped my indicator. My breathing became fast and laboured. 'Bye!' I yelled, hoping it would make them move faster. 'Have a great day!' And then I was off again, down the road and around the corner, desperate to return to the safety of whichever piece of furniture I could find to sit under that day. I had hoped it would make me feel better. Empowered. Like I could do it again tomorrow. But it didn't; I was just reminded that I couldn't.

A couple of times a week, Gaz would try to get me to the supermarket. First, we would climb into my car, which was parked on the street in case I needed to make a quick getaway.

'Okay,' he would say. 'Let's drive to that tree.'

And I would creep forward four or five metres to the tree on the corner.

'Great. What about driving to *that* tree?'

And I would go again, slowly, flooded with uncertainty, to the neighbours' tree.

'I know what you're doing,' I'd say.

'What?'

'Tricking me into going to the supermarket.'

'Nope,' he'd say. 'We're just going to the next tree.'

And we would go the whole way like that, crawling tree to tree around the back streets until we had driven the entire 500 metres to the supermarket. For months he did this, making jokes so I would laugh, which was a kind of breathing. A hand on my knee, or turning the air conditioner vents in my direction. He made me feel like I was *doing it* – bravely going all the way to buy tomatoes and eggs – without ever telling me it was easy. I will always be grateful for that.

When I could no longer leave the safety of indoors even to go into the backyard, we moved house. I had decided the house was the problem. If I could change that part of it, the other parts would fall into line. I would stop seeing penguins at the end of the street. I would emerge, victorious, from the black sludge that had become my brain and start doing normal things again, if only we could find the right place.

In our time living together, Gaz and I had got further and further away from the beach. This was my chance to go back there. To stand above the water and look *out*. Not at the person who was standing right next to me or the identical windowless townhouses or the gridlocked rows of white Toyotas, but at *distance*. If I could be near the water, I would breathe again.

Mum inspected the house for us on a Saturday morning while I was playing a game on my phone to forget I was made of stardust. 'You'll really like it,' she said.

It was a weatherboard place with pretty shutters and a tree that filled the entire yard and a little room that was just the right size for my writing desk. She was right: I did like it. But also I would have liked any other place. I would have lived in a sewer inside a volcano if it promised not to devour me.

When it came time to pack, Gaz video-called me (in the study) from where he was sitting (on the kitchen floor), so I could point at the pans I wanted to keep. I could scarcely breathe while giving my attention to his digital face instead of the games that would protect me.

'This one?' he said, lifting a small saucepan and smiling. He has always done that – acted as though the maze of my brain is perfectly normal.

'Yes,' I said, choking to death. 'But not that big one.'

He moved it to the side.

'This one?'

I squinted at his pixelated self. He was five metres down the hallway, but he could have been anywhere. 'I think so?' I said. 'I can't really see it.'

'Do you feel like you could come and have a look?'

The earth moved under me. Not much. Millimetres. I breathed in through my mouth. 'Sorry,' I said. 'Sorry.'

Gaz's face came in and out of focus.

'That's okay. Hey ...' He picked up a cupcake-shaped pan. 'This one?'

On the first night, after our furniture had been moved and our keys to the old house returned, when there was no way to unmake the decision and no other home to go to, I sat in my car outside the local pool and I howled. It was dark out. Gaz and the kids were at the new place, unpacking and pottering around and becoming familiar with it. The beds were made. The heater was on.

It was too far away. How was I supposed to stay there – *live* there – if I couldn't even drive past without panicking? For hours I went back and forth between the two buildings, neither of them safe, waiting to exhaust myself into going inside to sleep.

The lights were on in the new bedroom. Gaz's silhouette moved behind the blinds.

I lay stiffly on the bed. Slept for an hour. Woke with the fists of time around my throat. Slept another hour. Stopped and started until the sun came up, and there, I had done it, the first night was over. Nine o'clock, wait for the daytime panic to begin.

All the water was poisoned. I knew lead was seeping into the old pipes under our new house, and I was going to become delirious and then die. I began to buy slabs of bottled water. Every time I was thirsty, I took a new bottle from the cupboard and drank from it. At the end of the day, half-full bottles went in the bin in case someone broke in and poisoned them during the night. If I couldn't remember which one was my current bottle, I put them all in the bin. If I left the house, I believed people were breaking into my car, poisoning the water bottle inside, then carefully locking it up again without taking my wallet.

On Friday nights, stiff with weekend panic, I bought extra bottles in case I ran out and died of thirst.

Some part of me knew it wasn't poisoned; I let my children drink it and used it to cook my own meals. But paranoia knows little about logic.

For three years, I drank only the same brand of bottled water and nothing else. I could tell which batch it was by the flavour; I could tell by the faint staleness which water had been bottled earlier; the small bottles tasted different from the larger ones. I would stop in at a petrol station on a hot day and they wouldn't have the brand I knew was safe, and I would pace back and forth in front of the fridges, trying to figure it out. Sometimes an attendant would come over and ask if I needed any help and I would think, You did this on purpose so you could make me sick.

It spilled into other purchases. I went to the supermarket to buy extremely normal things like dried pasta and popcorn and knew only certain packets were safe. I had to buy products in order from left to right. If there were two products on the left, I had to make a decision about which was the poisoned one. Often I left the shops without the things I had come for because

I couldn't risk eating something laced with cyanide. On the really bad days, I sat on the floor in front of the fettucine, put my head on my knees and just cried.

Beep*. This was supposed to make you better. Moving house was meant to fix it.*

Establishing anxiety triggers is so easy. Even once I was feeling a little better, I still thought of the penguins every time I drove down my street. I still took a beat at the entry to the shops, remembering that they had been dangerous and might be still. Wherever I went, there I was.

Every fortnight I went to my therapist's house and looked at her old dog and said hello to her husband. On Friday nights, Gaz and the kids and I went to the local shopping centre to have dinner right on the edge of the food court, as close as possible to the escape hatch (door). Eventually there were other patterns. I began to sleep through the night. There were small joys in cooking meals in my new kitchen, buying flowers for the hall table, choosing a fancy hand soap for the unfamiliar bathroom.

One day I realised I was brave enough to get up and put a tray of frozen sausage rolls in the oven. That was the moment. We ate sausage rolls that were mostly sawdust and I realised I was close to heading out the other side.

I drank water from the tap. I did not die.

A disproportionate fear of public places

In my bedside drawer I have a book my dad gave me.

I had given it to him first, decades ago. It's ten or so pieces of yellow paper stapled together, and on the front it says *The Little Bird*, and there's a drawing in crayon of a small parrot. He has dozens of these 'books', from when I was in kindergarten right through to when I started hiding them from him in my teens.

I have always wanted to be a writer. In a mind packed with untrustworthy information, this might be the truest thing I know about myself.

When I realised I had become a 'real writer', I felt both elation and sadness. I had always imagined I would travel the world – or at least the country – sharing my stories, speaking in libraries, visiting vibrant writing communities. I wanted so much for that to be true. When literary festivals asked if I would come and speak, I said yes, but before the invitation was even fully issued, my cogs whirred. It would be a cold, a minor car accident, trains not running, dropped a milk carton on my foot, house caught in a tornado. Then, closer to the time, I said no. Sobbing, I wrote emails to my heroes with lies in them: *I have the flu, my kid is sick*. Anything but the truth, which was: *I'm too scared*.

In the end I asked my publisher to stop forwarding the invites. The pressure to find a new excuse, to make up a reason they hadn't heard before, was destroying me. Each time I said no, I felt I was letting down my four-year-old self. *The Little Bird* indeed. What a fucking hack.

In April 2016, when we were settled in the new house and I was still afraid of the weekend but no longer seeing penguins, I started driving.

Every morning I got in my car and, at the risk of revealing exactly where I live, drove past the 7-Eleven, around the roundabout, through the petrol station and then as far as my brain would carry me along the beach before it yelled at me to turn around again.

Day after day, I drove a little further. Along the foreshore. Past the bathing boxes.

I went so much further than I ever imagined I could.

My first novel, *The Paper House*, was a couple of months away from being published. It's about a mother–daughter relationship that's been whacked by mental illness. It is not, I assured my own mother when she asked, a story about her. The mother and daughter are both me, in the way fiction is often autobiographical.

I had been waiting my whole life to have a book launch. I had to get there.

On the night of the launch I went to get a fancy blow wave. I had bought a new dress and a new yellow cardigan and new shoes. I was an hour early to the hairdresser. It can become too much to bear, the pressure inside my chest. I had to be moving, to hold my nerve. I had practised so hard, all those days of driving along the beach. A little further, a little further. I would do it. Nine kilometres in a straight line. Down one road, bit of a dogleg, turn left. Easy.

I sat in my car outside the salon and the sun went down. I bought myself a box of noodles and I ate three of them and looked at Twitter and took deep breaths. Two hours. Two hours and nine kilometres.

My hairdresser talked to me about how excited I must be. I tried to mirror her. *So excited! I've been waiting for this my whole life!* She used a round brush and sprayed some volume into my hair. Her apprentice brought me a cup of tea. *Thank you*, I said, but I couldn't risk the caffeine injection. *So excited!* I said again. The launch would start in an hour. I laughed. I admired my shiny locks. I paid my bill.

I sat in my car.

I sat.

'Go on, car,' I said.

Move. Let's go.

I drove to the next intersection. Eight kilometres.

Around the bend and past the pub. Seven kilometres. Ahead, the city skyline was lit up in all its blues and reds.

'I can't,' I whispered to the car.

Turn around. Eight kilometres. I sat on the side of the road, staring at it. Staring at the road like I could turn it into a conveyer belt, and bring the bookshop to me.

A text from Gaz: *How are you getting on?*

A little shaky. *I'm OK.*

You can do it!

Forward again. Seven kilometres. Past the fish-and-chip shop. Yachts knocking together in the marina. Six kilometres. Time for a break, pull over. Glossy navy night.

Dad called. I tried not to answer it. Stop, fingers, don't press the button!

'Hello?'

In the background, the sound of a bookstore. That beautiful page-flipping, shelf-clunking humdrum. 'Are you on your way?' he said.

Did sitting on the side of the road count as being on my way? Is *being on my way* an action or an intention?

'I think so,' I said.

'We've saved you the park right out the front.'

My heart leaped. Five kilometres. Four-and-a-half kilometres. Alongside the beachfront mansions on their half-acre blocks. Four-and-a-quarter kilometres. The buildings shook and shifted. My breaths came out short and fast. A house might leap from its foundations and land on me. Stop that, houses. I have to get to my book launch. They bent and twirled. I stopped at the red traffic light. Breath-breath-breath. Quick, short, sharp. Just enough oxygen to stay technically conscious.

Go green, light. We gotta go. Keep moving.

Four kilometres.

Shit. About to die. ABOUT TO DIE. IN THE ACTIVE PROCESS OF DYING. Do a U-turn here, chuck the car around, back through the intersection. Don't die don't die don't die.

Six kilometres.

I stopped the car. Found a quiet spot in a car park outside the yacht club with the restaurant attached. I watched the people going inside to have dinner with friends, to laugh and compare lives.

My phone rang. Dad again.

'Everyone is waiting,' he said.

'I'm trying.' I tried to push the edges of the car away. I tried to become absorbed into the steering wheel.

His voice grew a little louder. 'They've come a long way.' Louder again. 'You don't want to let them down.'

My body was collapsing. I was an oil slick.

Call waiting. My friend Erin. I jammed my finger into the screen. Erin would know what to do.

'Hello?'

'Are you alive?' she said.

I checked each limb for blood flow. Pink fingers. Toes wiggling. 'I think so. My dad says I'm letting everybody down.'

'Where are you?'

Fifteen minutes to curtain call.

Having a panic attack in the car park at the yacht club. 'At the yacht club.'

'Do you think you'll get here?'

No. 'Maybe.'

'It's okay if you can't.'

I can't. 'I can't.'

Five, six, seven kilometres. Out on the sea, a ship steamed towards the port. A single light glowed in the water.

'Everyone is going to be so angry.'

'They're not angry.' I could hear them in the background, shouting my name, lighting their torches.

'I thought I could do it,' I said. I didn't know if this was ever true.

Erin talked in her soft voice. I listened to the broad vowel sounds Queensland gave her. 'Hey, you did really well,' she said. 'Stay there.'

'Okay.'

'I've told your parents to stop calling you.'

'Thank you.'

My parents called anyway. There was a long, long sigh. Years of sighing. 'That's a bit disappointing,' one of them said.

'Sorry.' Inside me, simultaneous waves of relief and self-loathing roared. Oil and water.

I turned off my car.

'Sorry,' I said again, to no one.

I climbed out. The night was dark and cool. My favourite kind of night, a winter briskness. I kicked my rear driver's-side tyre. Kick. Again, *kick*.

Upstairs, the restaurant was humming but not busy. I sat at the bar on my own. I caught my reflection in the window and I wanted to punch that person in the head. Loser. Failure. Why did you ever think you could do this, you big fake? Fuck you.

Cars started arriving. I could see them from the window. People tumbled out of them, faces I recognised. It was so warm by the fire. Footsteps on the stairs. There was Bethanie, Ben, Laura, Joe, Kathryn, Janine, Megan, Sam, Marlee, Adeline,

Jane, Justin, Mat, Belle, Robyne, Caroline, Lisa, Cat who had come all the way from Sydney. Gaz's mum and dad. My siblings and their families. My mum and dad. Then Erin. Gaz, my love. My children. Old friends and people I had never met before.

Suddenly, instead of sobbing in an armchair, I was on a throne.

Woman of the hour.

Someone bought me a lemon squash. People talked and laughed and the room was far too warm, with all of us roasting in the radiant kindness.

They lined up to see me. Sign your book? Ha ha – how do I do that? Just kidding, I bought a new pen especially for it.

It was like a movie.

An incredible display of compassion and love.

I wrote a book! I *wrote* a *book*.

The little girl who lives inside me was laughing. The decades-older gal outside was laughing too.

(And yet – and *still* – my brain goes: Five kilometres. Five kilometres. Five kilometres.)

I wish I had a nice redemption story to go with this. That when my next book was released, I had conquered my fears and we all drove to the bookshop together and had the most lovely time. That's how I would write the novelised version, right? But it doesn't work that way. Devastated I hadn't found the miraculous shot of courage, I went to bed for three days. I was so angry with myself. All those people I had let down. All those smiling faces who had had to make an exception for me, an abrasive no-good book-launch failure.

I sent apology flowers to the store's marketing people and my publisher: I'm so sorry I screwed it up. I wish I could tell you how much I wanted to be there. I wish I could explain to you how hard I tried.

I'm writing this on the anniversary of that day. Isn't that funny? I didn't plan to, but some of these things stick in your mind and pop back up without you really knowing why. Every year I think about it. What a terrible disappointment I was and am.

But just now I ducked over to Facebook and there's my dad, reposting a memory from years ago. It's a photo from the bar on the night of my book launch. My family, all of us: me and him and Mum and Gaz and my children and my siblings and their children. We're smiling. I'm flushed with the warmth of the room and the people in it. Through the window are the lights of the city. A glimpse of the night my childhood dream came true. Sort of.

And above the picture, Dad's written: *proud proud proud.*

Right before Christmas of that same year, my sister drove out to Collingwood on a weeknight. She had been at work all day. Inside an office building, the headquarters of Aesop, a room full of strangers probably wondered why she was there. She took a seat at a long white table. My seat.

I had been shortlisted for the Horne Prize, then in its first year. An award for long-form non-fiction, it had been established by *The Saturday Paper* and Aesop was the sponsor. The paper's then-editor, Erik Jensen, had called me a few weeks earlier and said, 'Your essay is shortlisted!' I assumed there must have been hundreds on that list, so I squeaked, 'Amazing!', but didn't think for a moment that I might win. I had written what I imagined was a dreary, introspective bit of personal sorrow, about my grandfather and his identical twin brother. 'The Suicide Gene' had been a university assignment. There were so many other stories worth telling and, honestly, my morale was pretty low.

There were five writers on the shortlist, including me. People I admired and others I would come to. All of them had written powerful, beautiful pieces. And all four were there in the room, sitting with my sister at the table.

I wanted to go. Of course I did. But I could not.

On the night my sister was at the Aesop headquarters, I made pizza for my family. A kind of meditation: knead the dough, fold it, let it rise. I let a Napoli sauce simmer on the stove all day; the house filled tomato-rich. I pretended it was a normal night. Knead the dough. Fold it. Let it rise. No one is shortlisted for a prize, don't be ridiculous. Toss the dough, spoon the sauce. Ham, garlic, olives, salami. The pizza sizzled and oozed.

My sister texted: *It's starting, someone is making a speech.*

Whatever! No prizes being won here. If I was really going to win, they would have insisted I attend in person. No one would give a prize to a proxy. I pulled the pizza from the oven. I took a bite.

'This is all totally normal,' I said to my family, plying them with pizza. More and more pizza, shove it down. Don't talk about the shortlisting. Tell me about school, work, dog poo, anything else.

One of the kids said, 'Did you give Julia an acceptance speech?'

'Ha ha! Of course not.' An acceptance for what? Ignore it. Prize schmize.

Barely two minutes passed before my phone rang.

I answered it. 'Hello?' I willed her not to say it. Don't say it!

'Um …' Julia's voice trembled.

Don't say it!

'You won.'

I put the phone on the bench. My family stared at me. 'You won,' Gaz said. 'Didn't you?'

My mouth was open. I nodded. I let my body fill with disappointment at not being there, embarrassment at having someone else speak on my behalf, then gratitude for their understanding and for my sister's love. I sat loose-limbed at the table. I thought about my grandfather and wondered if he would have liked my essay.

I put a bit of pizza in my mouth but I couldn't eat it. Each time I tried it got stuck there, between my outsides and my ins.

Julia tells me she got two sentences into this acceptance speech before she started crying. That she had even written one tells you everything you need to know about my sister – the enormous space she has in her heart, the way she believes in the people she loves. I did not think I would win, but she did.

> My sister spoke in her essay 'The Suicide Gene' about doppelgängers; a spiritual double.
>
> This could not be more relevant to me, as I see my sister as two people: the, smart, witty and kind sister who I speak to every day

on my way to work and laugh endlessly with at awful jokes, but also the anxious and vulnerable sister, who calls me when she can't move from the side of the road, and can't work up the courage, as hard as she tries, to make it to her own award ceremony or book launch.

From a young age, it was hard for me to understand how she felt because it was not always a familiar feeling for me and I never felt the same immense burden. I looked up to her, at five years my senior, and until I was much older I never even recognised this other side.

Sometimes I think to myself that perhaps I could have fixed her; that I should have been the older sister so I could have protected her from the demons she encountered so early on. I felt constant guilt, that maybe there was something I could say or do to make her feel better, but I could never find the words.

Depression rarely ever just affects one person. I know Anna has always felt immense guilt for imposing it on her family and often feels like a burden. Just like I know how she will be feeling about not being able to attend tonight.

I can't take away my sister's pain or change the way she feels about life; I could sooner change her eye colour or DNA. But I don't want to change her, because she is a wonderful person; a truly deserving person. Her depression doesn't define her (she often tells me that she is 'functionally mental', and we laugh), but it has shaped her thoughts, words and feelings and made her the writer that she is today.

The Horne Prize is about 'Australian Life', and I'm so proud that my sister was brave enough to speak to all of you about hers. I hope that her braveness can inspire other people to be true to themselves, just as she has always inspired me to do the same.

I could not be more thrilled to accept this award on behalf of her.

Thank you.

The awesome irony of failing to collect an award for my writing on mental illness because of my mental illness. And my incredible luck, knowing people who love me this much regardless.

I read about women who are writers now, writing about their journey to writing, being young and finding ways to go to literary parties and make stories about all of their feelings and experiment with poetry and get a by-line and work on the student newspaper together and how embarrassing to have published that essay before they were even self-aware and before they had even learned what intersectional feminism is. I think about how I was twenty-four and I didn't know there was such a thing as literary parties because I was getting divorced and I couldn't bring my little children when I left on account of no one would lease me their one-bedroom flat because what can a single mother contribute except her walnut-shell beaten-up womb. Oh, close the curtains, what if someone sees you and realises you are only a hieroglyph, you have sold yourself for nothing, and when did your hair get so thin. It doesn't matter, it's not a competition, it's just the years of someone saying *you didn't amount to much* and *you didn't live up to your potential*, and *no one needs your words* and you say, I'm sorry for the decisions I made, you are right to devalue my contribution.

While I was writing this I was lying down on the modular couch in my lounge room on a very cold May night, after eleven o'clock, with my dog Rupert snoring nearby, and one of my children laughing at their computer behind me. I thought of the absolutely perfect way to describe the feeling of having your words erased by your life choices. How I had chosen a path that meant I could never be a whole self again. That, because I am this jittery, quaking person trying to make sense of things, I only ever have the loosest hold on words.

I had the perfect phrasing for this in my head. It went down my arms, into my fingertips on the keys, and then my kid yelled, 'Do you want to see a meme?' And it was gone.

The words flew into the atmosphere and never came back. And this is what it is like for me to be a writer.

I was once asked to speak about agoraphobia at a conference in Brisbane, 1700 kilometres away. I thought it was a joke.

'Mm, I can't, though,' I said.

'Why not?'

'Well, because I have agoraphobia.' Awkward laugh.

'Oh,' they said flatly. 'But – but that's why we want you to talk about it.'

I sort of waited for them to hear themselves. A hint of recognition. Nothing.

There's a degree to which people imagine mental illness is performative, I think. It can't be as bad as all that. You must be exaggerating! You *say* you can't leave the house, but what do you *mean*? Even my parents used to say things like, 'I bet you'd manage to go to the other side of town to get a new kitten.' (I've tried this trick on myself. It does not work.) People who have read my writing on anxiety are often surprised to find that I have – I know – anxiety. People who write to share their own experiences with depression are angered when I don't reply right away because I'm depressed.

I'm not separate from this. The words I put on paper exist because I wrote them with the frayed ends of life as I know it.

Recurrent and persistent thoughts, urges or impulses

Sometime after that I found a cluster of tiny brown mushrooms growing in the bathroom.

Well, Gaz found it. He was cleaning the shower and then he was shouting, 'Anna, what the *fuck*?' I thought he had found my collection of expensive half-used moisturisers, or that the cat had pooed there, or that maybe I had left my undies in the bath again. But, no: fungus.

'This is disgusting,' he said, waving a roll of paper towel in my face. 'This is the most disgusting thing I've ever seen.'

Our exhaust fan was too small for the space, so it didn't extract efficiently. And my younger kid always has very hot showers and forgets to open a window, leaving a layer of damp on every surface. It seemed inevitable to me that mushrooms would eventually grow there.

The thing is: I did not care. I will concede that allowing your bathroom to get into such a state that it would support plant growth is pretty gnarly, but I was completely unfazed. I picked the little mushrooms, thought briefly about whether they were edible, then apologised to them and chucked them in the bin. I wasn't grossed out by the state of the bathroom. I did not imagine all the germs swarming around my immense untidiness. I didn't even mop. In fact, at some level, I fully expect mushrooms to eventually grow there again.

I'm telling you this not because I want you to call Human Services but because I need to tell you something about obsessive-compulsive disorder.

I knew the feeling of compulsion and fixation years before I had a word for it. When I was in primary school I was sometimes tasked with hanging out the washing. We had a basket of clothes pegs that had been collected over many years: wood and metal and plastic, red and white and yellow. I could only use 'matching' pegs to hang clothes. In the beginning, this meant using two of the same colour; as I got older and more frightened it evolved to using the same colour and brand, and later the same colour and brand that were also the same colour as the clothing item I was hanging out. Red shirt? Identical red pegs. If I didn't have the 'right' pegs, someone else had to finish the chore for me.

I don't know what I thought would happen, only that I knew it was *something* and it would be *bad*. It wasn't only a cognitive worry, either: I felt the tension of my error in my body. Using the wrong pegs made my arms tight, my throat hurt. Occasionally I would go against my instinct and use blue pegs on a black shirt, only to rush outside again later to correct the error.

No one set these rules for me. I just knew that I needed to follow them to be safe.

OCD is an anxiety disorder; the diagnostic criteria are very clear about the distress associated with it. Performing rituals can alleviate fear but only insofar as the obsessive thought or compulsive behaviour is bound to be repeated later. Many mental illnesses and their symptoms operate this way – the temporary relief of self-harm, of purging, of shrieking. A valve that briefly releases the tension.

OCD is defined by a complex set of both obsessive and compulsive patterns. A person can be obsessive or compulsive or both together.

Per the *Diagnostic and Statistical Manual of Mental Disorders, Fifth Edition* (DSM-V), *obsession* is:

> Recurrent and persistent thoughts, urges, or images … that in most individuals cause marked anxiety or distress.
>
> The individual attempts to ignore or suppress such thoughts, urges, or images, or to neutralize them with some other thought or action (i.e., by performing a compulsion).

So: something 'bad' is going to happen to my family, but I can neutralise the threat by trying to suppress the thought or putting the TV volume on a multiple of four.

Compulsion is:

> Repetitive behaviors (e.g., hand washing, ordering, checking) or mental acts (e.g., praying, counting, repeating words silently) that

> the individual feels driven to perform in response to an obsession or according to rules that must be applied rigidly.
>
> The behaviors or mental acts are aimed at preventing or reducing anxiety or distress, or preventing some dreaded event or situation; however, these behaviors or mental acts are not connected in a realistic way with what they are designed to neutralize or prevent, or are clearly excessive.

The behaviour is not connected to reality. It's not logical or consequential. It isn't: If I lock the doors, robbers won't be able to get in. There is zero real-world evidence that it neutralises the threat.

Except that there is. Each time a behaviour is performed and nothing 'bad' happens, its power is reinforced. I have completed this ritual every day for decades and, so far, no sharks have climbed out of the ocean and eaten my loved ones – therefore, it works. I can't take the risk and stop doing it. What if using the right spoon is the only thing stopping a full-scale marine takeover?

The reverse also holds. If I perform this ritual and something bad *does* happen, I haven't done it right. The ritual hasn't failed, I have. This anxious reiteration is self-serving and cyclical – I have missed a step, I must try harder to do it properly, it's my fault. As anxiety increases, so do the obsessive-compulsive symptoms. Breaking the pattern requires treating the anxiety, not manipulating the behaviour.

Sometimes, the neutralising ritual is unclear. When I was in the midst of my nervous breakdown and standing in the supermarket, paralysed by not knowing which packet of chips was the 'correct' one to buy, I didn't have a tonic. I was simultaneously certain I *had to* do this, and also that I didn't know what action to take. I would often just leave behind the food my family needed because I couldn't figure it out. More recently, I was rearranging my medicine cabinet and was hit by total shutdown. I knew *something* needed to be done to the various tablets and tapes and Band-Aids, but I didn't know what it was. I tried all kinds of things – no boxes touching the sides, boxes in order of size, boxes facing in the same direction, boxes in alphabetical order – but nothing soothed the intrusive thought that I was putting my family at risk by not getting it right. So, there can be a step before the compulsive behaviour, which is figuring out what the fuck is your brain's problem.

Or, there can be multiple, mutually exclusive rituals. This is the most exhausting of all. You have to set your car's climate control to twenty-three degrees, but you *also* have to increase the temperature in sets of two. It can only be even numbers. But it also has to be twenty-three. If you don't meet both of these conditions simultaneously, *something bad* will happen and it will be all your fault.

At its worst, OCD can restrict a whole life. The obsession and compulsion *become* the life. Time-consuming, debilitating – and absolutely essential.

The first place I saw OCD represented in the media was on seminal beach soap *Home and Away*. A young Sally Fletcher (Kate Ritchie) is putting away the dishes and she becomes fixated on making sure all the forks are facing the same direction in the cutlery drawer. It's so critical to her. She absolutely must do it or something horrible will happen. I remember feeling like: That's me, I think. I know that I don't care about the direction the forks are pointing, but I recognise the feeling of being somehow responsible for keeping things in order.

This kind of representation is exquisitely rare. People with OCD are, culturally, neat freaks who panic about visitors putting their feet on the table. They are not middle-aged women who let mushrooms grow in their bathrooms but also have to unlock their house in a certain order. They are people who enjoy having a tidy kitchen, not champion tennis players performing a ritual before every point.

(OCD is *also* many of these things: a fear of contamination is very common, but the 'solution' tends to be excessive hand-washing [that is, not only the amount required to be rid of germs], compulsive disinfecting, throwing things away and cleaning areas that are definitely, objectively, clinically clean. For a couple of years, when we'd moved into the new house and I thought the water was poisoned, I also had to wash my hands in repetitions of four – rub four times, rinse four times, dry four times, then repeat that process four times. If I touched any part of the sink or tapware, I had to start again from the beginning.)

Hannah Horvath, Lena Dunham's character in *Girls*, got it right twenty-odd years after Summer Bay. In that show, Hannah realises her OCD symptoms are returning; as she loses control of her life, she's simultaneously reintroducing systems of control. The psychological symptoms precede or coincide with the OCD behaviours – they're not a logical fix for an issue but a way of soothing distress. Eventually, Hannah pushes a Q-tip too far and ruptures her eardrum, and she ends up in the ER.

This is the OCD I know. A nebulous, erratic and ultimately calming ritual that changes nothing but must be performed at all costs.

From an early age, in many cultures, we're taught to internalise repetitive and avoidant behaviour as protection. Obviously, my nanna is an absolute expert at this. If you grew up in a white Anglo-Celtic household, like I did, you may have been encouraged by someone to knock on wood, not step on cracks, and to hold your breath when passing a cemetery. You might know to never walk under a ladder or open an umbrella inside or break a mirror. Throw a pinch of salt over your shoulder, lift your feet when you're driving over railway tracks, never put new shoes on the table, put a coin in with a knife if you give one as a gift, duck when you go through a tunnel. If you lie, your tongue will split. If you make a face and the wind changes it will become permanent. In my family, if you hear a siren you must touch a button (preferably your bellybutton); no one knows where it started, but my siblings and I do it still, as adults.

Mental illness and superstition have been proven to be closely tied. Studies have shown that the propensity to engage in superstitious behaviour (as distinct from beliefs) is associated with a wide range of psychological symptomology, including anxiety and depression, and more specific diagnoses like OCD and schizophrenia. In 1984, researcher Roy King hypothesised that superstition and paranoia exist in schizophrenic patients because of 'chaotic changes in the firing rate of mesolimbic dopamine neurons', which 'mimic the conditions under which animals develop superstitious behaviour.'

We're taught magical thinking – that our thoughts can and will change reality. We grow up believing that we can change the future with our minds. Wish on eyelashes, on shooting stars, on dandelion seeds, when we glance at the clock at 11.11. Read *The Secret*. Manifest your dream job. Carry a rabbit's foot, nail a horseshoe above the door, wear your lucky undies. On our first birthdays, some people who probably love us put a cake on the table and tell us to make a wish. Don't tell anyone, or it won't come true! If you touch the bottom or let the knife come out dirty, [insert miscellaneous consequence of your choice here – usually something to do with red-headed children, the ultimate punishment].

Magical thinking has also been clinically linked to mental illness. Danielle Einstein and Ross Menzies' research found: 'Large and significant relationships between Magical Ideation scores and the measures of OCD were obtained even when alternative constructs were held constant; the findings suggest that a general magical thinking tendency may underpin previous observed links between superstitiousness, thought action fusion and OCD severity.' Throughout history, psychological symptoms like hallucinations, speaking in tongues or hearing voices have often been associated with predicting the future or knowing something unknowable.

In many ways, the outcomes of failing to abide by superstition are very similar to the arbitrary, all-encompassing nature of obsessive-compulsive disorder. Superstition is designed to make you fear a poorly defined threat. 'Bad things' might happen. A generic 'harm' might befall someone you love. Talismans are for 'good luck', but the nature of the luck is uncertain. Apotropaic magic wards off 'evil influences' without giving any of their names or email addresses. Unless you engage in a highly specific behaviour, a non-specific ill will befall an unspecified person or persons you may or may not know.

Easy, isn't it, to see the overlap with OCD.

My dad worries, but he is not negative. He truly believes everything will work out in the end. He thinks the worst will happen, but also that the universe has a way of figuring things out. He has lived a life of coincidence and universal meaning, led in his worry by a larger sense of magical thinking and superstition. This is, I assume, the Irish in him (and me).

When my anxiety is better managed, the OCD dissipates. It no longer seems absolutely critical to perform certain behaviours. I don't feel the profound discomfort of setting the volume to seventeen instead of sixteen. I believe everything will work out in the end.

But as the anxiety waxes again – which it always does to some degree, no matter how often I turn up at therapy with clean hair – the compulsion returns. It can be small at first. A tic. Touching the leaf of a tree and immediately feeling like I should touch every other leaf. This is a warning. I am at risk: both of being responsible for the untimely demise of everyone I love, and of letting fear wash me out to sea.

Mental time travel is here in this rigid space. I can see myself in a future event where I have failed to properly complete the ritual and everything has gone to shit. I can see myself in past events, where I have accurately completed the ritual and everything is fine. Now I am here, in the in-between space, and I need to make a decision about whether or not to perform the ritual. What does the time machine tell me? Perform the ritual, Anna. Do not hesitate.

It starts with counting. I hug my kid and, after we've been standing there for a minute, I realise I've been rubbing her shoulder in fours. Pat pat pat pat. She doesn't notice because she's not counting. I put the dishes away four at a time. I wipe my hands on my jeans four times. I walk to and from the letterbox and I don't know how many steps it takes but I do know it was a multiple of four. Take a step back from the front door, another step, march forward. Four steps. Sixteen steps. Sixty-four steps. Two hundred and fifty-six steps.

The paranoia demands increasingly irrational behaviour. If I don't count in fours, I will definitely die. If I make a mistake while typing and don't delete the entire word and start again, I will die. If I eat a Tic Toc biscuit without looking at the time first, I will die. If I lose a level of *Homescapes*, I will die. If I fail to unlock my phone on the first attempt, I will die. If I watch television and afterwards realise the volume was on a multiple of three, I will die. I sit at my desk and count to four, and count to four and count to four, to protect myself from the meteorite that is about to plummet through the ceiling and puncture my brain, and won't everybody be relieved.

There's so much crying. I don't mind because it's good for my skin, the salt. And I don't mind because sometimes parts of me that are inside are required to come outside. And I don't mind because it's impossible to count tears so I can just let them rush out without worrying about how many there are, until I start thinking about whether I can figure out how many there are, and then I count breaths instead, every deliberate exchange of carbon dioxide for oxygen, until my head is spinning.

My head is spinning because I forgot to count. Or because I left the tea towel slightly crooked on the sink. Or because I unlocked the front door differently. Or because I –

In the mornings I wake up and there are two of me. There is the one who is calmly getting the dog food from the cupboard (FOUR SCOOPS. FOUR. DO YOU WANT TO KILL US ALL?) and the one who hangs out in the back and doesn't get how this person grabs the Science Diet or how she drives the car or why a stranger's kids are here or how she knows which school to take them to FOUR SCOOPS, JESUS CHRIST.

There's a beach, so I sit there. A bird is shouting and I can't understand its voice and all the other sounds at once so I drown out the other sounds and just listen to the bird. It tells me about the time I forgot to pick up the stranger's kids from school and was ten minutes late and how when they are adults they will tell their therapists all the different ways I failed them. I tell the bird to fuck off.

My parents are going to have me killed. They told me this morning. Not in words, but in the tone of voice they used when they said 'we're so proud of you'. They know I forgot to count how many times the car bumped over the train tracks.

An inexhaustive list of what I've done to protect my family from indeterminate dangers:

1. Washed my hands in four sets of four times each. If I touched the tap or the basin, I had to start again.
2. Only pegged up washing in matching peg pairs; if no pairs remained, no more washing could be hung out.
3. Set the TV volume to multiples of four.
4. Distributed cutlery equally among the dishwasher basket compartments. If there were an indivisible number, they could acceptably be uneven but only in a clockwise direction.
5. Only taken items from shelves from left to right.
6. Not let characters in video games step on cracks.
7. Pulled off dozens of sheets of toilet paper until I got a clean line with no torn bits.

Things I have never done:

1. Cleaned

And I never will.

(Just kidding: maybe if animals start living in my wardrobe. But never before.)

I quit smoking in my late twenties. I had been a devout smoker. I had smoked elegant ivory with gold paper seals, stolen one-milligram menthols from a friend's mum's drawers and picked the butts out of last night's beers to roll a brand-new cigarette.

We had been such good friends, me and nicotine. Mornings on the verandah, watching clouds curl into the trees. Taking cover under an awning while the rain came down, enveloped in its chemical earth smell. The hiss of using the end of one cigarette to light the next. Passing one between you and a lover. Waiting for a train. Connecting with a stranger.

Sometimes I had even used it to keep me alive, like that time when I was pregnant at my nanna's house; nicotine has actually been shown to 'diminish negative psychotic symptoms and lessen distress' and 'improve cognitive deficits in individuals with psychosis'. Please don't cite this when your mum busts you smoking at the park. Pulmonary and cardiovascular disease is still very real. But there was something about the physical act of smoking that kept me pinned to the earth.

Then, in my late twenties, I woke up in the night and my chest was rattling. Each breath burbled like a stream. In the morning, I put my half-empty packet in the bin, and never smoked again. Never *nearly* smoked, even though I was still living with a smoker at the time.

People were amazed. How about my resilience! How tough was I! Jesus Christ, just quitting like that without any patches or gum or self-help books.

'How did you do it?' they asked, showing me their collection of imported vape juices.

'Cold turkey,' I said.

They were so impressed by my ability to take charge of this addiction. What a ferocious brain I had, so powerful, so in control.

In reality, it was the opposite. I had swapped one compulsion for another. Whenever I thought I might buy a sneaky pack at the local service station, the same intruders arrived – if you smoke, something bad will happen. I don't know what, exactly. Your family will die; not of the second-hand poison but of some other unnamed killer. An asteroid will land on them. A murderer will follow them to the park. They'll be swept away by a tsunami. I'm not going to tell you what it is, but you should know that it will be Very Bad Indeed.

If you've ever been an ex-smoker, you know how hard it is to break that habit. I had quit six times before, and I had caved the very moment anyone even said 'Peter Stuyvesant' within earshot. But not the last time. As it turned out, the only thing more powerful than my nicotine addiction was my obsessive-compulsive disorder.

Extreme avoidance of situations that might cause panic

I was once in a therapy session with a boyfriend and the psychologist asked him where he felt his feelings.

'In my head,' he said.

'You experience pain in your head?'

'No. Like, as thoughts. In my head.'

'But,' said the psychologist, 'where do you feel *in your body*?'

'Nowhere,' he said. 'I don't understand the question.'

That night I lay in bed and pushed my fingers into the gaps between my ribs. I let my throat close with worry and reopen with sadness. I noticed my heart strain under its rapid beat, the effervescence in my knuckles and wrists, the knots of fear in my shoulders. I felt my feelings in every part of my body. I could not be extricated from them; we were one and the same.

I struggle to understand how we don't all go around in this permanent state of existential dread. Someone once told me our brains are designed to protect us against it, that they don't *allow* us to focus too hard on it all of the time. I wonder if it's true. Sometimes I'm walking down the street (not often – mostly I'm driving/hiding) and see other people and look for facial expressions that reveal they are also thinking about how:

1. our sun will explode;
2. history will be consumed by matter;
3. one day time will cease to exist.

And then they're gone and I've walked into the supermarket, and the thought of the heat death of an infinitely massive universe is replaced by saying no to plastic toys with purchase and trying to remember if there's any milk at home.

SHOPPING LIST

eggs

do flowers feel pain when we pick them for our own enjoyment

milk??

brownie mix

dog food

who will remember us when existence itself ends

onion (brown)

I remember years ago I climbed out of my car to go to the supermarket, and when I closed the door a thought forced its way into my mind: When I die, I'll really miss listening to classical music. Nothing was happening then to remind me, it just popped in. And then I was through the whoosh of the automatic doors and wondering where to find fresh bay leaves.

Every night, I listen on repeat to rain-sound videos. There are so many options: rain on a tin roof, rain on a car roof, torrential rain, gentle spring rain, distant thunder, nearby thunder. There is a relaxing weather event for every taste; they even dim the screen to black, so you can sleep peacefully without a bright screen shining back at you.

Sometimes the fear is so acute I put on multiple videos at once to drown it out. Soothing Rain Sounds for Cats *and* Thunderstorm Rain Sounds for Sleeping. When that isn't sufficiently calming, I add another layer of relaxation: Japanese ASMR cooking, the full-fat sound of someone slicing through couverture chocolate and stirring it into butter. I add an American woman eating only pink foods for a whole day; a couple of pseudo-celebrities photoshopping each other into increasingly weird situations; an expert chef facing off against a rank amateur. Rain on a BuzzFeed cook. Rain on a buff nerd.

Underneath their sponsored content, the rain plays. If I turn up the volume enough, I can't hear my brain. I can drift off to the artificial trickle, imaginary rivulets, and a YouTuber getting kicked in the balls.

In the night, I stir and hear the water and first think, with joy, Oh, it's raining. Then I see my laptop keyboard light up, betraying the false storm, and remember that not only is it not actually raining (climate change, the desertification of our planet) but I'm also desperately playing twelve-hour videos to help me forget. And so, in trying to forget, I necessarily remember. Panic rises in my throat (this is the way it travels: from my knees quickly into my hips, to my shoulders, my chest and into my throat; it takes the air in one morbid grasp), and I reach across to Gaz and shake him. *We're all going to die.* And he says, *We've got food, we've got a house, we won't die.* And I say, *I don't mean of this, but of something.*

I listen to these rain sounds all night, layer upon layer, soothing and calming and comforting. And I still wake up already thinking about dying.

This is how I panic: one Monday, I felt a depression stirring. For several days I had been on top of things, productive, light-hearted. I've learned to be wary of this feeling. To find a little joy in the ease of it, but also to recognise it as a warning sign. And there I was, day four, sitting at my kitchen table feeling absolutely furious. Agitated. Irritated. Stop emailing me! Why do people always need stuff from me! My writing was no good. The words didn't flow, filtered like krill through baleen. I typed them and then I hated them. I deleted them and then I hated myself.

Depression has long taken a back seat to my anxiety. They are comorbid, but anxiety takes so much energy that I sometimes don't notice how flat I am. Often, depression only reveals itself when the anxiety is falling on the downward slope of a very nasty spike. And I had had a panic attack on the previous Friday, so I was coming down.

I have a panic attack most days, but they are usually the kind that squeeze your oesophagus for a few seconds and let go. *You're gonna die!* one-two-three *Oh, no, sorry, you're fine.* You're in a bookshop and for a moment the shelves might fall and kill you!!! But they don't and you go on. Put a few things in your *New Yorker* tote bag and it passes.

But on that Friday I was driving my kids to a friend's house to play *Dungeons & Dragons*. This friend had moved house to somewhere I didn't know very well. I noticed, when I drove out of my street, that I was a bit nervous. I pretended I wasn't. I said to my kids, *Got your snacks?* and, *Can you bring up her house on Google Maps?* We drove and laughed. Down the highway, past the hardware stores and car dealerships, under the rail bridge. Drove and laughed. Laughed so my body would know we were having a good time. Ha ha, anxiety armour. Where did you say to go? Up this street? And then around the corner and, oh, three dead-end streets in a row? You're playing Dungeons & Dragons inside a labyrinth? Ha ha, no, that's perfect. Will I be able to find my way out again? Ha ha, just a joke, I'm your parent and I know how to navigate this maze of cul-de-sacs and I definitely won't die here. You're safe with me, a regular mum who can protect you.

We pulled up outside the house and the panic found me. I needed to move. I needed to *be moving*. This is how I know I'm still alive. Foot off the brake pedal just a bit but still stationary. Quickly, get out of the car. Hurry, hurry. If I don't leave now, I don't know what will happen. I don't know. I won't be able. I can't. I will never get out. Please hurry. HAVE FUN, CHILDREN!

I left them in the wake of ghost dust my car made. End of the street, turn left, left again, it's so far to the exit, how do I get out, which way did they say. Three dead-ends in a row, left left left. Can't see the intersection, watch for that car, turn up the air conditioner, take a breath, two breaths, there's the roundabout, is your chest still inflating, don't cry, don't cry, give way to the right, you're not going to die but you *might*, you might die, probably not, but you still might.

I started talking out loud to myself. 'Get to the traffic lights. You'll be okay when you get to the traffic lights. Then it's left and down the road – you know that road. Get to the traffic lights.' Aloud, in my car, on my own. 'Come on, grown woman, just another two hundred metres down the road and you'll be safe again.' Heart racing, hands shaking. It sounds clichéd but it's true, that's how it goes. An overdose of adrenaline. Let it go on too long and it heads the other way, a deficit, can't go in any direction but staying still isn't right either, so you have to move. Keep moving. Get away from the danger (the danger is inarticulable).

At the end of the street, I called my dad, jabbing my car's touchscreen with my fingertip until his name lit up.

'Hi, my sweet,' he said. (He always says this.)

'Hi,' I went. 'Hi, what are you doing?' Tell me what you're doing. Something normal. The most normal thing a person can be doing. Paying a bill. Making some toast. Pushing in a chair.

'Not much. What are you doing?'

'Me? Me, Anna? What am I doing?' Heart's a Gravitron, spinning like a top, and all the kids inside it are puking, bang bang bang, let me out, Kieran spewed in my mouth! 'Just driving the kids to a friend's place and now I'm on my way home gotta do some work this afternoon have a meeting get ready for the meeting make some notes I think I have to send a few emails.'

He paused. His brain whirred. I knew it was doing this. I knew he was calculating the velocity of my words and putting them into the Is Anna Panicking equation. *Panic = displacement over word count.* Sixty words a square metre. Cube it if you can hear the air conditioner fan running. 'And,' he said, carefully enunciating each word, 'what else are you doing?'

Run. RUN. 'Might stop at the shops and get soup, you know from the fridge at the supermarket because it's winter so they bring all the soups back, do you ever eat those, do you ever ever eat them, what do you think of them, I might get two maybe we can have them for dinner the kids are going to their dad's.'

'What flavour do you like?' he said slowly.

I stopped to think. 'Broccoli,' I said. 'Yeah.' An extra beat. 'I like broccoli the best.' That's the trick. Slow me down with a specific topic and the panic will end. Everyone in my family knows this trick. They have all been on the other end of this conversation.

Once I went to a shopping centre with my brother and his daughter. She was only little, maybe she hadn't started school yet. I wanted to take her for an ice cream. There's a gelato shop in this centre and it makes milkshakes with as many flavours as you want to put in it, and next door there's an arcade with games that flash in bright colours. I wanted to go there with her. I wanted to be an aunty who gets an ice cream or a milkshake and buys you tokens to win a prize.

We went into the shopping centre. There were so many people. The three of us walked towards the ice-cream shop. One tile at a time, don't step on the cracks. People talked and laughed. They swung their shopping bags and pushed their trolleys. Step, tile, step, tile. We walked for maybe fifty tiles. And then I stopped. I couldn't get past this one square. An invisible wall had been erected around it. The ice-cream shop was twenty-five tiles away, but it didn't matter as long as this one tile was blocked off.

'Fuck,' I muttered. I stepped back from the tile. I went forward again, hit the wall. Back again, forward. Invisible wall. My niece started running off towards the gelato shop, but my brother kept standing there with me. My little brother, six inches taller than me. My tough, sweary, kind brother.

He looked at me. 'Are you stuck?' he said.

'Yeah,' I said.

'Really stuck, or just a bit stuck?'

'Really stuck.'

'That's okay.' He went with my niece to the shop and brought an ice cream back for me. We sat on the safe side of the Indiana-Jones-danger-trap tile. We ate together, the three of us, and he didn't say it. He didn't say, *Are you okay?* He just asked me if my ice cream was good.

Here's how a panic attack works.

You're in a situation that may or may not be threatening. That is, you might be picking up some delicious takeaway, or driving a train for the first time. Suddenly, you experience intense fear. Your body reacts the way it does to a real threat: you hyperventilate, your heart races, your hands shake, your palms are sweaty (mom's spaghetti). Maybe your chest hurts, or you feel dizzy or out of your body or like you're going to spew. WHAT IS HAPPENING? IT MAKES NO SENSE!

It can feel – literally, physiologically – like you're dying. The warning signs of heart attacks and stroke? Also symptoms of panic attacks. It's like rehearsing to die.

Usually, the symptoms don't last that long, and then you're left with the residual heart-fluttering outer-space tiredness. Sometimes for a few minutes. Sometimes for days. Months. Years.

Researchers still don't really know why this happens. They think it involves the amygdala (the part of your brain that regulates emotion – or doesn't). Studies have implicated dysfunction of the hypothalamic-pituitary-adrenal axis. During panic attacks, adrenaline in the body more than doubles. Blood sugar spikes. Carbon dioxide levels drop.

I think there is a moment before the panic, before bile shoots into your throat and your fingers try to fall off, when the mental time machine grabs you. An instant in the past, a nanosecond in the future. Warning. There is danger here. Maybe not *here*, at this burger shop, but on the space-time continuum. You are at risk. Now. Then. Always. Remember to be afraid.

I had felt the early signs of a big panic attack a couple of days before the broccoli-soup incident. I went to pick up my kids from school. They had exams so I was collecting them at the wrong time of day; any change in routine can be a trigger. I drove the other way you can go, past the park and down through the winding streets to the beach. When I was nearly at the beach I thought I might die. I had clicked out of the moment. One minute I'd been driving along perfectly normally, here I go, picking up my children, and then I was somewhere else for a second, and then I was back in the car again. A minor dissociation.

I knew where I was literally: on this street that connected to the other street. But *when* was I and *who* and *how* was I?

It takes effort to collect the pieces of my psyche that are scattered across the bitumen and wrestle them back into the body that's supposed to contain me.

I did do that, though, because I had no choice. I had to collect my children from school. My heart rate slowed a little. The beach was right there. As I've said, I love the beach. Not the actual beach, which is terrible because of sand and childhood trauma, but being near it. In a city like Melbourne – which has a population of five million people – it's so rare to be able to see out to the horizon, to be anything other than right next to some other dickhead. I took a deep breath. I had enough in reserve to get me to the kids' school. On I went.

I parked by the gate. I read my Twitter feed. I sent an email. On the whole, I was pretty relaxed. But there was this seed of anxiety sitting under my solar plexus, sprouting fronds into my lungs. It said, *You're not in danger yet, but you're about to be.*

'Hurry,' I whispered to the car and my very slow children. '*Hurry*.'

I tapped my foot on the accelerator pedal without depressing it. I could see my kids through the window, picking up their bags the way a Greenland shark might (with prehistoric lethargy).

'Come on.'

The radio barked at me. Too loud, turn it down. Too soft, turn it up! *Tap tap tap.*

A couple of teenagers meandered towards the car. Familiar, but irritating. Their lack of urgency seemed to be putting me at great risk. Is that my heart or just a muscle spasm? I pressed the button to unlock the boot.

'Hi!' I aimed for brightness. 'Hop in!' Big smile. 'Isn't everything just fine!'

I patted the little one's leg, reached behind me to squeeze the hand of the other one. Then I chucked a U-turn across the empty street and immediately, right then, the stems that had sprouted from this anxiety seed closed tight around my organs and roared.

'Fuck,' I whispered. (My kids were teenagers, so I was allowed to swear in front of them.) 'Fuck. Sorry. Just a spot of anxiety!'

'It's okay,' Quinn said.

'Sorry about this.' Smile. *Make a joke!* 'Probably had too much chocolate, over-caffeinated.' Also the world is collapsing. Can't you see it? Folding in like a paper fortune teller. *Get to the end of the road.* 'How do you think your exams went?' *Talk to me about a specific topic.*

'Alright,' Georgia said.

Take a deep breath. Shallow breaths make you dizzy makes you anxious makes you more dizzy. 'Sorry!' I said again, still smiling. 'Sorry, it's just been a bit of a day.'

'It's fine,' said Quinn, through gritted teeth.

'How was maths?'

'Fine.'

Drive. Around this corner, down this street. How far now? Need to get *out* – out of where? Back to the main road. Drive. Turn down the radio. Turn up the air conditioner.

Now there was the beach, the God-awful sand but the comforting distance. My heart was still racing but my hands had stopped shaking. Take a breath. Another breath. Slowwww dowwwwwn.

'And how was physics?'

'Fine.'

I indicated to turn into the street that would take us home.

Panic can be very long. It is long like the elastic seconds you spend outside an automatic door while your child is having an operation. It is nothing, an instant, but every one of those moments is your entire life.

Recently, after I had met my new therapist and learned about my Schemas and started putting my puzzle back together, my kids needed to go back to that house where they had played *Dungeons & Dragons*. Their friend was having a birthday party. It was on a Saturday night, which, if you'll recall, was once the most terrifying prospect I could imagine. But I said I would take them, partly because I was raised by overprotective parents but largely to prove that I could.

I did a dry run on the Thursday before. Drove down the highway and up the street. Had a tiny adrenaline spike and turned at a roundabout and went home. It felt so far away. I wanted to do it, but each time I tried, my body spat its reminders of last time, when I had panicked all the way out of my head. It said, *Remember, you can't do this.*

On the Saturday, I thought about it all day. I would do it, I knew. I was sure I could make it. But would I be alive at the end? Impossible to say.

At six o'clock I shoved the kids into the car and we set off. Down the highway, past the hardware stores and car dealerships, under the rail bridge. They laughed. I laughed. We went down the street where my heart had tried to explode, then through three dead-end streets, right, right, right. I stopped the car outside the house. Put on the handbrake. Paused a moment longer, looked around to notice that I had done it, I had made it and I hadn't vomited up a single internal organ, not even the ones you don't strictly need. Then I made a right-hand turn and went the long way back, past the park and the train crossing, all the way to the beach and home again, where I let the dam of success fill up.

Sometimes when you don't panic for a while, your body sort of loses a bit of muscle memory. You rebuild some of the neural pathways, so *fight or flight* isn't the only one you can access. You learn to cope a little better. Maybe you even forget exactly how it feels to be in anxiety's fist.

'Hey,' you say to strangers in the street. 'Look at how well I can breathe. In *and* out!'

Sometimes it comes back. Out of nowhere, like a drunk ex-boyfriend who's suddenly decided you need to hear from him (you don't). Your body remembers immediately. It knows the way to bend, to pulse, to rush, to twist. It surges through you.

The work starts again. But sometimes you notice you're not exactly the same as last time. Your tools are slightly different. Sometimes there is courage there, too.

SEPTEMBER

Gaz and I go to a discount store to buy trackpants. He is very particular about trackpants (no elastic around the ankle, no weird shiny bits) so we go to a number of different places. The shops are busy. Melbourne has finally been allowed out of lockdown for the sixth time and everyone is urgently making up for lost days they didn't spend buying t-shirts made in a Bangladeshi sweatshop.

It is a Saturday afternoon. There's a doughnut shop and kids screaming on a two-dollar ride and a line to get into Aldi. It's like being at an agricultural show. There's so much stimulus my ear starts ringing a bit but I feel brave. I think about what my new therapist taught me about Wise Mind. If I focus, I can make the two parts of my mind merge together to make Wise Mind.

'Let's go in here,' Gaz says.

We are in the bowels of the shopping centre. This is as far away from the exit as it is possible to go but I am still brave. I tell myself I'm great at being trapped and surrounded at the shops on a Saturday afternoon. I tell myself it's okay that I'm still learning.

The racks of trackpants are right at the back of the shop. If I want to get out of here, I will have to sprint. I will have to go chaotically at the speed of light to the escalator, and then to level two, and then past the games shop and the movies and up another escalator and out to the car. But I won't have to. I can be very, very far from the exit and still be brave.

Gaz picks up some navy blue trackies. He screws up his face. He picks up some orange trackies and puts them in a 'maybe' pile. I go to another rack. I flick through the coathangers to find trackies without elastic around the ankle.

Then the ground shifts a bit.

No one else has noticed.

The rack I'm holding sways like it's on wheels. A sharp breath comes out of me. My feet start trying to make me go towards the door. I am a marionette under the control of Big Anxiety and my legs are moving even though I am telling them to be still. 'Be still, legs!' I hiss.

Gaz's head pokes around the corner. He can't even see my legs but he knows.

'Are you okay?' he says.

'Yes!' I say, in my most relaxed voice. 'What about these trackpants? They have elastic around the ankle but it's not tight elastic, not the gathered kind you don't like it's more like stretchy fabric, so-it-might-do?' My body tries to dance towards the cash register.

Gaz's hand slides into mine.

'I'm fine,' I say.

He squeezes my knuckles between his knuckles.

'I really am.'

His other hand finds my shoulder. His fingers slide under the fabric of my shirt until his skin is against my skin.

'I'm *fine*.' I smile to make it true, except it kind of is true. The rush of panic has subsided. I feel clear and tough. 'You don't have to worry about me.'

He says, 'I don't know how.'

We go to the next shop. It is still far from the door but I hear my therapist's voice remind me that thoughts aren't facts. We pick over the shelves. This shop has some grey trackpants so I buy them to say thank you.

Recurrent aborted sudden cardiac death

After four decades of worrying, catastrophising and therapising, I had a pretty good handle on the nature of my anxiety. I didn't like it, but I knew more about it. I had learned that it was irrational. My brain telling me lies. My out-of-shape memory. The people I love weren't going to suddenly die for no reason! No one I loved would abruptly abandon me!

By the time I was in my late thirties, I knew these lies intimately. I finally believed my therapists when they explained I couldn't always trust my thoughts. I had developed techniques to acknowledge and dismiss them, to sit with the discomfort they created, and to rationalise them out of my mind. I was prepared for almost anything they could throw at me, any falsehood, any paranoia, any slip-sliding in and out of time.

I was not prepared for them to be true.

On a cool May morning, when I was 17, the phone rang as I was leaving for school. That wasn't unusual in itself, but when I answered, Gramps's deep voice boomed out.

He had never called before, and he never called again. It was always Nanna's voice, pitched and cheerful. His tolled like a warning bell.

'Is your mum there?' he asked, and I realised he was crying.

I have never run so fast to pass the phone to someone else.

I eavesdropped. I listened to my mum break into a howl.

My uncle, who was thirty-nine, had hosted a dinner party the night before for his wife's birthday. They had eaten good food, drunk good wine, and when the festivities ended they had gone to bed. And he had died.

Early in the day – too early, the wrong kind of early – my mum sends a text. *I'm at your front door!* Smiley face. And immediately, another: *I have a baguette!*

Half-dressed, I take the bread from her. It is still warm. I wait for her to rush off, as she usually does, but she pushes past me and sits at the kitchen table.

'Hi?' I say.

She's unfolding some paper. My children are still asleep.

'I have to talk to you about a medical issue,' she says, as though they are not the most terrifying words that exist. 'But don't worry, it's not about your dad.' This is always her way, to simultaneously reassure us and diminish herself.

She had been to hospital a few weeks earlier with chest pains. I had collected her myself, afterwards. I had carefully packed her into my car while the angiogram bruising spread across her skin. She seemed in good spirits. Her arteries had been clear, she said at the time; there was nothing wrong with them.

Technically, this is true. She is a lawyer, after all.

Now she backtracks. There is something wrong, actually. She knew this then, when I picked her up. She had let me drive her home and complain about my own minor problems, and she had listened and helped. *Don't worry, you're okay, I'm here.* This is her way, too – to always make space for other people.

She sits in my kitchen, at a table she bought for me. 'It's no big deal,' she says, which is a lie. 'I didn't even know if I should tell you.' She turns the paper face up. It is a mess of crests and falls I recognise as an echocardiogram.

She points to a place where the line shifts. 'It's called Brugada syndrome.'

I don't know who taught me to say, 'See you in the morning.' Even as a child, well before my uncle died, I was fixated on it. Paranoia told me if I didn't tell someone I would see them in the morning, I wouldn't. Over time, the obsession evolved – it would have to be the last thing I said to them before they went to sleep. When I moved out of home, I would call my parents and shout it down the line.

See you in the morning. A demand. Promise me I will see you in the morning.

Many things can take you in the night. There are monsters

under the mattress, in the wardrobe, scratching at the window. A house might land on you, or a loose tree branch. In the dark you might eat a poisonous spider, sleepwalk into a bear trap, be taken by a wild dog. The earth might be peppered with ancient rocks from an asteroid belt.

> The Brugada syndrome was described in 1992, in patients presenting with recurrent aborted sudden cardiac death (SCD) and a typical electrocardiography sign of ST-elevation in leads V1 to V3.
>
> It was later shown that patients die of ventricular tachycardia or fibrillation, often during sleep.

Brugada syndrome also comes in the darkness. In the Philippines, they call it *bangungut*: to rise and moan in sleep.

See you in the morning. *Seeyouinthemorning.*

When I was about twenty-one, I called my mum late at night. I can't remember why, but it seemed very important that I do so. The first time, the call rang out. The second time, she answered, yelled, 'I'M AT THE HOSPITAL WITH YOUR DAD!' and hung up. When I called back, her phone was off. I called all the emergency departments I could think of to find the one they were at. Receptionists must have heard the panic in my voice, breaking privacy rules to tell me there was no one there by my dad's name, until finally someone put me through to a cardiac ward. He had life-saving heart surgery the next day.

Fifteen years later, I rang my dad. It was late afternoon, and I had just dropped home one of my kids' friends. I could hear that Dad was in his car, which was not strange in itself but something to talk about.

'Where are you?' I asked, without expectation.

He stumbled, so briefly, barely perceptible except to someone who always expects the worst.

'Getting a coffee,' he said, a second too late.

I glanced at the time. 'At five o'clock? Where from?'

'Westfield.'

As it happened, Quinn and I were also headed there to buy stuff for dinner. 'Why don't we meet you there?' I said.

He tripped again. 'Oh, no, I'm just leaving. I *was* there, but now I'm not there.'

'Dad,' I said, for reasons only the misfiring synapses in my brain can know, 'you're at the hospital, aren't you?'

'No,' he said. 'I'll call you back in fifteen minutes.'

Forty minutes later, I tried him again. He sent a text: *In a meeting*.

It was 6 pm. I was in the Aldi car park, crying into my steering wheel because I knew – I *knew* – something had gone horribly wrong.

'Don't search for it.' Mum tries to peer at my phone. I have eaten the end of the baguette without realising. 'I did,' she says. 'Just don't.'

The screen blinks back from my hand. I have six tabs open already.

> Brugada syndrome: a rare inherited cardiac arrhythmia syndrome that is characterised by a 'coved-shaped' atypical right bundle branch pattern on a 12-lead ECG. [Melbourne Heart Rhythm]

> Brugada syndrome: a potentially life-threatening heart rhythm disorder that is sometimes inherited. [Mayo Clinic]

> Brugada syndrome: also known as Sudden Unexplained Nocturnal Death Syndrome. [Wikipedia]

I ask her every question I can think of. What does it mean? Are you in danger right now? Do I have it? Why didn't you know about it before? Does it hurt? Are you scared? Are you *scared*?

Brugada syndrome is new – it is only in the past fifteen years or so that doctors have seen and described it. When my uncle died, no one knew about it. In retrospect, the doctors say, there's a very high likelihood he died because of this; my mum's other brother has since found out he also has it. It is inherited in an autosomal dominant manner: you only need one abnormal gene from one parent. The average age of an 'episode' – a nice word they use to describe your sudden massive heart attack – is forty.

In a month I will be thirty-seven.

'Try not to worry,' Mum says. 'There's a fifty per cent chance you don't have it.'

There is no cure. The treatment options are having a tiny defibrillator implanted in your chest, or 'watchful waiting'. The only symptoms are fainting and death.

Mum touches my arm again; her skin is so soft, like wax paper. She says, 'I'm sorry.'

My uncle's death is ever-present in our family. He was handsome, talented, gregarious, bold and fervently loved. It was so unexpected, so inexplicable. I think about him often. I think about him as I drive to the heart specialist. I think about him as I call my ex-husband to explain gently that our children – *my* children, my own children – might have inherited a sudden death disorder.

'We'll worry about it if we need to,' he says. I have never done this in my life.

Because I am an anxiety-stricken mess of a human, I've had many ECGs. I've run into hospitals and shrieked about chest pain. I've explained to my doctor the fluttery, breath-catching palpitations. I've scrubbed the sticky residue left by dozens of leads, worn twenty-four-hour Holter monitors and carried the reports around with me for reassurance. So there is, the specialist explains, a good chance someone would have found it by now. But, he muses, I have something called an incomplete right branch bundle block – a different kind of electrical fault. It's probably not related. Except, you know.

Even if you don't have it, you can be a carrier. Even if you don't have it, your children can.

Your children – my children – can have *Sudden Unexplained Nocturnal Death Syndrome.*

The specialist is a man too jovial for his beige office. He immediately recognises me as someone who panic-searches for information; I have come to the appointment with just enough to be a danger to everyone.

I say, 'I read that in Japan they just call it "sudden death syndrome".'

'Yes!' he says brightly. 'That is what it causes.'

He checks my heart with his stethoscope. I resist the urge to wonder jokingly if I have one at all. I fill the time with leading questions based on my Google-fed micro-facts and mixed-up presumptions.

'You know a lot,' he says, bemused. 'But remember to be discerning.'

I will not remember to be discerning. Instead, I will remember him saying, 'A past history of fever and fainting puts you at high risk.' I will remember holding my daughter when she was three years old while she went limp and blue in my arms, and the way my hands shook as I called an ambulance. I will remember the way her body burned as her knees collapsed in the middle of a Blockbuster, and the long line at the emergency room.

I know this about myself: I will not remember to be discerning. I will take in every skerrick of non-peer-reviewed speculation from every website I can find.

Brugada syndrome is a rare, distinctive but oft-missed wave on an ECG. It rises, then it falls strangely and dips at the bottom ('coved ST segment elevation >2mm in >1 of V1-V3 followed by a negative T wave'). The heart muscle is structurally normal but the electrics are dodgy. It's different from other heart disorders because it's still present when you're resting or asleep, not exacerbated by exertion. The risk is not reduced by exercise or diet. It doesn't cause chest tightness, breathlessness, shooting arm pain or any of the other signs the TV tells us to watch for. It has absolutely no impact on a person unless they have an episode.

The heart just beats and beats, and one day it might stop.

A sudden, unexplained death.

Each night, when my kids get into their pyjamas and have their skin all soft and clean, we chat for a few minutes. Usually they say things like, *I'm feeling a bit sick* or *I think I'm getting a headache* – a set-up for when they try to get out of going to school the next day.

When that's done, I hug them and I say, 'See you in the morning.' I make them say it back to me. They mumble, the way teenagers do. 'SEE YOU IN THE MORNING,' I yell, and they go to bed and dream about K-pop or whatever, and I think about how I've defended them from night-time yet again.

On a Friday I take them to have their hearts monitored in a weatherboard house. We sit in plastic chairs and wait our turn. They say they're not nervous, but their questions betray them: Will it hurt? Can you come in with me? When will we find out?

A strip of paper delivers your child's heart function from a machine. It comes in waves and spikes. The muscle you created with your own body, the same beats you heard in the ultrasound room, and later with your ear pressed to their tiny chests. The nurse prints it out in a small dim room and hides it from you. No, you're not an armchair cardiologist. No, you don't know how to interpret the results. No, if we give you a copy, you'll google it and scare yourself.

I am a pro, I say. The only thing I know is how to google and scare myself.

The internet tells me CPR is the only course of action if you wake and find a person in cardiac arrest.

Start cardiopulmonary resuscitation as soon as possible.

Place your hands, one on top of the other, at the bottom of the breastbone; push down one-third of the depth of the person's chest; thirty compressions followed by two breaths, aiming for about 100 to 120 compressions a minute. A good way to keep the rhythm is to think of the Bee Gees song 'Staying Alive'. *Ah-ah-ah-ah.* Remember to reflect on the irony throughout.

Without CPR, it takes three to four minutes for a person to become brain dead. CPR does not guarantee that person's survival, but it creates a chance where there would have been none.

Start cardiopulmonary resuscitation as soon as possible.

Don't let the whole night go by without starting it. Sit beside your loved one while they sleep. Lie there until your eyes are swollen with fatigue. Watch their nerves twitch with their dreams. In a quiet voice, reminisce about the times you ate picnics at the beach and the times you bought golden jonquil bulbs and the time when you were born, and your slippery eel body was safe with their arms around it.

If you drift off and their heart stops, start cardiopulmonary resuscitation as soon as possible.

Quinn sends me emails from school. *Have you got the results yet?* they ask.

Not yet. Try not to worry, I tell them.

I'm not worried, they write.

Me neither, I reply.

We are liars.

In the afternoon, I call the medical results number. My whole body is quaking. My fingertips sweat. The nurse needs a minute to find our records. It is longer than any other minute there has ever been. The phone line quietens, just a low chatter in a corridor.

'Are you there?' I say.

My heart is slamming against the bones that protect it. It is a propeller about to lift me into space. It constricts, fights, pukes. What does it know?

The nurse clicks whatever nurses click to reveal fates. Finally, she says, 'The note says they are all normal.'

By some miracle, against the odds, it appears for now as though none of us have inherited it. My brother, my sister, my children have normal ECGs. They might change as we get older. Sometimes the pattern isn't revealed until a person is in their forties. I can't think about this. I cannot.

My mum sleeps while Dad's radio plays upstairs in a room with a balcony that overlooks the park. Her bedcovers are made of material printed with petals, bees, fish. She leaves her glasses on the bedside table. Downstairs she always has fresh flowers and she keeps expensive individually wrapped ice creams in the freezer, in case her grandchildren visit. She texts in emojis. She sends me messages like, *How is my beautiful girl?* and *So proud of my girl.* Sometimes she just sends me a photo of my face that she's secretly taken sometime in the past.

When I was a teenager, we fought every single day. I think about how much we fought. All the years we could have spent being mates. I think: *You will lose her.*

At night, I pull out my phone and text her. I imagine her hazel-grey eyes flicking across her screen as she reads my words. I want to type, See you in the morning. I want to demand it. But it no longer seems fair to insist. Instead I type, *Love you lots.*

I wait, watchfully.

After a minute, her reply comes: *Love my girl!!!*

Don't we make a lot of assumptions about time? How we learn from the past and take that information into the future, but never in the other direction. How something that happened to us as a child couldn't be informed by a temporal slipstream, information being fed back to guide us. How we are afraid of suddenly losing our family 'for no reason'.

How 'now' means something absolutely different to each person who experiences it.

How the present can be a future echo.

How being *right* can be so exquisitely bittersweet.

When my mum was forty, at the apex of the average age of death from Brugada syndrome, I was eight. And I was sitting in Mrs Gill's classroom, panicking because Mum was about to walk down the steps and tell me Nanna had just died.

Senseless. Worrying for nothing. Irrational. Lighten up! Chill out! Your family won't suddenly and inexplicably die! Stop crying during maths!

Except, you know.

And then I think of my nanna and this grief she has been forced to carry. How she tried and failed to keep her family safe with her endless rituals. How only a year after she lost her youngest child I rocked up at her door and she, broken-hearted, opened it to me and nourished me. How she showed me the rituals again and again, the tiny protections that weren't.

At least three of Nanna's four children were born with this deadly electrical fault in their heart. It is likely to have come from Gramps's side – he had a brother who suddenly died in his sleep on his way to war. No one has told Nanna this. She has never heard the words 'Brugada syndrome'. She will never know that she could have woken one morning to find all her loved ones gone, or that her protection would have made no difference.

Part 4

To want something to be true

On a Friday afternoon, a couple of years after we had moved house and I hadn't been poisoned by the water and I had been doing okay, actually, mostly, I left home and drove to the local emergency department. Everything had got so heavy. Walking from my car to the automatic doors was like pulling a whale from the ocean. I stood at the ER check-in window. It was like a drive-thru, a pane of glass with a hole in it. I thought about why the glass must have been there, who must have threatened somebody. I thought, I'm holding it together quite well, comparatively.

It was still this. After all these years, it was still *going to the ER on a Friday afternoon.*

A triage nurse glanced at my Medicare card and confirmed my phone number. I took a seat by the entry to the outdoor playground. I had sat there many times. This time, I was alone.

The triage nurse called my name and I dragged my whole body back to the window. I dragged my legs and my arms and my head. We all fell into the chair; we were one of those wooden toy animals where you press the bottom and the whole thing collapses. Every part of me was joined by elastic and cellophane.

I tried to be upright. I made my eyes look right at her. *Eyes, look forward*, I said in my head. *Act normal. Be friendly. Make a joke.*

'How are you today?' Her face was soft and open.

I went, 'Yeah, fine!' I tried laughing.

Half her mouth curled up in pity, and then her hand was on my arm. This was a kindness; I knew the hospital had no psychiatric facilities and the nurse was within rights to turn me away. The nearest mental hospital was thirty-five minutes away, even from here in suburban Melbourne. They don't put treatment facilities where I live, in case the nice middle-class families are forced to accidentally see a sick person.

'Are you feeling bad?' she said.

My skin blushed warm where her fingers touched it. Goodness ran out of her and into me. I nodded. And then, I cried. 'I can't do it anymore,' I told her.

'Do what?'

'*It*.' It: get up in the morning, take a breath, carry oxygen around my body, synthesise proteins, exhale, urinate, love, shit in a bowl.

She put a band around my wrist. It said ANNA SPARGORYAN and my birthday. 'How do you pronounce that?' she said. '*Spah-gore-ian*?'

I didn't correct her. Who gives a shit? Kids with broken arms watched me cry out all the fluid that made me. Their parents watched too, and whispered, *fucking hell* and *poor woman* and *psycho*.

There were no beds for someone with my affliction so the nurse took me to a small room. I knew what the room was for. It had grey carpet and a window with venetian blinds. It was the room they take you to if something horrible has happened, so they can tell you in private.

'I have to go back to the desk,' she said. 'But you don't have to worry. Don't worry. Just for a little while.' She was definitely somebody's grandmother. 'A doctor will come. Are you okay here by yourself?'

'Yes,' I said.

I was not okay there by myself. If I sat up, I was too close to the sky. I felt all the parts of me tearing away from my bones and shooting at the window. *Pew pew!* Flesh and tendons. I put my bag under a chair and then I got on the floor and crawled under the chair as well. If I curled up small enough, my body would come back together. I was a T-1000; I was Alex Mack; I shapeshifted into different versions of myself. I melted into the carpet. I thought that when the nurse came back she would think it was funny that I'd disappeared but my bag was still there, me just swimming around under the floor so I didn't float away.

The door opened. 'Anna?'

A doctor. I suddenly thought, Sitting on the floor under a chair is something a crazy person would do. They're going to think I'm insane! There were so many exclamation marks in my head!

I rolled away from the chair and sat up and thought, Make a joke!!!

'Sorry, it's just the floor is so comfortable.'

The doctor smiled thinly. 'What seems to be the matter?'

I slid my liquid arm back into its socket. 'I feel like I need to die,' I said.

'Tell me more about that.'

'I feel like that's what's supposed to happen.'

She paused, and I waited for the question: 'Do you have a family history of mental illness?'

'Yes,' I said. 'My grandfather killed himself.'

The door was wide open then, and in the corridor two men in paramedics' uniforms were talking about sandwiches. I wondered what might have happened if they had brought me in. If I had called triple zero and explained how parts of my body were disintegrating and it simply wasn't possible to keep stapling them back together.

The doctor tried to find other ways to say, *What's wrong with you?* 'Do you have a diagnosis?' she asked eventually.

'Various,' I said. 'Mostly I have dissociative symptoms, including derealisation and depersonalisation. I also have chronic depression and generalised anxiety, and acute periods, which is what's happening now.'

'Are you a nurse?' she said, with some surprise.

'Ha ha, no,' I said, pleased that she had noticed how excellent I was at being mental. 'I just have to know a lot about it because otherwise I can't advocate for myself.'

We sat there for a second. She said, 'I'm going to call someone.'

Through the open door I could see a bed with a girl in it; maybe she was fifteen. She was lying as still as possible on the gurney while a doctor talked to her dad. 'She says she's dizzy,' the dad explained. 'Her head is spinning.' She was so pale there might not be any blood in her at all.

'My head is spinning, too,' I said to the small room. My dad didn't arrive.

The nice nurse came back with a cordless phone.

I put it to my ear. 'Hello?'

A high voice: 'Anna, is it? How are you feeling, Anna?'

She said my name like it should bring me some comfort. Like, *Remember, you're a person*.

'Bad,' I said, uncertain.

'I'm from the CAT team. Do you know what that is?'

My throat grew tight. 'Yes.'

'The doctor tells me you're not feeling very well. Is that right?'

The cords for the venetian blind swung in the air-conditioning.

'Well, Anna. *Anna*. The thing is, they can't treat you in this hospital. I'm sorry. They don't have psychiatric facilities there. Did the doctor explain that to you?'

'Yes.'

'So, the only thing we can do is bring you into the hospital out here. But I don't think it's the best place for you. Do you think it is?'

I didn't know how to answer. 'I was hoping you might tell me,' I said, watching the cord move.

'We think you'll be alright. Don't we?' A deeper voice in the background agreed. 'We think you'll be alright until Monday. It's Friday now, isn't it?' She waited for me to confirm that it was Friday. 'So, here's what I propose: you will go home from the hospital tonight, and not do anything too strenuous over the weekend. And then, on Sunday night, I'll give you a call and see how you're going. How does that sound?'

I said, 'But I feel like I want to die.'

'Okay, Anna. That sounds really tough. But like I said, the only other option is to admit you to the public psychiatric ward. Do you want to go there?'

'I don't know?'

She took a breath. 'So I will call you on Sunday. Okay?'

The phone was so heavy in my hand it must have been marble. I used all my might to hold it. 'Okay,' I said.

The nice nurse gave me a single-serve orange juice. On the way back to my car I pulled the band from my wrist and threw it in the bin. I had forgotten how to drive. I sat in the car until it was dark and then I remembered I had to go home and feed my children.

On Sunday, the woman from the CAT team called as promised. 'How are you feeling, Anna?'

I had made a sandwich. My dog circled around my legs, waiting for a piece of ham to fall. 'Better,' I said. *Make a joke.* 'Not dead yet!'

A pause. 'I'm glad.'

'Thanks for calling.'

'Sure. Do you want me to call again tomorrow?'

'Nah.' I gave the dog a rub. She rolled in a pool of sunlight on the floor.

My body was wafer-thin pages: stagnant, dried out. But if I flipped them, it gave the illusion of motion.

I called a suicide hotline. I had called suicide hotlines before, but not for many years, and I didn't want to call it now but I was knee-deep in my own shit.

'I'm so sad,' I said to the woman on the other end. 'Can you die of sadness?'

She made a clucking sound like a grandmother. 'You should wear pink to attract love,' she said.

'Pardon?' I said.

'Pink is the colour of love. Wear it and it will come to you.'

'What the fuck?' I said. 'I have a psychotic illness.'

She was not deterred. She explained the crystals I could buy, how I could string them up in my bedroom and put one under my pillow. 'And eat a cup of vegetables,' she suggested. 'Bake muffins.' If I followed her advice, she assured me, before long I would be absolutely drowning in love.

'I'm fixed now,' I said, and hung up.

Many years earlier, when Georgia was a baby, I had been watching TV in my parents' kitchen when I realised my brain thought Homer Simpson was my dad. Not that he and my dad were the same person, but that I had been sired and raised by a cartoon. I can only speculate that in some crossed neurological pathway, I'd heard Dan Castellaneta's voice so many times that I figured it must have been significant in this way.

I didn't have any money so I went down to a bulk-billing medical clinic under a railway bridge. It was one of those old ones with brown carpet and vinyl chairs that hiss when you sit down. I said, 'I think Homer Simpson is my dad.'

The doctor I saw was frightened of me. She opened her digital rolodex and started phoning psychiatrists while I sat there. 'This patient is psychotic,' she hissed. 'She's disconnected from reality.'

The shrink I ended up seeing worked from a converted garage in his house in a nearby suburb. As I drove there, my brain flickered in and out of the present. The road I was on looked like a road from my childhood, then didn't. The shops were familiar, then not. When I arrived at the house I wasn't sure exactly where I was but it was too unsafe to drive home again. This old man sat across from me and asked questions about what was happening in the world: Who is the US president? What month is it? What are your children's names? I gave him the answers he wanted and then I panicked and the ceiling collapsed and I leaped at him, gasping, shaking. He swatted at me. He shook his head. He told me to sit down.

'Come back in two days,' he said, but I didn't, and no one called to follow up.

When you spend as much time as I do thinking you're moments from gruesome death, a hospital can be a place for calm. I have rocked up in emergency rooms many times and been grateful for the chance to be hooked up to a machine, taken seriously, and for the order of getting lunch on a tray, dinner on a tray, breakfast on a tray. I like the nature of them: saving lives, birthing babies, helping people. I like that when you're in one, someone is always keen to know how you're going and they get paid to find out.

I am extraordinarily lucky in this way. Sometimes – often – people go to hospitals to get help for their brains and someone takes everything away from them. Their phone, their family, their agency, their freedom. Sometimes people are strapped to a bed and left there for months, or are obliged to take medicine against their will, or forced to surrender control of their own life. It is a fine line, the one between not helping someone (neglect) and not helping someone (brute force).

A couple of years after the hospital called the CAT team (the seventh or eighth time someone had called them), I went back to the local emergency department because my heart felt like it had stopped, even though I could put my fingers to my neck and feel it bouncing away there. I had said to the triage nurse, 'I have chest pains.' They usually take you in if you have chest pains. Which isn't to say I didn't have chest pains, because I did. An invisible hand was twisting all of the organs from my throat to my bellybutton.

It was quiet that day. There was only me and a boy with a fever and an old man with an oxygen mask strapped to his face. A woman sat next to him. I put on the white gown and lay in bed by myself, reading a book. Coincidentally, the book I was reading was set in the hospital where I was trying to panic to death, which made things much worse (the protagonist of the book was committing a series of murders), but it was still better than being at home, trying to figure out if I was dying.

Because it was quiet, the nurses came over periodically to chat to me about my kids and my cats, and to make sure I was still alive. One of them took my blood to test for heart attack enzymes. It would take three hours for the blood test to come back, so I was welcome, they said, to just hang out until then. I read my book, thought about being murdered, and periodically flinched at the very tight cuff of the automated blood pressure machine. I didn't have to worry. Someone would let me know if I stopped being alive.

After a few minutes, a rapid beeping began above my head. My heart surged. The machine shouted furiously, a sound I had never heard before. The nurse looked up from her station.

'What does it mean?' I shouted. 'WHAT DOES IT MEAN?'

'The machine thinks you've stopped breathing.'

'*Have* I stopped breathing?'

'Dunno, have you?' She smiled.

'I don't think so?' I took a long breath in and let it out through my mouth. 'Is this breathing?' I said to her. 'Am I doing it?'

She got me a fridge-stale egg sandwich. 'You're totally fine,' she said.

A couple of beds over, the old man coughed like he'd got a bird stuck there. After an hour, they told me I could put my clothes back on and go home, and I thanked them for letting me have a rest.

At the end of a very hard year – after my mum had been diagnosed with sudden nocturnal death syndrome, and my elderly cat had had lung cancer and died, and my brain had become so tired it was a lump of chalk – I asked my doctor for a referral to a new therapist. I liked my old therapist very much. I had been seeing her for ten years, from the first time I noticed I was a going a bit mental at the Grand Prix, but I felt like it was clinically irresponsible to keep seeing her. I needed some fresh perspective. It had been years since I had felt that I was actually making progress – or even that anything had changed at all, for better or worse.

I walked into the nearby medical centre and I felt Deeply Uncertain. Cheating on my old therapist. Secretly trying something new. Also, there was absolutely no way that after all this time – after decades of therapy that had only made me feel up and down and never stable – anyone could do anything that might actually help me. I was certain: if something could be done, they would have done it by now.

That day, I wore my loudest thongs. They slapped against the floor as we walked to her room, which was at the back of the building. I had let her down before we even started. She would refuse to see me again. I would be blacklisted from all therapists in the state. Maybe I wore the thongs on purpose, as an act of sabotage. A wall. Therapise *this*, I dare you.

I sat on her terrible, awful, black vinyl couch and she pulled out her legal pad. And everything changed.

OCTOBER

I sit on my new therapist's black vinyl couch. There's going to be a new couch soon but I won't sit on it. I have progressed, emotionally, to a point where I can say to her, 'I don't like sitting on the couch.'

She says, 'How are you feeling?'

For the whole morning, I have been thinking about how she would ask me this and I wouldn't know how to articulate it. How there is calm inside me. Joy. Liberation. How I think about who I am as a person and it doesn't make my heart hurt. How the words people used to describe me as a child aren't connected to my nervous system right now. I push my tongue against the roof of my mouth. I roll it over my teeth.

'Good.'

She writes on her pad.

'Tell me about that,' she says.

I lean forward and put my elbows on my knees. 'I was thinking about all those words I remember people using to describe me when I was a kid. Like, self-centred. Mean. Ungrateful. And I realised I didn't believe them anymore.'

She starts drawing a little diagram.

'And this hard thing happened with work but I didn't get angry with myself about it.'

'Mm-hm,' she says, drawing.

'And I don't blame myself for all of it. Anymore.'

She turns the pad around. She's drawn a line across the top, then a dip down, and another line across the bottom.

'This is you before,' she says, pointing to the top line. 'Self-loathing. You were full of self-loathing. When I first started seeing you, you were really angry.'

Bubbles start bursting in my chest. 'Was I?' I think about how carefully I had tried to stay calm, measured, successful.

'But now ...' She traces the line with the tip of her pen. 'You've gone down this line and crossed over.'

'Crossed over into what?' I say, ignoring the bubbles. Ignoring the way my eyes are stinging for no reason, definitely not because of crying, how stupid!

'Compassion,' she says. 'Empathy.' She draws a little squiggle on the bottom line. 'Self-acceptance.'

The power of using supernatural forces to make impossible things happen

I workshopped this book as part of a creative writing course. I was the only Australian student alongside five writers in the US, all of whom were also writing on various aspects of their lived experience. When we got to my experiences on the medical side, they were *astonished* ('flummoxed,' said one) by the lack of due diligence in the care I received, both from the system I was trying to penetrate and from the family who seemed not to hear me. In the comments someone typed: *I don't understand why no one is* helping *this narrator??*

For as long as I can remember, I have had a degree of understanding that this is 'just the way I am'. I have been led to believe – first by my parents, later by doctors, and all combinations of these relationships – that I should just get on with things. They have, at times, made me feel that my condition wasn't serious enough to warrant serious mental health care, or that I should be prioritising other things in my life. That is, how can you demand someone take your suicidal ideation seriously if you also have to take the kids to school in the morning? How can you expect – desire, even – a paramedic to give you medical attention when they could be responding to someone who has something *actually wrong with them* and isn't just being dramatic?

When I didn't tell my parents I was psychotic it was because I thought – assumed – I would be punished for 'admitting' to this failing. I felt I was meant to be embarrassed by it and keep it hidden. It was shameful not to be tough and resilient; it was a waste of everyone's energy to demand they take care of me. I was being ridiculous, intense, 'a lot'.

I felt so deeply burdensome that I wanted to avoid making it worse at any cost. I didn't want to ask for help, or tell someone I needed support, or try, pointlessly, to articulate what was happening in my head. I was so afraid. I woke up each morning hoping it would be better, found I was praying for relief that never came. Most days I spent curled into the smallest possible version of myself, staring at the TV, trying to stay alive.

Then one day, my parents asked me to come for a drive with them down the Mornington Peninsula – an hour or so – and I realised I absolutely couldn't do it. I couldn't get in the car, couldn't be trapped inside, couldn't be so far from home. I remember sitting on the stairs inside their house and telling them the smallest bit of what was happening to me. Mostly I felt guilt. I apologised a lot. Sorry I'm like this. Sorry I did this. Sorry I did it to you. I don't remember what they said or whether they went on their drive; they did not point me towards anything resembling help. Once again, I went to the doctor on my own.

I believed what she told me because no one had explained that I could contest it, do my own research, become my own informed advocate.

When the first lot of treatment didn't work, I didn't know there was a next step I was *supposed* to take. No one – not a doctor, a nurse, a parent – ever indicated that I should seek out the next person up the rung. That when my GP couldn't help me, I should logically progress to a psychologist, a psychiatrist. This had never been explained. I only knew the language of 'don't make a scene' and 'don't take up so much space'. I was taught to be contrite and grateful. I had learned, over years and decades, that feeling bad was never about trying to feel better again but about not getting in anyone else's way while you did it.

It wasn't until very recently that I felt justified in needing the help I had sought decades ago. During that time, I invested a lot of energy in teaching myself how to appear okay from the outside – to mask. I have become a convincing liar. I know what you're supposed to look like when someone asks you how you're going, how to smile politely, how not to cry (mostly). I've been conditioned to hide vulnerability, not only by my well-intentioned parents but by being a woman in the world and knowing I could be sectioned, and having so much fear that someone would take my children away from me. What if they knew? What if I said to someone, *I think about leaving this planet every single day*, and forgot to laugh at the end so they knew it was a joke? A sad joke. Like: I'm joking, but I also want you to notice I'm not joking. You won't, though, because I'm laughing the exact amount I know will comfort you enough to ignore how serious I am.

People have only rarely tried to make me do anything more

than this. With few exceptions, I have taken the steps myself. I think I did wonder about it, to begin with – why isn't anyone helping me? Eventually I came to the conclusion that they weren't supposed to. I believed I wasn't as sick as I imagined. That I was, once again, just being overly dramatic. And then I was trapped inside, too anxious to leave, and I was self-harming and drinking heavily, and feeling like I wasn't a real person, and each time I asked for help, someone told me to Calm Down.

Here's a big thought: I'm still so afraid I might kill myself. I know, heavy. Even though I'm too anxious to contemplate it, even though I've done decades of therapy, even though I understand the impact it would have on people who care about me. I'm still afraid I might one day be so deeply sad and anxious that I won't be able to remember any of those things and I will suddenly realise I did have a plan after all, I had just written it in invisible ink and forgotten to mention it to my therapist.

That's only part of the thought, though. Can I tell you a secret? I'm afraid that if I don't die this way – if I find another way to die, from old age or climate change or cancer – that all the time I've spent talking about mental illness will have been a farce.

Sometimes people I know have said reprehensible things like, 'If I was as disabled as you, I would kill myself.' Obviously, part of me thinks, Never speak to me again, but another part wonders, Why are they telling me this? Are they challenging me? Do they not believe me? Does the fact of my still being alive prove that it is less serious than I'm making out?

I worry that one day someone will say, 'Just do it, then,' because they have grown tired of my wolf-crying and saying it's unbearable when clearly it *is* bearable, look at you, you keep on managing to be alive. If you were really so depressed, you would have done it by now. You would just be ashes on the wind, you phony.

If I don't do it – if I don't die by my own hand, pull up stumps, put stones in my pockets and walk into the sea – have I been bad at mental illness? Less committed? Can you even write these words down, legally?

I worry that on that very bad day, on a day when I have disconnected from the parts that know I'm too anxious to contemplate it, when I can't hear the voices of my therapist or my children or Gaz or my friends, I will feel the draw of its inevitability, and decide it's my time to go before the rational part of me has had a chance to speak up.

That I will ask my family, for my sake: *Please retain very happy memories of me.*

I'm afraid that I might, from the afterlife, read an obituary.

I'm afraid that it might say: 'after a long battle with mental illness.'

At the time I started thinking about writing this book, I was angry. I planned to jump into my word processor and rant about the fractured relationships I had had to bear as a teenager, and how I had made decisions before I understood the impact they would have on my life, and the abuse I had copped at the hands of terrible people, and how fucking tired I was. I was fully prepared to bare every rusted cog and sprung coil of my soul, and dare a reader to see me for all my wounded, battered grey matter.

When I was dealing with the most acute mental illness periods, Mum would often say to me (sometimes we would be yelling), 'I understand *better than you realise*.' It enraged me. How could she? I was sure no one else had ever experienced anything like this psychic agony, this internal warfare, this ego death. She said it time and again: *better than you realise*. And of course she was right. It took writing this book to understand what made that true. What it means for me. What it looks like to help. What the future can be.

There's a quote from literary theorist Paul de Man to which I have returned over and over during the writing: 'can we not suggest … that the autobiographical project may itself produce and determine the life …?' Through *writing* a narrative, he hypothesises, we can *create* a narrative. When we write the story, we can become the story.

The autobiographical narrative I have now is not the same as the one I had when I created this blank document. By remembering and contextualising, I have written and rewritten my identity. I have an improved understanding of what happened and why. I have come to a sense of forgiveness about many things, a better awareness of why I should consider my memories with scepticism. I've learned more about the reasons for my mixed-up self-awareness, and why I feel different from one moment to the next. So many times, I've read some research about identity or anxiety or depression and said *Ohhhhh* out loud. On these pages, I've addressed my mental illness to its face. I've been able to look right at it.

At the beginning of this process, an editor hinted at an impossible question. She apologised when she approached it: 'Sorry, Anna. I have to ask this.' Weighty pause. I guessed. I said, 'What if I kill myself while I'm writing?' And I sat a long time with that question. What if I retraumatised myself into oblivion? What if, in remembering, I became lost in the nooks and crannies of time?

But I haven't. I've taken my self-narrative from before and shaped it into a new way of looking at myself. I've remembered some things, and forgotten others. I am a more peaceful person than I was when I started. There is still time ahead, people to love, moments to savour.

I'm anxious and depressed and often a total mess, but that's not the same as saying I'm unhappy. Living with mental illness(es) doesn't make me miserable 100 per cent of the time. It doesn't mean I can't find comfort or experience love, gladness, fulfilment.

Actually, sometimes it's the opposite of that. I am anxious and depressed, but I'm optimistic. I try to look for the good in people. I plan for the future. I believe things will work out. And I don't mean *things will work out* like my brain will mend itself, but, like my dad, I believe that it will be okay in the end.

Sometimes I am overwhelmed by a kind of uncut joy, as though to penetrate my tired old skin it has been distilled into a thin and potent stream. I will find ways to feel like a whole person some of the time. I will find pockets of untarnished time and live through them.

I have rarely been hard done by. I am, to butcher the language, very easy done by. Besides being detached from reality, my life is as smooth a ride as there is. I have every possible means of support, family who love me, a safe home, access to education, literacy, money. That doesn't mean good help is available, but it does mean that if it *becomes* available, I'll probably be able to get it.

I have not had to contend with my psychopathy alongside racism, transphobia, poverty, isolation or violence. The seriousness of an illness isn't the main reason people die. It is the barriers society builds – *we* build. Welfare that doesn't keep people from homelessness. Disability support that requires a degree just to apply. Basic human needs that aren't met, people who are left behind.

Mental illnesses choose their targets based on many whims, but the treatment is more discretionary. It is reserved for a select few. I have been excruciatingly unwell under the best possible circumstances and that's a large part of why I have survived.

My life *is* full of a kind of magic: Coincidence, superstition, and luck.

The act or process through which something becomes different

That long-ago Sunday morning, home alone and staring down a gargantuan possum, I was not brave. When I looked again at the bathroom door, the tail was gone. I slammed it shut and hoped the creature was trapped inside, but I couldn't be sure. No breath went into my lungs, no blood through my veins. My body throbbed and ticked. I could feel the panic just over the verge. If I took one more step forward, it would all be over. The anxiety would consume me, and then the possum would eat me.

I called Gaz. It was 5 am. He realised it was Sunday and, because he is like a support animal who can smell my panic, he said, 'I'll come home.'

I couldn't sleep – what if the possum clawed my face off? What if I clawed my face off? Being so early in the morning, the only place I could think to call next was the twenty-four-hour vet.

The woman who answered was finishing her night shift in an hour. If I wanted, she could come by afterwards, she said, and take it to an animal welfare foster carer.

'I don't know what to do,' I said. 'What if it's loose in my house? What if my cats try to eat it? Should I call the police?'

I did not say: *Can you spare any horse tranquilliser?*

I did not say: *How do you deal with reality on Sunday mornings?*

I did not say: *Please just stay on the phone to me*, but she did anyway, for the full hour it took Gaz to get back. Distracting me from my existence.

Gaz was prepared. He pulled on his hardcore tree-pruning gloves and said, 'I'm going in!' like he was rescuing children from a cave. There was scuffling and growling, barking and yelling. He told me later that the possum had clung for dear life to the towel rack and refused to let go; he had to pry off its tiny possum fingers one by one. Then he opened the window and piffed it into the garden.

'It's gone,' I said to the woman from the twenty-four-hour vet. 'My boyfriend chucked it out the window.'

In the living room, the aluminium vases had been knocked from the mantelpiece and spilled onto the floor. Sooty footprints ran across the hearth, along the floorboards and up the white paint on the bathroom door.

'How funny,' the vet nurse said. 'It probably liked the smell of the flowers.'

There's a grate over the chimney now. Impossible to know if it keeps possums out, or me in.

When I was thirty-four, on 21 May 2017 – a Sunday – I decided to go outside. It's still hard to communicate just how bad it had got by this stage. I hadn't been outside on a weekend for more than five years. I don't mean it euphemistically, like I had been out the door but not *out the door*. I had not gone one step. For two of those years I had spent the entirety of Saturday and Sunday on the couch – Gaz called it my 'nest', a pocket of safety comprising my laptop, blankets, books, video games, chocolate and anything else that would occupy me. Some weekends were so bad I couldn't even cope with the fifteen seconds between TV episodes; on others I had to play three games at once to be sufficiently distracted. I couldn't get up from my nest even to go to the toilet, so I stopped drinking water altogether.

Those days had become another dimension, something I'd described to my therapist as 'like the world has stopped humming for forty-eight hours'.

The honest truth about that particular Sunday is: Gaz had moved out. He had been absolutely ground into powder by the situation with the weekend and gone to stay at his parents' house. My heart was a rattling bit of loose metal in my chest. I was alone in my house and I was just. so. tired. of myself. I felt like peeling off all my skin and setting fire to it. I felt like unscrewing my head and replacing it with a sandwich.

I was consumed by wanting to get better. Urgently. Rapidly. I got out of bed that day and I already knew I would do it. My heart thundered. I didn't wear shoes. I put on a jumper and walked (quickly, hurriedly, confusedly) from my front door to the nature strip. The day was cool and bright. I stood in the sunshine for thirty seconds, timing it on my phone. I took a photo, so I could post evidence of my achievement to Facebook.

Then I ran back inside and cried at my desk for two full hours. I heard an echo of someone saying, 'See? You *can* do it, you just didn't want to.'

The next Sunday, I did it again. I went across the road and stood under the neighbours' Irish strawberry tree for two full minutes. The Sunday after that, I got in my car and drove to the newsagent. I didn't go in; I just parked out the front and looked at it and thought, So that's what a newsagent looks like on a Sunday.

For two years, I pushed myself harder and harder. Social media provides a record of some of those days: I sat in the garden with my dog, went to the hardware store with my brother, bought a succulent from a pop-up plant sale. I went out for breakfast, drove to the beach, took my dogs for a walk. Every single Sunday, however I felt (and sometimes I felt very bad indeed), I put on both legs of my pants and walked out the door. After a while, I stopped wondering if I could do it. I knew I could do it. I began to make plans on Sundays, certain that they would come to fruition even though I was scared. And, after that, I began to look forward Sunday morning, knowing it would contain breakfast and laughter and a sense of achievement.

And I did take my kids to the park, eventually. We made a plan with a friend and his family, and in the morning I went to the supermarket to buy bread, cheese, cold cuts, juice, tubs of berries. We took the dogs with us. I remember looking at all the families gathered together and realising I'd thought families didn't go to parks anymore but, actually, it was just me who didn't go. Kids crawled over the play equipment like bugs. Parents yelled and laughed. And I was just like them, sun-licked at a picnic table, using my hands to grab rotisserie chicken from a bag. A bona fide human being on a Sunday afternoon.

For all that time, I was still paralytic with fear on Saturdays. It was as though the anxiety I had felt across the whole weekend had been condensed into that one day. I barely stopped hyperventilating from midnight to midnight. But, somehow, I knew I eventually would. Sunday morning breakfast told me it was possible. In the recesses of my brain, there was a pool of courage forming.

It was *Pokémon Go* that did it. Remember when we all did that for a few weeks? Something about the connection and community made me feel like part of the world again. Also, I like winning, and there was a special stone you could only get if you played the game for seven days in a row. I would tap the screen for six days and then bam, Saturday, trapped inside, unable to win.

For a couple of weeks I'd been practising walking to the end of the verandah with Gaz, who had come back and left again and come back (this would not be the last time). Together, we walked literally eight steps from the front door. My therapist had set me the task of spending fifteen seconds outside, and I counted every one of them before racing back in.

Did I really want a digital stone from a mobile app? Impossible to say, but what I did long for, deeply, was a good enough reason to try something new to conquer my fear. That morning, I walked to the letterbox. I stood there for a minute, maybe. A whole minute, exposed to the universe. I felt the pull of my car as strongly as I had ever felt anything. Drive me! it shrieked.

Take me to the PokéStop! The courage pool swelled. I was going to do it. I could feel it. But I had left my keys inside.

Gaz was standing beside me, presumably admiring the incredible bravery I was demonstrating. 'Your keys!' I shouted at him. 'Can I borrow them?' And then I was climbing into his car, with no shoes or bra, a too-spontaneous act of bravado. And then I was driving down the street, convulsing with fear, and then I was at the train station where the PokéStop was. And then I was driving home again and pulling into the driveway and running, sprinting, hyperventilating back inside, where I immediately burst into tears.

Fuck, yeah, said a little voice, which was Gaz's.

For two years after that, every Saturday morning I went out to get Gaz a coffee from whichever neighbourhood espresso machine I could make it to that day. Some Saturdays, it was the hole-in-the-wall almost visible from our house; others, it was a busy cafe by the bay, kilometres away. It was different every time. Some weekends I felt emboldened by the progress I had made the week before, while others felt like starting the whole thing again from the beginning. But I did not waver. I knew the fear wouldn't fix itself. And every Saturday, when I took that paper cup home, Gaz said, 'This is the best coffee I've had all week.'

When I started writing this, back in 2019, I was still so afraid. But the weekend is okay now. Finally. It feels bizarre to say that;

I had spent fully a third of my life internalising this fear. The fear dissipated because of self-belief and compassion. Gross. Like a self-help book. But the change was a side effect. No longer so angry with myself, I could finally hear the quiet voice of encouragement from within.

Now I've been to farmers' markets and discovered banana bread with brownie pieces baked into it, and I've gone to buy my dog a little tweed coat, and to get my glasses fixed, and to fetch a loaf of fresh bread from my favourite bakery. I've been to Spotlight with my mum, and taken my family out for lunch, and gone to the supermarket and the bookshop and the petrol station. I've been out for dinner and swum laps in the local pool and wandered aimlessly in shopping centres. I've even done hard things, like taking my old sick cat to the vet and my kid to have medical tests, and getting vaccinated in a pandemic. I have done all of this on days when I sincerely, with all of my heart, imagined I would never do anything again.

The fear is still there, a little. I still wake up on Saturday mornings and think, It's Saturday morning. I don't do that on other days. I don't wake up on Tuesdays and think, Shit, Tuesday. In the wee hours, the dream pre-wake pink-dawn moments, I go through a thought process like: I'm awake, oh it's Saturday, shit, is that my heart, is it still beating, can I breathe, do I need to go to the hospital, what if I die, wait five minutes and see if you die, are you dead? No, get out of bed, grab a blanket in case you fly off the world, can you get a drink, what about a bit of toast, you're okay, it will pass.

Every now and then, still, I get to the very end of the day – 11 pm, wrapped up in bed with some relaxing telly on – and the fear attacks me. Maybe my chest pinches a little, or my breath catches. I don't know how to get away from it. I don't know how to fix it except for it to not be Saturday, which defies the laws of physics.

So I have to trust that it will abate. I have had to learn to wait. I have learned to be patient with my fear.

NOVEMBER (AGAIN)

At the end of the second year of the pandemic, I have to go back to my GP to explain why I need to keep going to therapy again the following year. Exactly the same as I have every other year in living memory. Here is no checkbox to tell the government I need it indefinitely or I will die.

'So,' my doctor says, adjusting her mask. 'What progress do you feel you have made this year?'

I'm so tired I'm not sure my feet are even attached to my body anymore. I think about the days spent refreshing the *Covid-19 cases near you!* map and watching every press conference and crying because I couldn't find the fork I really like. 'I did not die,' I say.

She doesn't know if she's supposed to laugh, so she coughs in a way that could be a laugh. I laugh too and she is relieved. Now it's a joke and I'm not going to set myself on fire during our extra-long appointment that costs $186. 'And do you think you need to continue with your therapy?' she says.

'Yes.'

'Tell me about that.' She seems sincerely interested. I want to hug her. Or, I want her to hug me. My body feels tight and sore from lack of human contact.

'Well ...' I explain how I need to go to therapy, even if I don't feel like it, or else I start to lose my grip on things. I explain how, if I don't go to therapy, I will wake up one morning and not get out of bed, and I will keep not getting out of bed, and I will shrivel into an empty shell before I have even noticed that I haven't been going to therapy. And that actually, *at this stage of my life*, I don't even expect or need to make progress anymore, I just need to maintain the level of wellbeing I currently have. I need a new mental health care plan, so I can use the subsidy to avoid getting any worse. The measure of my progress, of my success, I say, is that I can still come to your office, wearing clothes and shoes, and no one visibly recoils when I walk past. That's why I need to continue with my therapy: because I need it to stay alive. I don't say the thing I'm always thinking with the secret parts of my brain, which is, Maybe I'll get better, even though I won't.

'Right,' she says. 'Yes.' She hands me a form with boxes on it. 'You've probably done this lots of times. The K10 questionnaire?'

'Yes.' Every year for a decade, I have filled out the Kessler psychological distress scale. They need the answers to decide whether you're anxious and depressed. They can't simply believe you when you tell them. To get more mental health care, you have to prove to the government that you're mental but, like, mathematically.

Next to *About how often did you feel nervous?* I circle *All of the time*. But as I go down the list, my body is different. I can lift the pen without faltering. When I look over my answers, some of the numbers are zeroes.

I hand back the paper. The doctor says, 'That was quick!'

I don't care about winning at the K10 questionnaire. I'm more complex and interesting than that.

'How is your psychologist?' she asks while she prints my new referral. 'Good?'

I think about how my new therapist didn't chuck me out when I wore thongs to a place full of sick people. And the other stuff, too – being able to stand in a shopping centre without screaming, letting go of guilt, finding peace in my heart. I think of being in a park with the sun on my face. I think of buying an avocado, of reading a book, of saying 'no'. I think of self-acceptance.

'She's excellent,' I say. A long breath slides out of me. 'She's really, really helping.'

'I'm glad.' The doctor prints me a copy of my new mental health care plan. 'It's hard to find good ones.'

In the car, I unfold the sheet of paper. *MENTAL HEALTH CARE PLAN – ANNA SPARGO-RYAN*. For Anxiety I have scored 28 (Severe). But for Depression I have scored 4 (Normal). I have never scored so low. I feel the relief in my hands first, my arms, my elbows. It traverses the span between my shoulders and down my back and into my knees. It is both gentle and electric. It is familiar and novel. My heart is in my throat and I let it sit there, remembering the drumbeat of it.

I adjust my sunglasses. I reach into my chest and touch the hot stones that live there. Onwards.

References

Part 1

Page 33. 'if we begin to call our memory into question …' Shaw, J., *The Memory Illusion: Remembering, Forgetting, and the Science of False Memory*, Cornerstone Digital, 2016.

Page 35. 'Those who are significantly affected by it …' Atkinson, M., *Traumata*, University of Queensland Press, 2018.

Page 36. 'evidence that the world is a place of unremitting danger …' Erikson, K.T., 'Notes on trauma and community', in *Trauma: Explorations in Memory* (ed. Caruth, C.), The Johns Hopkins University Press, 1995.

Page 54. 'intense distress in the event of actual or perceived abandonment …' Palihawadana, V. et al, 'Reviewing the clinical significance of "fear of abandonment" in borderline personality disorder', *Australasian Psychiatry*, 2019.

Page 55. This research found that social exclusion stimulates the same parts of the brain as physical pain. Eisenberger, N.I.

and Lieberman, M.D., 'Why rejection hurts: a common neural alarm system for physical and social pain', *Trends in Cognitive Sciences*, 2004.

Page 55. This research hypothesises that we can learn a fear of abandonment from our parents' behaviour, and their own fear of abandonment. IJzendoorn, M.H. van and Bakermans-Kranenburg, M.J., 'Bridges across the intergenerational transmission of attachment gap', *Current Opinion in Psychology*, 2019.

Page 55. 'patients with [Crohn's Disease] exhibit …' Agostini, A. et al, 'Adult Attachment and Early Parental Experiences in Patients With Crohn's Disease', *Psychosomatics*, 2010.

Page 60. These papers speak to the consistent finding that genetics play a role in heritability of anxiety. 'Post-Traumatic Stress Disorder', *Psychiatry Neuroimaging Laboratory*, Harvard Medical School, 2017 together with Gottschalk, M.G. and Domschke, K., 'Genetics of generalized anxiety disorder and related traits', *Dialogues in Clinical Neuroscience*, 2017.

Page 61. 'genetic contributions toward neuroticism …' *ibid.*

Page 61. 'enhances our ability to extinguish fear …' University of Queensland. 'Extinguishing fear memories relies on an unusual change to DNA', *ScienceDaily*, 2019.

Page 62. 'Over a lifetime, comorbidity of mood disorders …' Hofmeijer-Sevink, M.K. et al, 'Clinical relevance of comorbidity in anxiety disorders: A report from the Netherlands Study of Depression and Anxiety (NESDA)', *Journal of Affective Disorders*, 2012.

Page 72. 'We tell ourselves stories …' Didion, J., *The White Album*, Simon & Schuster, 1979.

Page 73. 'If memory is not a tape recorder …' Savage, E., *Blueberries*, Text Publishing, 2020.

Page 75. 'retention of classically conditioned emotional relationships …' Baars, B.J. and Gage, N.M., 'The Fear System', *Cognition, Brain and Consciousness: Introduction to Cognitive Neuroscience, Second edition*, Academic Press, 2010.

Page 78. 'our memories are built to forget …' Shaw, J., *The Memory Illusion: Remembering, Forgetting, and the Science of False Memory*, Cornerstone Digital, 2016.

Page 81. 'Instead of seeing the brain as rigid …' Sacks, O., 'In the River of Consciousness', *The New York Review*, 2004.

Part 2

Page 99. This paper explores the potential impact of cannabis use on developing brains. Yasgur, B.S., 'Cannabis-Induced Psychosis in Teenagers and Young Adults: Risk Factors, Detection, Management', *Psychiatry Advisor*, 2019.

Page 101. This paper reports on suicidal tendencies of people who have delusions or delusional disorders. González-Rodríguez, A. et al, 'Suicidal Ideation and Suicidal Behaviour in Delusional Disorder: A Clinical Overview', *Psychiatry Journal*, 2014.

Page 116. This paper quotes research relating to the suicidality of twins. Zai, C.C. et al, 'Genetic Factors and Suicidal Behavior', cited in *The Neurobiological Basis of Suicide*, Taylor & Francis, 2012.

Page 117. This study followed the lives of surviving twins to compare suicide rates of identical and fraternal twins. Roy, A. et al, 'Attempted suicide among living co-twins of twin suicide victims', *American Journal of Psychiatry*, 1995.

Page 127. This analysis reports various psychotic symptoms in patients with borderline personality disorder, also citing studies that include self-reported symptoms, and the impact of childhood trauma. Schroeder, K. et al, 'Psychotic symptoms in patients with borderline personality disorder', *Current Opinion in Psychiatry*, 2013.

Page 129. This research articulates one of the ways personality disorders are differentiated from mood disorders. 'Some research describes personality disorders …' Skodol, A.E. et al, 'Personality disorders and mood disorders: perspectives on diagnosis and classification from studies of longitudinal course and familial associations', *Journal of Personality Disorders*, 2010.

Page 133. 'Pain is difficult to communicate …' Maslen, K., *Show Me Where it Hurts: Living with Invisible Illness*, Text Publishing, 2020.

Page 133. 'I think every doctor in Australia …' Gibbs, E., (personal communication, 2021).

Page 137. 'I must be defective.' Mason, P.T. and Kreger, R. *Stop Walking on Eggshells*, New Harbinger Publications, 1998.

Page 138. 'fragmentation of the narrative self …' Fuchs, T., 'Fragmented Selves: Temporality and Identity in Borderline Personality Disorder', *Psychopathology*, 2007.

Page 141. 'But why bother with diagnoses …' Nelson, M., *Bluets*, Random House, 2017.

Page 186. 'Soon they will be teenagers …' Spargo-Ryan, A., 'The mother who never does anything', *ABC RampUp*, 2013.

Page 201. 'the underlying belief that one must strive …' Young, J.E. et al, 'Schema Therapy: Conceptual Model' in *Schema Therapy: A Practitioner's Guide*, Guilford Publications, 2003.

Page 208. 'Some people find that they have no memory …' Bernstein, E. and Putnam, F., 'Development, reliability, and validity of a dissociation scale', *Journal of Nervous and Mental Disease*, 1986.

Page 208. This paper looks at the impact of stress on dissociative symptoms. Krause-Utz, A. et al, 'Reduced amygdala reactivity and impaired working memory during dissociation in borderline personality disorder', *European Archives of Psychiatry and Clinical Neuroscience*, 2018.

Part 3

Page 254. 'Recurrent and persistent thoughts …' *Diagnostic and Statistical Manual of Mental Disorders, Fifth Edition*, American Psychiatric Association, 2013.

Page 254. 'Repetitive behaviors (e.g., hand washing, ordering, checking) …' *Diagnostic and Statistical Manual of Mental Disorders, Fifth Edition,* American Psychiatric Association, 2013.

Page 258. 'chaotic changes in the firing rate …' King, R. cited in Shaner, A., 'Delusions, superstitious conditioning and chaotic dopamine neurodynamics', *Medical Hypotheses*, 1999.

Page 259. 'Large and significant relationships between Magical Ideation scores …' Einstein, D.A. & Menzies, R.G., 'The presence of magical thinking in obsessive compulsive disorder', *Behaviour Research and Therapy*, 2004.

Page 264. 'diminish negative psychotic symptoms and lessen distress …' Quigley, H. and MacCabe, J.H., 'The relationship between nicotine and psychosis', *Therapeutic Advances in Psychopharmacology*, 2019.

Page 274. This study in part analyses the role of the hypothalamus in panic attacks. Fischer, S., 'The hypothalamus in anxiety disorders', *Handbook of Clinical Neurology, Therapeutic Advances in Psychopharmacol*, 2021.

Page 285. 'The Brugada syndrome was described in 1992 …' Brugada, P. and Brugada, J., 'Right bundle branch block, persistent ST segment elevation and sudden cardiac death: A distinct clinical and electrocardiographic syndrome: A multicenter report', *Journal of the American College of Cardiology*, 1992.

Part 4

Page 315. 'can we not suggest … that the autobiographical project …' Man, P de., 'Autobiography as De-facement', *MLN Comparative Literature*, The Johns Hopkins University Press, 1979.

A version of 'Injuring oneself with the intent to die' was originally published as 'The Suicide Gene', in *The Saturday Paper*, 24 December 2016.

A version of 'Recurrent aborted sudden cardiac death' was originally published as 'Coved-shaped Waves', in *The Saturday Paper*, 16 and 23 November 2019.

Acknowledgements

Thank you to every person who has made the path to mental health care a little simpler, whether by increasing funding, conducting research, writing good policy, busting stigma or just believing someone's testimony.

A book that strips naked your entire brain is not easy to write, and I owe so many thankyous. Thank you firstly to Alex Craig, who has never wavered (as far as I know) in her belief in my writing and in me, and to the amazing Ultimo team. Thank you Tara Wynne and Caitlan Cooper-Trent, agents extraordinaire, for dealing with my reckless tweeting. Thank you Ali Lavau for knowing how to end it.

I think you're supposed to pretend not to recognise your therapist in public, but I would simply not have made it without mine.

Thank you to the editors who set me in motion: Jonathan Green, Erik Jensen, Svetlana Stankovic, Sophie Kalagas.

Thank you to everyone who helped this be a book and not just rants in the group chat: Mathilda Imlah, Cassandra Atherton,

Indigo Perry, Kirstie Bedford, Eleni Hale, Amy Jasper, Gwen Luscombe, Cat McGregor, Kate Murdoch, Hala Alyan, Raechel Lee, Rebecca Shalomoff, Kristina Martino, Lesley Heiser, Tommy Mira y Lopez, Libby Turner, Michael Livingston, Lauren Béldi, Christian McCrea, Sam Van Zweden, Eloise Grills, Roz Bellamy, Fiona Wright, Kylie Maslen, Katerina Bryant, Jessica Friedmann, Gemma Carey, Vanessa Jones, Melanie White, Lilly Dancyger, Clementyne Howard, Amy Estes, Bex Pachl, MeiMei Dennis, Mel King.

And thank you especially to the people who have loved me when I have been a brain on a stick: Mum and Dad, Julia Spargo-Ryan, Jono Spargo-Ryan, Erin Van Krimpen, Allison Tait, my extraordinary children Georgia and Quinn, Gaz and, now, me.

If you or anyone you know is in need of support for mental health concerns, help is available, 24 hours a day, seven days a week, anywhere in Australia.

Lifeline
13 11 14
lifeline.org.au

Suicide Call Back Service
1300 659 467
suicidecallbackservice.org.au

Beyond Blue
1300 224 636
beyondblue.org.au

Headspace
1800 650 890
headspace.com

Head to Health
headtohealth.gov.au

MensLine Australia
1300 789 978
mensline.org.au

In an emergency, call 000.

Anna Spargo-Ryan is the author of two novels, *The Gulf* and *The Paper House*, and an acclaimed non-fiction writer and teacher. She was the inaugural winner of the Horne Prize and is the current Non-fiction Editor at *Island Magazine*.